The Gods and Technology

SUNY series in Theology and Continental Thought
Douglas L. Donkel, editor

The Gods and Technology

A Reading of Heidegger

Richard Rojcewicz

State University of New York Press

Published by
State University of New York Press, Albany

© 2006 State University of New York

For information, address State University of New York Press,
194 Washington Avenue, Suite 305, Albany, NY 12210-2384

Production by Diane Ganeles
Marketing by Susan M. Petrie

Library of Congress Cataloging-in-Publication Data

Rojcewicz, Richard.
    The gods and technology : a reading of Heidegger / Richard Rojcewicz.
        p. cm. — (SUNY series in theology and continental thought)
    Includes bibliographical references (p.   ) and index.
    ISBN-13: 978-0-7914-6641-4 (hardcover : alk. paper)
    ISBN-10: 0-7914-6641-8 (hardcover : alk. paper)
    ISBN-13: 978-0-7914-6642-1 (pbk : alk. paper)
    ISBN-10: 0-7914-6642-6 (pbk : alk. paper)
    1. Heidegger, Martin, 1889–1976. 2. Technology—Philosophy. I. Title.
II. Series.

B3279.H49R625 2005
193—dc22

2005003401

10 9 8 7 6 5 4 3 2 1

Contents

Preface

This is a lengthy study attempting to reopen and take a fresh look at a brief text in which Martin Heidegger projected a philosophy of technology. What is offered here is a careful and sympathetic reading of that text in its own terms. I do situate Heidegger's philosophy of technology within his overall philosophical enterprise, and I follow to their end certain paths that lead not infrequently into ancient Greek philosophy and at times into modern physics. Moreover, never far from the surface is the theme of piety, a theme especially characteristic of Heidegger's later period; in play throughout this study is what Heidegger sees as the proper human piety with respect to something ascendant over humans, with respect to the gods. Nevertheless, the focus remains intensely concentrated, and the goal is neither more nor less than a penetrating exposition of a classic text of twentieth century continental philosophy.

That such a reading could be urgent, or even called for at all, might seem highly doubtful today, fifty years after the appearance of "Die Frage nach der Technik." Has not Heidegger's philosophy of technology already been exhausted of its resources? Was it not time long ago to pass beyond exposition to judgment, perhaps even—in view of Heidegger's unsavory political leanings—to dismissal? In any case, surely everyone is already familiar with this philosophy of technology in its own terms: the "Enframing," the "saving power," the "objectless standing-reserve," the "constellation," the redetermination of the sense of essence as "granting," and so on and on. Or are all these terms, if they do genuinely express Heidegger's ideas, still largely undetermined and deserving of closer examination? Have we mastered, not to say surpassed, Heidegger's philosophy of technology, or are all readers of Heidegger, the present one included, still struggling to come to grips with what is thought there? The modest premise of this book is that the latter is the case.

Thus I do not pretend to speak the last word on Heidegger's philosophy of technology, nor do I even purport to offer the first word—in the sense of a definitive exposition that would set every subsequent discussion on sure ground. On the contrary, I merely attempt to take a step closer to the matters genuinely at issue in Heidegger's thought. In that way, the following pages, even while claiming a certain originality, merge into the general effort of all the secondary literature[1] on Heidegger.

Introduction

The original turn in the history of philosophy, from pre-Socratic thought to the philosophy of Socrates and of all later Western thinkers, can be understood as a turn from piety to idolatry. In a certain sense, then, Cicero was correct to characterize this turn as one that "called philosophy down from the heavens and relegated it to the cities of men and women."[1]

Cicero is usually taken to mean that Socrates inaugurated the tradition of humanism in philosophy, the focus on the human subject as what is most worthy of thinking. In contradistinction, the pre-Socratic philosophers were cosmologists; they concerned themselves with the universe as a whole, with the gods, with the ultimate things, "the things in the air and the things below the earth." Socrates supposedly held it was foolish to inquire into such arcane and superhuman matters and limited himself instead to the properly human things; his questions did not concern the gods and the cosmos but precisely men and women and cities. Thus his questions were ethical and political: what is virtue, what is friendship, what is the ideal polity?

The Ciceronian characterization, understood along these lines, would have to be rejected as superficial, even altogether erroneous. As for Socrates, he by no means brought philosophy down to earth, if this means that the human world becomes the exclusive subject matter of philosophy. Socrates did not limit his attention to human, moral matters. On the contrary, even when the ostensible topic of his conversation is some moral issue, Socrates' aim is always to open up the divine realm, the realm of the Ideas. That is, he is concerned with bringing philosophy, or the human gaze, up to heaven; more specifically, he is occupied with the relation between the things of the earth and the things of heaven. To put it in philosophical terms, his concern is to open up the distinction between Being and beings. That is his constant theme, and the ostensible moral topic of discussion is, primarily, only the occasion for the more fundamental metaphysical inquiry. As for all later thinkers, Cicero's characterization seems even less applicable. The entire tradition of metaphysics, from Aristotle down to our own times, concerns itself precisely with the things of heaven, with Being itself, and even calls this concern "first philosophy" in contrast to the secondary philosophical interest in men and women and cities.

Understood in another sense, however, Cicero's characterization is perfectly correct. From Socrates on, philosophy is indeed withdrawn from the gods and relegated, completely and utterly, to men and women, with the result that the human being becomes the exclusive subject of philosophy. This statement holds, and it expresses the Socratic turn, but only if "subject" here means agent, doer, and not topic, not subject *matter*. Socrates makes philosophy a purely human accomplishment and Being a passive object. In other words, for the Socratic tradition philosophy is the philosophy "of" Being, or "of" the gods, *only* in the sense of the *genitivus obiectivus*; in philosophy Being merely lies there as an object, awaiting human inquiry. This is indeed a turn, since the pre-Socratic view is the pious one that humans, in carrying out philosophy, in disclosing what it means to be, play a deferential role. The proper human role in philosophy is then something like this: not to wrest a disclosure of the gods but to abet and appropriate the gods' own self-disclosure. While we might be able to see the piety in this pre-Socratic attitude, it will strike us much more forcefully as enigmatic. The turn taken by the ancient Greek philosopher Socrates was the removing of the enigma. The turn taken by the German philosopher Martin Heidegger, two and half millennia later, reverses the original one and restores the enigma—as well as the piety.

Consider the Socratic versus the pre-Socratic notion of truth. For the Socratic tradition, truth is an unproblematic, though no doubt arduous, human affair. Truth is the product of the human research which wrests information from the things. For the pre-Socratic philosopher, Parmenides, on the contrary, truth is a goddess, one that leads the thinker by the hand. As Heidegger emphasizes, Parmenides does not speak of a goddess *of* truth, a divine patron of truth, but of truth itself as a goddess:

> If, however, Parmenides calls the goddess "truth," then here truth itself is being experienced as a goddess. This might seem strange to us. For in the first place we would consider it extremely odd for thinkers to relate their thinking to the word of a divine being. It is distinctive of the thinkers who later, i.e., from the time of Plato on, are called "philosophers" that their own meditation is the source of their thoughts. Thinkers are indeed decidedly called "thinkers" because, as is said, they think "out of" themselves. . . . Thinkers answer questions they themselves have raised. Thinkers do not proclaim "revelations" from a god. They do not report the inspirations of a goddess. They state their own insights. What then are we to make of a goddess in the "didactic poem" of Parmenides, which brings to words the thoughts of a thinking whose purity and rigor have never recurred since? (*P*, 7/5)

That is the sense in which Socrates brought philosophy down to the men and women in the city: he made their own meditation the source of their thoughts. Philosophy becomes a human affair, not in that it becomes primarily ethics and politics, but in the sense that it arises exclusively out of the spontaneity of the human faculty of thinking. Humans are the protagonists in the search for truth, they take the initiative, they exercise the spontaneity, they think "out of" themselves, and Being is the passive object. For Parmenides, and the pre-Socratics generally, on the other hand, philosophy is a response to a claim made upon the thinker by something beyond, by a god or goddess, by Being. The pre-Socratic philosopher does not take up the topic of the gods; on the contrary, the gods take up the philosopher.

This last statement indeed strikes us as extremely odd, not to say nonsensical, since we recognize no claim coming from beyond and nothing more autonomous than our own subjectivity. Therein lies the idolatry. The post-Socratic view is the narrow, parochial view that humans as such are above all else, are sovereign in their search for knowledge, subject to nothing more eminent. This is an idolizing of humanity, a kind of human chauvinism, our epoch's most basic and pervasive form of chauvinism. It is humanism properly so-called, and the unrelenting domination of modern technology, which is entirely motivated by it, attests to its pervasiveness.

Now Heidegger's philosophy is emphatically not a humanism, at least not the usual chauvinistic one. For Heidegger, there is something which holds sway over humans, is more eminent, more autonomous, and it would be utterly parochial to regard humans as the prime movers. This applies especially to that most decisive of all accomplishments, the disclosure of truth. To consider humans *the* agents of truth, to consider truth a primarily human accomplishment, would amount to hubris, a challenging of the gods, and would draw down an inexorable nemesis.

From Socrates on, in Heidegger's eyes, there has been a "falling away" from the great original outlook,[2] a forswearing of the attitude that led to the view of truth as a goddess, and so the entirety of the intervening history basically amounts to *Ab-fall*, apostasy (*P*, 79/54). For Heidegger, this apostasy has culminated in metaphysics, humanism, and modern technology, and for him, as we will see, these are all in essence exactly the same. They are merely different expressions of the same human chauvinism. They all understand the human being in terms of subjectivity and in particular as *the* subject, the sovereign subject.

For example, metaphysics defines the human being as ζῷον λόγον ἔχον (*zoon logon echon*), "the animal possessing language." Heidegger's quarrel here is not primarily over the words ζῷον and λόγος. Those terms do signify something essential, namely that humans are unique among living beings in enjoying an understanding of what it means to be in general. This understanding is especially manifest in the use of *language*, inasmuch as words are general expressions; they express universals, concepts, essences, the Being of things. Thus to be able to speak is a sign that one is in touch with the realm of Being or, in other words, that one is "in the truth." To that extent, the metaphysical definition points to something valid and is unobjectionable. The definition goes further, however, and in Heidegger's eyes it does not simply make the observation that humans enjoy a relation to truth but also stipulates that relation as one of "possessing." Now that *is* objectionable to Heidegger, and so his criticism bears on what, to all appearances, is an utterly innocuous word in the definition, ἔχω, "possess."

To possess is to be the subject, the owner, the master. Heidegger's concern here is not that the metaphysical definition implies humans are in *complete* possession of the truth; it does not imply that at all. But the definition indeed intends to say that humans are the subjects of whatever truth they do possess. Humans are the possessors of language in the sense that the understanding of the essence of things, and the expression of essences in words, are human accomplishments. Humans have *wrested* this understanding; it is a result of their own research and insight. Humans are then, as it were, *in control* as regards the disclosure of truth; humans are the subjects, the agents, the main protagonists, of the disclosure. That is the characteristic stance of metaphysics; metaphysics makes the human being the subject. In other words, the human being is the subject *of* metaphysics: again, not in the sense of the subject *matter*, but in the sense of the agent of metaphysics, that which by its own powers accomplishes metaphysics, wrests the disclosure of truth or Being.

From a Heideggerian perspective, the "possessing" spoken of in the metaphysical definition ought to be turned around. Accordingly, Heidegger reverses the formula expressing the essence of a human being: from ζῷον λόγον ἔχον to λόγος ἄνθρωπον ἔχων (*EM*, 184/137), from humans possessing language to language possessing humans. Humans are not the sovereign possessors, not the subjects of metaphysics, not the primary disclosers of truth. Instead, humans are the ones to whom truth *is disclosed*. Referring to the metaphysical definition, Heidegger asks: "Is language something that comes at all under the discretionary power of man? Is language a sheer human accomplishment? Is man a being that possesses language as one of his belongings? Or is it language that 'possesses' man and man belongs to language, inasmuch as language first discloses the world to man and thereby [prepares] man's dwelling in this world?" (*PT*, 74–5/59)

The attitude motivating these questions is the pre-Socratic one whereby the gods (or, equivalently, truth, Being, language, the essence of things in general) hold sway over human subjectivity. The full sense of this holding sway is a nuanced one and will emerge in the course of our study of Heidegger's philosophy of technology. It is certain at least that Heidegger does not merely reverse the direction of the "possessing" while leaving its sense of mastery or domination intact. Nevertheless, for Heidegger, the human powers of disclosure are indeed appropriated by something ascendant over them, something which discloses itself to humans—or which hesitates to do so. Thus Heidegger makes it clear that the apostasy he finds in history is not *human* apostasy; it is not a matter of human failing. Humans are not the ultimate subjects of this apostasy; they are not the apostates, the gods are. That is to say, humans have not forsaken the beginning, so much as the beginning has forsaken humans. Humans have not foresworn the gods; on the contrary, the gods have on their own absconded from us. Humans have not been unobservant or careless in their pursuit of the truth; instead, the truth has drawn over itself a more impenetrable veil. Humans do now speak superficially, but not because they have been negligent, have neglected to preserve the strong sense of words; on the contrary, language itself has emasculated the terms in which it speaks to us. Most generally, humans have not overlooked Being, so much as Being has become increasingly reticent in showing itself.

These inverted views are altogether characteristic of Heidegger's philosophy, especially in its later period. His philosophy cannot then but seem countersensical or mystical to someone in the metaphysical tradition. For Heidegger, the human being is not the subject of metaphysics. The prime movers of metaphysics, the main protagonists of the disclosure of what it means to be in general, are the gods or, to speak less metaphorically, Being itself. Since metaphysics and modern technology are essentially the same, we will see that for Heidegger humans are not the subjects of this technology either; the gods are the prime movers of modern technology and indeed of all technology. Technology is not merely, and not even primarily, a human accomplishment.

If humans are, in some way, possessed by language, *led* to the truth, if they are primarily the receivers rather than the agents of the disclosure of Being, that does nevertheless of course not mean for Heidegger that humans are sheer receivers, utterly passive recipients. Humans do not receive the self-offering of the gods the way softened wax receives the impress of a stamp. Humans make an active contribution to the disclosure of the meaning of Being. Humans co-constitute that disclosure and are co-responsible for it. Humans are therefore called upon to exercise all their disclosive powers; humans must be sensitive, thoughtful, creative, resolute. There is no disclosure of truth without a human contribution, and the genuineness of the disclosure depends to some necessary extent upon that contribution. In other words, truth, the goddess, may take the thinker by the hand, but the thinker must actually be a thinker, must actively attempt to disclose the truth, must, as it were, reach out a hand toward the truth for the goddess to take up.

Heidegger never loses sight of the necessary and necessarily *active* role humans play in the disclosure of the meaning of Being. Nevertheless, for him the human role remains ancillary, and the primary actor, the primary agent of the disclosure of truth, is Being itself. The proper human role is therefore not to wrest a disclosure of Being but to abet Being's own self-disclosure. Humans are not the prime movers, and neither are they merely, passively, the moved. Humans are, rather, something like shepherds or, perhaps better, midwives; they play a creative role within a more general context of receptivity. Heidegger attempts to express this role in the name he proposes as the proper one for humans, when viewed specifically with respect to the disclosure of Being. That name is not "possessor," but *Dasein*.

This German term is to be understood, in accord with its etymology, as designating the place, the "there" (*da*), where a disclosure of Being (*Sein*) occurs. Taken in this sense, the term is applicable to humans alone, and so it indicates, first of all, the privileged position of humanity. Only humans are Dasein, the "there" of Being. Only to humans is it revealed what it means to be in general. Only humans speak. Only humans are in the truth. Furthermore, humans are privileged in the sense that Being, as inherently self-revelatory, *needs* a place to reveal itself; and so Being can even be said to *require* humans. Being needs its "there" as a ground just in order to come into its own as Being. These privileges accorded to humans, and expressed in the name Dasein, do then mark Heidegger's philosophy as a humanism, though not a parochial one.

What is most decisive, however, in Heidegger's understanding of humans as Dasein is the precise meaning of the "there," the exact sense in which humans are called upon to be the place of a self-revelation of Being. This sense of "there" (as also of *da* in German) is expressed very nearly in a colloquial use of the word in a context admittedly quite foreign to the present one. In the interpersonal domain, a parent may promise a child, or a lover a beloved, to "be there" always for her or him. That is of course not a promise simply to remain at a certain place in space. Nor, at the other extreme, is it a claim of domination. Instead, it is a promise to be available in a supportive way; it is an offer of constant advocacy and nurture. To be "there" in this sense is not to dominate, but neither is it at all passive; it requires an active giving of oneself, a mature commitment of one's personal powers, all while respecting the other person's proper autonomy. For Heidegger, humans are called on to be Dasein, to be the "there" of Being, in an analogous sense. To be Dasein is to be a place of reception, but not of passive reception. To be Dasein is to be pious, but not obsequiously pious. Being cannot and does not *impose* itself on humans. To be Dasein is not to take in passively but to abet the self-offering of Being by exercising one's own disclosive powers. To be Dasein is thus to be a sort of midwife or ob-stetrician to the self-revelation of Being; it is to "stand there" (*ob-stare*) in an abetting way.

It is thus impossible to be Dasein passively. No one is Dasein simply by occupying a certain place. All receiving (not only of the self-offering of Being) requires some degree of giving, some amount of going out of oneself or active opening of oneself. As regards the human reception of the meaning of Being, Heidegger is calling for the highest possible giving on the part of the receiver, the most dedicated reception, the most active reaching out toward the giver. To be truly Dasein is to be "there" *with all one's might*, with full diligence, with the exercise of all one's disclosive powers.

On the other hand, Dasein's abetting must not be understood as a compelling or even an *invoking*, to which Being or the gods would *respond* with a self-disclosure. The abetting does not *call forth* the self-offering of the gods. The gods are always the motivat*ing* and never the motivat*ed*. They offer themselves, to the extent that they do offer themselves, on their own initiative and not on account of our reaching out to them. To be Dasein is not to be a supplicant. Thus Heidegger is exhorting humans to be watchful and ready out of his mere *hope* that Being will return, that another beginning, one rivaling the first, more wholehearted, self-disclosure of the gods, might be at hand. A new beginning will not take place unless humans are ready for it; but human readiness will not cause it.

In other terms, to be Dasein is to be theoretical, provided we take "theory" in the original sense, i.e., in the sense of the Greek θεωρία (*theoria*). In Heidegger's analysis, this word expresses a two-fold looking (*PS*, 63/44; *P*, 152–160/103–09). The one look, θέα- (*théa*), expresses the "looking" at us of the goddess, θεά (*theá*), or, in other words, the self-disclosure of the gods, θεοί (*theoi*), to us.[3] The other look, -ὁράω (*horao*), refers to our human disclosive looking back upon the gods. Thus to be theoretical, thea-horetical, means to have some insight into the gods, to be in the truth, to understand, more or less, the meaning of Being in general. And that understanding is precisely what is constitutive of Dasein. The decisive moment in theory, however, is not *looking* as opposed to other modes of disclosing, e.g., feeling and handling. Theory is not empty speculation, mere gaping. Theory is intimate acquaintance, no matter how acquired; it is only later ages that take theory to be "mere" onlooking, in distinction to real knowledge acquired hands-on. What is decisive in the Greek concept of theory is, rather, the *relation* between our human disclosive looking and the self-disclosure of the gods, their "looking" at us. Originally, the gods were given the priority. Their self-disclosure was understood as the primary determinant of what we see and that we see:

> The Greeks experience the human look as a "taking up perceptu-
> ally," because this look is determined originally on the basis of a look
> that already takes up man and . . . has the priority. With respect to
> the [gods'] primordial look, man is "only" the looked upon. This
> "only," however, is so essential that man, precisely as the looked
> upon, is first received and taken up into a relation to Being and is
> thus led to perceive. (*P*, 160/108)

This passage says that the Greeks experienced themselves as the looked
upon, the ones to whom a self-disclosure of Being is addressed, not ones
who by their own efforts *wrest* a disclosure of the meaning of Being.
Human looking is not original but is a *response*—to a more original
being-looked-at. Thus the Greeks were not chauvinistic as regards theory.
For them, the main protagonists with respect to theory, with respect to
the disclosure of truth, or of the meaning of Being, are not humans but
the gods. Therefore, according to Heidegger, the word "theory" ultimately breaks down into θεά- ("goddess"; specifically, the goddess truth)
and -ώρα (*ora*, "pious care"). Theory then names not merely a responsive
looking back upon the gods but a specifically deferential, solicitous looking back. Theory is the "disclosive looking that abets truth" (*das hütende
Schauen der Wahrheit*) (WB, 47/165).

  To be Dasein and to be theoretical are therefore equivalent—these
terms both refer to humans as the "there" of Being, as active, abetting receivers of the self-disclosure of truth. The theoretical is, of course, only
one characteristic of humans, but Heidegger's philosophical concern with
humans does not extend beyond it. Heidegger's is exclusively a first philosophy, an ontology, a study of the meaning of Being, and not second
philosophy, not philosophical anthropology, not the study of humans *as
such*. Heidegger's single philosophical theme, which he pursues with un-
precedented concentration, is Being (or its avatars, namely, the gods,
truth, essence, language, etc.). Only secondarily does Heidegger's philosophy attend to humans, and then only in a restricted way, i.e., merely as
Dasein, merely as the "there" of Being, merely as thea-horetical. Heidegger thematizes humans only insofar as they relate to the gods, only as
privileged places for the self-disclosure of Being. He thematizes the place
of access only inasmuch as he is interested in the thing accessed, Being.
Heidegger's philosophy then disregards the full phenomenon of the
human being. But that should occasion absolutely no reproach. Heidegger does not deny that second philosophy is worthwhile. He simply does
not get beyond the more foundational questions, the ones of first philosophy; he does not get beyond theory, in the original sense.

  Then what are we to make of Heidegger's writings on technology?
Technology would seem to be a theme of second philosophy. Indeed, if
ever there was a purely human affair, it is technology. Technology is a

matter of human inventiveness, and it is a way humans accomplish practical tasks. Technology seems to be absolutely human and instrumental, rather than god-like and theoretical. Technology has nothing to do with the gods and is not theory but, quite to the contrary, is the practical application of theory. Technology is concerned simply with ways and means, not with ultimate causes, and certainly not with Being itself. Technology would then seem to have no place in Heidegger's theoretical philosophy of Being. Yet all this merely seems to be so, and for Heidegger the philosophy of technology is actually *equivalent* to first philosophy, since, for him, technology is nothing other than the knowledge of what it means to be in general. Like all ontological knowledge, technology is accomplished primarily by the gods, by the self-revelation of Being. Thus, to be Dasein, to be thea-horetical, to be technological, and to be ontological all mean exactly the same. They all mean to stand in a disclosive relation to Being itself.

This concept of technology as theoretical knowledge is not simply a new, idiosyncratic use of the term on Heidegger's part. Quite to the contrary, it is a return to the old Greek understanding of *techne*:

> What is wonder? What is the basic attitude in which the preservation of the wondrous, the Being of beings, unfolds and comes into its own? We have to seek it in what the Greeks call τέχνη [*techne*]. We must divorce this Greek word from our familiar term derived from it, "technology," and from all nexuses of meaning that are thought in the name of technology. . . . *Techne* does not mean "technology" in the sense of the mechanical ordering of beings, nor does it mean "art" in the sense of mere skill and proficiency in procedures and operations. *Techne* means knowledge. . . . For that is what *techne* means: to grasp beings as emerging out of themselves in the way they show themselves, in their essence, εἶδος [*eidos*], ἰδέα [*idea*]. . . . (GP, 178–79/154–155)

Heidegger is here identifying *techne*, in its original sense, with wonder, the basic disposition of philosophy. For Heidegger, individual beings may be astonishing, marvelous, remarkable, but only Being itself is worthy of wonder. If *techne* has to do with wonder, then it is related to Being and to first philosophy. Furthermore, it is in *techne*, the passage says, that Being comes into its own, i.e., fulfills its self-disclosure. *Techne* is the human looking back in response to a more primordial "look" or self-disclosure. Thus *techne* does pertain to the gods; it is thea-horetical. What Heidegger means by "technology" (*die Technik*), or by the "essence of technology," is *techne* in that sense.

Technology is then not the application of some more basic knowledge but is itself the most basic knowledge, namely, the understanding of what it means to be at all. On the other hand, technology itself can be applied. For example, science is an application of modern technology. Science is the research motivated by the self-disclosure of the essence of beings as orderable through calculation. Science *presupposes* this understanding of the Being of beings, and so science presupposes modern technology, which is nothing other than the theory of beings as essentially calculable. In turn, science itself can be applied, and that application issues in a certain sophisticated manipulation of beings, which is "technology" in the usual sense, namely, "the mechanical ordering of beings."

Whence arises this theory of beings as orderable through calculation, a theory that leads to science and to modern, high-tech machinations? According to Heidegger, "in the essence of *techne* . . . , as the occurrence and establishment of the unconcealedness of beings, there lies the possibility of *imperiousness*, of an unbridled imposition of ends, which would accompany the absconding of the [original deferential attitude]" (*GP*, 180/155).

Modern technology accompanies the absconding of the original attitude. Modern technology is not the cause of the absconding but is simply the most visible aftermath of that withdrawal. Modern technology is the theory that is motivated when humans no longer experience themselves as the looked upon. In other words, when the gods abscond, when they look upon humans not wholeheartedly but reticently, then human disclosive looking presents itself as autonomous, as subject to nothing of greater autonomy. An imperious theory thereby fills the void left by the deferential one, hubris replaces piety, unbridled imposition supplants respectful abetting, and the understanding of humans as possessors displaces the one of humans as Dasein. Humans thereby become subjects, *the* sovereign, imperious subjects. The theory of beings as orderable through calculation is a correlate of this imperiousness: to be imperious is precisely to take beings as submissive to an ordering imposed by humans. The imperiousness of modern technology is therefore evidence of the self-withholding of the gods, and it is as such that Heidegger takes up modern technology. He pursues the philosophy of technology out of his interest in the relation between humans and the gods, i.e., out of his sole interest in the disclosure of the meaning of Being. Consequently, Heidegger's philosophy of technology is an exercise in first philosophy.

According to Heidegger, history has seen two basic forms of technology, two theories of the essence of beings in general, namely, ancient technology and modern technology. The history of these theories, the gradual supplanting of the first by the second, is grounded not in autonomous human choices but in what is for Heidegger a *history of Being*, namely a relative absconding of the gods after their original, more wholehearted, self-disclosure. The history of technology is thus, fundamentally, a history of Being. The latter history is the domain of the autonomous events, and these motivate a certain technology, a certain outlook on the essential possibilities of beings, which in turn issues in a certain practice with regard to those beings. The practice that arose from the earlier theory was ancient handcraft, whereas modern, high-tech machinations derive from the subsequent technology. The essential difference in the two practices, however, does not lie in the sophistication of the means employed; that is, the difference is not that one practice uses simple hand tools, and the other one high-tech devices. The essential difference resides in the theory, in the attitude that underlies the use of the means: namely, a pious attitude toward the object of the practice, versus an imperious, hubristic, "unbridled imposition of ends." By way of a preliminary illustration, let us consider counseling and farming, two practices offered by Aristotle as paradigms of the so-called efficient cause.

The ancient farmer and the ancient counselor were midwives. They respected the object to which their practice was directed, and their creative activity amounted merely to finding ingenious ways of *letting* this object come into its own. Thus the ancient farmer respected the seed and merely nursed it toward its own end. This "mere" nursing, of course, is not at all passive; farming requires intelligent, hard work. As to counseling, the prime example is, significantly, a father counseling his child, according to Aristotle. Counseling used to respect the one to be counseled and so required intimate acquaintance, such as a father might have of his child. Counseling took direction from the one counseled, took its end from the counseled, and was thereby a matter of "mere" rousing or abetting, instead of imposing.

In contrast, today's farming and counseling are imperious; they are unbridled in imposing their own ends. Farming is becoming more and more not a respect for the seed but a genetic manipulation of it, a forcing of the seed into the farmer's own predetermined ends. And counseling is being degraded into a casual dispensing of psychopharmaceuticals to almost complete strangers. Instead of respecting the counseled, counseling now imposes the counselor's own ends on the other. Farming and counseling have indeed today become "efficient causes," impositional causes, but they were not so for Aristotle.

In Heidegger's view, it is not because high-tech drugs are available that modern counseling looks upon the counseled as an object to be imposed on. On the contrary, it is because the object is already disclosed as a *patient*, as something meant to undergo (*pati*) the imposition of the agent, that we are motivated to synthesize those drugs in the first place. Modern counseling is not impositional *because* it uses high-tech drugs; instead, it summons up such drugs because it is already impositional in outlook. More generally, modern technology does not disrespect the things of nature *because* it uses impositional devices. On the contrary, the disclosure of nature as something to be disrespected and imposed on is what first calls up the production of those devices. Things do now look as if they were subject to our unbridled imposition of ends, but that is not *because* we now possess the means to impose our will on them. On the contrary, it was our view of ourselves as unbridled imposers that first motivated the fabrication of those means. It is the imperious theory that calls up the imperious means, and it is precisely this theory, and not the practice or the means, that embodies a challenging of the gods. It is as a theory that modern technology harbors the threat of nemesis.

For Heidegger, the prime danger of our epoch does emphatically not lie in the effects of modern technology, in high-tech things. In other words, the prime danger is not that technological things might get out of hand, that genetically manipulated crops might cause cancer, that laboratory-created life-forms might wreak havoc on their creators, or that humans might annihilate themselves in an accidental nuclear disaster. Something even more tragic is imminent; human beings are not so much in danger of losing their lives as they are in danger of losing their freedom, wherein lies their human dignity. That is the disintegration which accompanies arrogance. It is a threat deriving from the *essence* of technology, from the theory of ourselves as unbridled imposers and of nature as there to be imposed on.

This theory, according to Heidegger, places humans on the brink of a precipice. It is bound to bring disillusionment, most basically since it will eventually become obvious that humans, too, are part of nature and so are themselves subject to the same impositional causality they claimed to be the agents of. Then humans will view themselves as outcomes of environmental forces over which they have no control whatsoever. If imposition presents itself as the only possible mode of causality, then humans will either be the imposers or the imposed on, the controllers or the controlled. In either case, humans will be oblivious to genuine human freedom, unaware of the threats to that freedom, and therefore unable to protect it. The nemesis would then be to become enslaved to the very technology that promised freedom. Heidegger's first philosophy is indeed concerned with obviating this slavery, and so, again, it can be called a humanism, though not an idolizing one.

The antidote to the danger of modern technology, according to Heidegger, is a return to ancient technology or, more precisely, to the *essence* of ancient technology. That is to say, Heidegger is not at all urging a return to the practice of ancient handcraft; he is not advocating an abandonment of power tools or high-tech things; he is not a romantic Luddite. But he is advocating the pious, respectful outlook, the nonchauvinistic theory, which is precisely the essence of ancient technology. In that theory, human freedom does not amount to imposition but to abetting, nurturing, actively playing the role of Da-sein. Ancient technology is the theory of abetting causality, and it is that theory, rather than the practice of handcraft, that Heidegger sees as possessing saving power.

Theory is for Heidegger, to repeat, primarily a matter of the self-disclosure (or self-withholding) of truth or Being.[4] Thus a particular theory is not to be achieved by sheer human will power, and Heidegger is not, strictly speaking, urging us to adopt the ancient outlook. He is not urging humans to seize this viewpoint as much as he is hoping that it might *bestow itself* once again. That will indeed not come to pass without our abetting, and we need to prepare ourselves for its possible bestowal. Indeed, the preparation, the waiting, advocated by Heidegger will demand what he calls the most "strenuous exertions." The proper human waiting is not at all passive. Nevertheless, the other beginning, the return of the ancient attitude, is *primarily* in the hands of the gods. It will arrive, if it does arrive, primarily as a gift of the gods. That is the meaning of Heidegger's famous claim that "Only a god can save us." And it is also the theme of his philosophy of technology.

◆

All the above is, of course, only meant as a thread of Ariadne; it is obviously abstract and merely programmatic. My task is to bring it to life. That I propose to do through a close reading of the principal statement of Heidegger's thinking on technology, his essay, "Die Frage nach der Technik," first delivered as a lecture in 1953.[5] Since Heidegger's time, a great deal of ink has been spilled over the philosophy of technology, but his work remains unsurpassed—indeed unequalled—in its radicality, in its penetration down to the root, the essence, of technology.

"Die Frage nach der Technik" is carefully crafted; it is highly polished and follows a path that has been well staked out. At the very outset, Heidegger insists on the importance of this path. Heidegger likes to appeal to the image of meandering country lanes when describing the course of thinking, but here the path is practically a straight road. There are indeed a few side paths that need to be pursued, but the main directionality is clear and intelligible. By following it, my commentary will receive its own intelligible organization and will begin accordingly with ancient technology, approached through the correspondent Greek understanding of causality. Part II will then be devoted to Heidegger's characterization of the essence of modern technology and of the role played by science in manifesting that essence. For Heidegger, however, the task is not simply to *characterize* the essence of modern technology but to prepare for a proper relation to that essence. The preparation requires that we first see the danger in modern technology (Part III). Heidegger then proposes *art* and, specifically, poetry as that which might save us from the danger, and the connection between art and the saving gods will have to be drawn out (Part IV). Finally, Part V will suggest a sympathetic response to Heidegger's philosophy of technology. His essay is, so to speak, open-ended. It issues in an invitation and needs to be carried on; I will thus conclude by asking about the most proper response to that invitation. Here the guide will be Heidegger himself, who, in another of his writings, proposed contemplative thinking and a certain form of detachment (*Gelassenheit*) as the activities, the strenuous exertions, to be practiced in response to the danger of modern technology. In the end, I hope to show that this response, which would produce a genuinely "lasting human work," namely, the safeguarding of human freedom, and would prepare for a return of the gods, should they indeed be willing to offer us a clearer view of themselves once again, is, most concretely, an improvisation on the example of piety still manifest in art.

Part I
Ancient Technology

It is especially significant, in Heidegger's eyes, that the epoch of ancient technology coincides with the time of the theory of the four causes. Indeed, for Heidegger, the distinctive outlook of ancient technology found its most explicit expression in that theory. Where causality is understood as it is in the theory of the four causes, there ancient technology reigns. Ancient technology, in essence, *is* the theory of the four causes; ancient technology is the disclosure of things in general as subject to the four causes. Heidegger's path to an understanding of ancient technology thus proceeds by way of the sense of the causality of the four causes. In particular, the delineation of ancient technology in "Die Frage nach der Technik" turns on the sense of the four causes in the locus classicus of that theory, Aristotle's *Physics*.

The four causes as obligations, as making ready the ground

Heidegger begins by repeating the names and the common way of viewing the four causes of change or motion. It is well known that the four causes are the matter, the form, the agent (or efficient cause), and the end or purpose (the final cause). The prototypical example is a statue. What are the causes of the coming into existence of a statue? First, the matter, the marble, is a cause as that which is to receive the form of the statue. The shape or form (e.g., the shape of a horse and rider) is a cause as that which is to be imposed on the marble. The sculptor himself is the efficient cause, the agent who does the imposing of the form onto the matter. And the purpose, the honoring of a general, is a cause as the end toward which the entire process of making a statue is directed. All this is well known, indeed too well known. It has become a facile dogma and bars the way to the genuine sense of causality as understood by the ancients.

Heidegger maintains that the ancients did in fact not mean by "cause" what we today mean by the term. Thus Heidegger's interpretation of the doctrine of the four causes is a radical one: it strikes down to the root, to the basic understanding of causality that underlies the promulgation of the four causes. Yet, Heidegger's position is not at first sight so very profound, since three of the causes, the matter, the form, and the end or purpose, are most obviously not what we mean today by causes. We would today hardly call the marble the cause of the statue, so there must of course have been a different notion of causality operative in Aristotle, or, at least, Aristotle must have had a much broader notion than we do.

Our contemporary understanding of causality basically amounts to this: a cause is what, by its own agency, produces an effect. Hence, for us, the cause of the chalice is not the silver but the artisan who imposes on the silver the form of the chalice. The silversmith herself is, for us, the one responsible for the chalice. She is the only proper cause of the chalice, since it is by her own agency, her own efficacy, that the thing is produced; the chalice is her product, and we even call it her "creation." Accordingly, the silversmith herself takes credit for the chalice; that is what is meant by saying that she is the one "responsible" for the chalice. She answers for it; it is entirely her doing, and she deserves the credit. For us, the silver is merely the raw material upon which the agent works; the silver does nothing, effects nothing, does not at all turn itself into a chalice. Therefore we do not think of the matter as a cause. The matter merely undergoes the action of the other, the agent; it is the patient, that which suffers or undergoes the activity of the agent. The matter does not impose the form of a chalice onto itself. The matter imposes nothing; on the contrary, it is precisely imposed *upon*. The matter is entirely passive; in the terms of the traditional understanding of the Aristotelian four causes, matter plays the role of sheer potentiality. It has no determinations of its own but is instead the mere passive recipient of the determinations imposed upon it. As utterly passive, the matter would not today be considered a cause. A thing is a cause by virtue of its actuality, and matter is precisely what lacks all actuality of its own. The matter is thus not responsible for what is done to it and does not receive the credit or take the blame for the forms some external agent has imposed upon it. The matter is therefore the complete antithesis of what we mean today by cause.

In fact, only one of the four causes, the so-called efficient cause, would today be recognized as a cause. The common interpretation of Aristotle, then, is that he did include in his theory what we mean by cause, but that is to be found only in his concept of the efficient cause. Aristotle, however, also included other factors of change or motion (the matter, the form, and the end) under an expanded concept of cause. On this understanding, the concept of cause is therefore not a univocal one in

Aristotle: the silversmith and the silver are not causes in the same sense. They do both contribute to the chalice, but the one acts and the other is acted upon; these may conceivably both be called causes, but only the efficient cause is a cause in the proper sense. The silver is a cause in some other, improper sense, a sense we today feel no need to include under our concept of cause.

Heidegger's position is that for Aristotle the four causes are all causes in the same sense. And that sense does not correspond to *anything* we today call a cause. In particular, Aristotle's so-called efficient cause is not in fact what we today mean by cause; that is, what Aristotle speaks of cannot rightfully be called an efficient cause: "The silversmith does not act . . . as a *causa efficiens*. Aristotle's theory neither knows the cause that would bear this title nor does it use a correspondent Greek term for such a cause" (FT, 11/8).

This says that even the so-called efficient cause is not understood by Aristotle and the Greeks as the responsible agent, as something that produces an effect by its own agency. The Greeks do not know the concept of efficacy or agency as that which imposes a form onto a matter. Correspondingly, change or motion does not mean for the Greeks the imposition of a form onto a matter by an external agent. Furthermore, since change is not the imposition of a form, ancient technology will not be an affair of imposition either.

What then exactly does Aristotle understand by a cause, such that all four causes can be causes in the same sense? In particular, how can both the silver and the silversmith be included in the same sense of cause? According to Heidegger, in the first place, the Aristotelian distinction between the matter and the agent is not the distinction between passivity and activity. Aristotle did not understand the matter as entirely passive nor the maker as entirely active. In other words, the matter is not that which is imposed upon, and the maker is not that which does the imposing. To put it in a preliminary way, we might say that the matter actively participates in the choice of the form; the matter suggests a form to the craftsman, and the craftsman takes direction from that proffered form. Accordingly, the matter is already pregnant with a form and the role of the craftsman is the role of the midwife assisting that form to come to birth. Instead of an imposed upon and an imposer, we have here something like a mutual participation in a common venture, a partnership where the roles of activity and passivity are entirely intermingled.

Heidegger expresses this interpretation of causality by saying that the causes are for Aristotle the conditions to which the produced thing is obliged. *Obligation* is the one common concept by which all four causes are causes in the same sense. The thing produced is indeed obliged to the various conditions for something different in each case, but the general relation of obligation is the same. What then does Heidegger mean by obligation in this context?

Heidegger's German term is *Verschulden*. This word has a wide range of meanings, but it is only one particular nuance that is invoked here. The term is derived from the ordinary German word for "guilt," *die Schuld*. Therefore Heidegger has to say explicitly that he does not mean *moral* obligation in the sense of being guilty for some lapse or failure. Furthermore, the term *Verschulden* also possesses the connotation of "responsibility." Again Heidegger rejects this sense: he does not mean here responsible agent, that which brings about an effect by its own agency and so personally takes the credit for that effect. We might say, then, that what Heidegger rejects is both the passive (being guilty for some failure) and the active (responsibility as effective agent) meanings. The sense he is invoking will in a certain manner lie between, or partake of both, activity and passivity.

Perhaps the nuance Heidegger is seeking is expressed in our colloquial expression of gratitude, "Much obliged." What do we mean when we say to another person that we are much obliged to him or her? We mean that that other person has fostered us in some way or other. Specifically, we do not mean that we owe everything to that other person, that that other person *created* us, but only that he or she has "helped us along." The other person has not been so active as to bear the entire responsibility for what we have done or have become, nor has the other person been totally passive. The other, in a certain sense, has neither acted nor failed to act. Our being obliged to the other amounts, instead, to this: he or she has provided for us the conditions out of which we could accomplish what we did accomplish, i.e., the conditions out of which our own accomplishment could come forth. We are much obliged to another not for creation, or for taking away our accomplishment by accomplishing it himself or herself, but for abetting us in our own accomplishment.

That is the nuance Heidegger is trying to express: the four causes are ways of abetting. The thing produced is obliged to the four causes in the sense that the causes provide the conditions, the nurture, out of which the thing can come forth. The causes make it possible for the thing to emerge out in the open, the causes may even coax the thing out, but they do not force it out. The causes are not "personally" responsible for the thing: that means the causes do not effect the thing by their own agency, by external force. All the causes do is to provide the proper conditions, the nourishment, the abetting, required by the thing in order to fulfill its own potential. The causes do not impose that fulfillment, do not force the desired form onto the thing, they merely let that fulfillment come forth, in the active sense of letting, namely abetting.

Thus the fundamental difference between Aristotle's understanding of cause and our current understanding is that between nurture and force, letting and constraint, abetting and compulsion. That is why for Aristotle there can be four causes and for us there is only one. A chalice can be obliged to the matter, the silver, but cannot be forced into existence by it. If causality is force, then there is only one cause—since the force must be applied by an active agent. If, instead, causality means nurturing, then not only the crafts-man, but also the matter, the form, and the purpose may all be causes—by way of providing required conditions. These each provide a different condi-tion, but the sense of their causality is the same: i.e., precisely the sense of abetting or nurture, of providing a favorable condition. The four causes, therefore, are all causes by virtue of being obligations of the thing produced; it is "much obliged" to all four of them. But the thing has *no* efficient cause in the sense of an external agent to which it owes everything, by which it was compelled into existence. Nothing external forced it into existence, but it did receive assistance in coming to its own self-emergence. That is Heidegger's radical understanding of the doctrine of the four causes: the causality of each of the causes, including the so-called efficient cause, is a matter of abetting only, not imposition.

Two general questions immediately arise regarding this reading. In the first place, where in Aristotle does Heidegger find this understanding of causality; i.e., what is the textual basis in the Aristotelian corpus for Heidegger's interpretation? Secondly, where in Heidegger do *I* find that this is in fact his understanding; i.e., what is the textual basis in Heideg-ger for this interpretation of Aristotle? These questions arise because the answers are by no means obvious, especially to anything less than the closest possible reading.

The so-called efficient cause in Aristotle

Let us begin with Aristotle. Heidegger simply does not say where in the Stagirite he finds this understanding of causality as abetting. We therefore need to look for ourselves and see if Heidegger's interpreta-tion is borne out. Since the central issue is the way of understanding the so-called efficient cause, we will make that cause the focus of our inquiry. If the "efficient" cause amounts to abetting, then the others do a fortiori.

As we read the passages in Aristotle's *Physics* where this cause is in question, we immediately notice that Heidegger was right about one thing at least, namely that the Stagirite does not at all use the term "effi-cient cause." In fact, Aristotle hardly gives this cause a name at all; any translation that settles on a definite name, such as "efficient cause," is merely an interpretation, one which may or may not capture the proper sense. I shall myself propose a name for this cause, but the name must come only after the attempt to grasp the sense. At the start, a defining name would merely prejudice the inquiry.

In Book II of the *Physics*, Chapters 3 and 7, Aristotle designates this so-called efficient cause seven times. The designation is somewhat different each time, but there is one key word that occurs in a majority of the formulations. This word is not really a name, or, if it is, it is the most indeterminate name possible. That is to say, the word leaves the determination of the nature of this cause open; it only points out the direction in which to look for the proper determination. This word, which is Aristotle's most characteristic way of referring to the so-called efficient cause, is in fact not a name, a noun, but a relative adverb used substantively. The word is ὅθεν (*hothen*), a simple term which means, as a substantive, "that from which" or "the whence."

Aristotle's various designations then become variations on the notion of this cause as "the whence of the movement" (195a8). For example, it is called "the first whence of the movement" (198a27), "the whence from which arises the first beginning of the change" (194b30), and "that whence the beginning of the change emerges" (195a23). By calling this cause merely "the whence," Aristotle indicates where we are to look for it, namely by following the motion to its source. But nothing is thereby determined as to how the source is to be understood. That is, it is not stipulated in advance how the motion proceeds from its source; in particular, it is not said that the source is the efficient cause of the change or motion. Our inquiry into the nature of causality in Aristotle therefore cannot stop at these designations; they are entirely open.

Aristotle also provides three designations (198a19, a24, a33) which do not employ the word "whence." We find there instead something closer to a proper name, namely the term κινῆσαν (*kinesan*). Yet it is quite uncertain how this word is to be taken. It is the neuter aorist participle derived from the verb meaning "to move, set agoing, stir up, arouse, urge on, call forth." The word κινῆσαν thus actually expresses little more than "the whence"; it means in the most literal and neutral sense, "the first setting into motion" or "that from which the motion first derived." The word then actually adds nothing to the initial designation as the whence, since it also leaves undetermined how the whence is related to the motion. It certainly does not say that the whence is the efficient cause of the motion, that the whence is a force imposing the motion. As far as the name goes, this cause is simply, in some way or another, at the head of the motion, the source of the motion. But a thing may be a source of motion in many different senses; for example, a thing may impose the motion or merely arouse it, urge it on. The efficient cause, properly so called, is a source in the former sense; it effects or imposes motion by its own agency. According to Heidegger, however, the proper sense of causality in Aristotle is the latter one: not efficiency (imposition by one's own agency), but abetting, fostering, encouraging, arousing. Since the name does not determine the issue one way or another, however, we shall have to have recourse to the actual examples Aristotle provides. It is precisely in his choice of examples that Aristotle expresses his sense of causality, his sense of the "whence."

Aristotle provides three main sets of examples of this cause. In the first introduction of it as the whence or the source of the motion, Aristotle explains himself as follows: "For instance, counseling is this kind of cause, such as a father counsels his son, and, on the whole, the maker is this kind of cause of the thing made" (194b31). The second set of examples occurs a few lines down: "The sower of seeds, the doctor, the counselor, and, on the whole, the maker, are all things whence the beginning of a change emerges" (195a22). The final example is introduced when this cause is called the first κινῆσαν, "the first setting into motion." Aristotle illustrates: "For instance, why did they go to war? Because of the abduction" (198a19).

These are the examples from which we have to gather the sense of the causality that has come to be called—but not by Aristotle himself—"efficient causality." The paradigm case of such causality was taken—after Aristotle's death—to be the maker, the craftsman, and, very often, in particular the sculptor. The other instances of this type of cause, for example, counseling, were indeed always recognized as belonging within efficient causality but as derived forms, remote ones, ones to be understood by reference to the paradigm case. The pure case is the sculptor, the one who, as it seems, by himself imposes a form onto a matter.

We see from Aristotle's examples, however, that such a maker is not at all the Stagirite's own paradigm case. He does not place the maker first; and we may suppose that Aristotle does place first that which deserves the first place, that which is the prime instance. In fact, Aristotle suggests that the maker belongs to the list of examples only if we speak roughly, generally, on the whole. The maker is the derived form, and the pure cases, the paradigms, are counseling, sowing, doctoring, and abducting.

Now it is only in one particular sense that these can be called "the whence" of the motion: they are that which rouses up the motion, or releases the motion, but not that which produces motion by its own efficacy or agency. To counsel someone is not to force him or her into action; it is not to be the agent of the action, for that remains the other's action. Nor, of course, is it to do nothing; it is to encourage the other, urge her on, rouse her up. To counsel is to appeal to the freedom of the other, not to usurp that freedom.

For Heidegger, counseling, in its genuine sense, is equivalent to caring:

> In the word "counsel," we now hear only the more superficial, utilitarian meaning of counsel: giving advice, i.e., giving practical directives. In the proper sense, however, to give counsel means to take

into care, to retain in care that which is cared for, and thus to found an affiliation. Ordinarily, to give counsel means almost the opposite: to impart a directive [or, today, to prescribe a psychoactive drug] and then dismiss the one who has been counseled. (*HI*, 41/34)

If Heidegger is correct, then Aristotle's example of the father as a counselor is especially well chosen. The father is precisely the counselor who takes the counseled one into his care, retains him in care, and never dismisses him. The father is the prototype of the counselor, so much so that to be a counselor is to be a father, and vice versa: to be a father is not simply to beget an offspring but to care for him (or her), raise him, counsel him, and so beget another man. Thus for Aristotle, a father, as a man who begets a man, is a cause of the type under consideration. But that does not make the father an efficient cause. On the contrary, "to beget a man" must be taken in its full sense: to beget a real man, a fully developed man, and that requires care, affiliation, counsel, all of which are matters not of force but of nurture. Thus a man is not the *efficient* cause of another man but the *nurturing* cause.[1]

To consider for a moment Aristotle's other examples, sowing seed obviously does not make the corn grow in the sense of forcing the corn up. Corn cannot be forced. To sow seed is merely to provide the right conditions for the corn to arise. To sow is, in a sense, to encourage the corn to grow, to call it forth into action, to release its potential for growth, but it is not to bring about that action by one's own agency. The corn has to have it in itself to grow, or else sowing and nurturing will be of no avail. Sowing is thus not an efficient cause; it does not impose growth but only prepares or abets it.

Likewise, doctors (at least the doctors of Aristotle's time) do not cause health by their own agency. The doctor merely prescribes the right conditions for the body's natural health to reassert itself. Nature heals; the doctor is only the midwife to health. Aristotle's example of doctoring is then not an example of efficient causality but of abetting causality.

In a perfectly analogous way, an abduction is not an efficient cause of war; it does not by itself force the offended parties to declare war. All it does is rouse them, stir them up, or perhaps merely release their latent hostility, but they themselves freely respond to this perceived provocation by going to war—or not.

It is then clear that Aristotle's paradigm examples of this kind of cause are by no means instances of imposing a form onto a submissive matter. For Aristotle, this so-called efficient cause is in fact not the responsible agent, the one which, supposedly, by its own efficacy brings about the effect. This cause is not an efficient cause but instead, as Aristotle's examples make very plain, a cause that is efficacious only by acting in partnership with that upon which it acts. There must be some change or product latent in the matter, and this cause amounts to assisting that change or product to come to fruition by releasing it or arousing it. Without the cooperation of the matter—i.e., without the potential for activity on the part of the matter—the efficacy of this cause would come to naught. Since this cause amounts to a releasing, there must be some latent activity to be released. Or, in terms of rousing, this cause requires some counterpart which can be roused. The point is that this cause does require a genuine counterpart, a genuine sharer in a common venture; both parties must be agents, both must play an active role. An efficient cause may perhaps impose a form onto a passive stone, but Aristotle's examples point in the direction of abetting, and that requires another agent rather than a patient. Abetting is directed at something that can actively take up the proffered aid, not at something that would passively undergo a compelling force.

In Aristotle's paradigm examples, the roles of activity and passivity are entirely intermingled. They are instances of genuine partnerships in which each party is both active and passive; each party gives direction to and takes direction from the other, and it is ordinarily extremely difficult to say on which side the absolutely first action lies. Consider the case of the abduction and the war. Is the abduction merely a pretext for going to war, or is it a genuine provocation, a genuine motive? That is, which side begins the war? It would be almost impossible to say, since there is no such thing as a provocation or a motive in itself. A motive obtains its motivating force only by means of the decision made by the motivated person to recognize it as a motive. A motive is *nothing* if it is not accepted as a motive. Nor is any action in itself a provocation; even an abduction becomes an abduction, i.e., a provocation, only if it is taken as such by the provoked party. Thus it is the reaction to the abduction that first makes it be an abduction properly so called (and not a neutral picking up and transporting). A provocation becomes a provocation only when the provoked party confirms that it has been provoked. When will the provocation be sufficiently grievous to call for war? Precisely when, by declaring war, the offended party takes it as sufficiently grievous. In other words, it is the declaration of war that makes the provocation a provocation, and we could say that the war makes the provocation as much as the provocation makes the war. Thus it is impossible to provoke into war a nation that refuses to be so provoked, and provocation can therefore not be an efficient cause of a war. It can only be a rousing cause, one which merely, as Shakespeare says, "wakens the sleeping sword of war." Only what is sleeping—i.e., potentially awake—can be wakened; wakening cannot be imposed on something that lacks the potential for it. The ones provoked into war, then, must be both passive and active; they must be presented with an occasion to make war, and they must actively take up that occasion and make it effective as a motive for war.

The same activity and passivity are to be found on the side of the provokers. What shall they do to provoke their enemies into war? Indeed they will have to act in some way or other. In one sense, then, they begin the war; they take the first step, and they are the source of all the motion which is the war. But in another sense, they take direction from their enemies, and their action is in reality a *response* to their enemies. Thus they are not the *absolutely* first beginners of the war. They take direction from their enemies in the sense that their provocative act must spring from a knowledge of their enemies. Their provocative act must be appropriate to their enemies. For example, whom shall they choose to abduct, or how many do they need to abduct? If they wish to start a war, they must know exactly how far their enemies can be pushed before those enemies will consider themselves sufficiently provoked to engage in hostilities. Thus the provokers are responding to their enemies as well as acting on them.

Abetting, too, presupposes such a genuine partnership, where activity and passivity occur on both sides. Abetting is not an efficient cause, where all the agency lies on the one side and all the passivity on the other. In the first place, it is obvious that, by itself, abetting or nurturing is nothing. That is, it is nothing to one who cannot respond to the abetting; it is not possible to counsel a stone. For there to be abetting, there must be activity on the part of both the abetter and the abetted. Likewise, there must be passivity on both parts; the abetted has to receive the abetting, but the abetting has to be appropriate. That is, the abetters have to receive direction from the possibilities of development on the part of the abetted.

Counseling is a prime example of this intermingling of activity and passivity. The counselor has to take direction from the one she is counseling, as much as she has to give direction to him. That is why Aristotle's example of the father counseling his own child is, again, very happily chosen. The counselor must know intimately the one she is to counsel. The counseling must be appropriate to the one counseled, which is to say that it must not only be directed *to* the counseled but must take direction *from* the counseled. Thus the counseled rouses up the counseling nearly as much as the counseling rouses up the counseled, and it is extremely difficult to say on which side lies the absolutely first beginning, the absolutely first whence.

Perhaps this peculiar intermingling of activity and passivity, agent and patient, directing and directed, is the reason Aristotle's formulations of this cause become so convoluted. For instance, while he begins by asking simply about the whence or the source of the motion, he comes to formulate this cause as "the whence from which arises the first beginning of the change" or "that whence the first beginning emerges." In other words,

Aristotle comes to ask not merely about the first source but about the source of that source. In seeking the whence *of* the first beginning, Aristotle is thus seeking the beginning of the beginning or the whence of the whence, an inquiry that obviously would keep getting deferred to an earlier whence. There is no absolute, definitive first whence—that is what is expressed in Aristotle's reflexive formulations of this cause. Now I maintain that there is reflexivity in these formulations precisely because there is reciprocity in the cause that abets. That cause does indeed have a whence of its own, since it must be appropriate to that which it abets, i.e., must receive its direction from the object's possibilities of being abetted. If the whence amounts to rousing or releasing rather than imposing, then to speak of the whence does inexorably lead to speaking of the whence of the whence. That is, it leads to the necessary partnership between the rousing and the aroused, in which the cause relates not to a passive matter but to an active one, whose possibilities of action must be taken into account by the rousing agent. With a rousing cause, it is well-nigh impossible to determine the absolutely first source of the action, since the actor and the acted upon are mutually implicatory and take direction from one another. The counselor has to take counsel from the counseled, and the motive has to take its motivating power from the motivated. Is it the nurturing that calls forth the nurtured, or the nurtured that directs the nurturing? The answer is both, and thus neither one is absolutely first, which therefore accounts for the reflexivity in Aristotle's formulations of the whence, where the whence gets deferred into a prior whence. By posing the question of the cause the way he does, Aristotle is suggesting that there is reflexivity or partnership in this cause. Thus both Aristotle's examples and his very formulation of this cause indicate that he does not mean an efficient cause but a rousing or nurturing cause.

Yet even if Aristotle's paradigm examples do involve a partnership, an abetting, which prevents us from taking the sense of causality in play there as efficient causality, nevertheless Aristotle also includes the maker in his examples. Then what about the maker, the artisan, the sculptor? Is such a one an efficient cause, or is she to be understood in the sense of a nurturing cause, as in the paradigm cases? Is there the same partnership between the artisan and her material? Does the maker impose a form onto the matter, or does the matter impose a form onto her? Who or what determines the form of the sculpture: the marble or the sculptor?

Today, by means of lasers, practically any form may be imposed onto any matter. A laser beam is indifferent to the matter; nothing can stop a laser from its predetermined, preprogrammed efficacy. The matter makes no difference to a laser, and it, or its program, is the absolute first whence, the absolute beginning of the motion or change. Here we encounter an efficient cause in its pure state.

But let us take a traditional sculptor, such as Michelangelo. Is he to be understood as an efficient cause or, rather, as a midwife? That is to say, does he impose a form onto a submissive matter, or does he take direction from the matter and merely assist at the birth of the statue with which the particular block of marble is already pregnant? We have Michelangelo's own testimony that the latter is the case. He claimed that the task of a sculptor is merely to chisel away the extraneous bits of marble so as to expose the statue already present within. The sculptor, in other words, does not impose form, he merely allows the form to emerge by *releasing* it. He takes direction from the marble, determining what the marble itself wants, as it were, to bring forth. His activity is then to nurture that form into existence. He is so little an efficient cause that it is impossible to say whether his action calls forth the statue or the latent statue calls forth his activity.

In this way, the maker, the artisan, the supposed paradigm of an efficient cause, can be understood as a derived form of the paradigm case of the abetting cause. An artisan can be understood as a midwife rather than an imposer. If we think of any maker or craftsman not as a laser beam but as a Michelangelo, as a respecter of the material on which she works, then the maker is not an efficient cause but is instead, like the counselor, a nurturer, an abetter. That is precisely Heidegger's interpretation of ancient causality; for the ancients, to be a cause meant to respect and abet. Furthermore, that respectful outlook constitutes the essence of ancient technology; ancient technology is the disclosure of things in general as there to be respected. The practice that issues from this theory then amounts to abetting or nurturing, as we will see when we examine Heidegger's account of handcraft. For now, we merely need to ask whether his interpretation is true to Aristotle.

Heidegger has been accused of violence in his interpretations of the ancients, but here the evidence points to his view as the faithful one. In contrast, the traditional imputation of the notion of efficient causality to Aristotle surely appears to be violent. After all, Aristotle himself twice places the maker last in his list of examples, and on the third occasion (the example of the abduction) he does not include the maker at all. Moreover, Aristotle also distances himself from the maker by stating explicitly that the maker fits within the list of examples only roughly, only if we speak in a general way or on the whole. In other words, Aristotle is expressing quite unmistakably his view that the maker is not the best example. The craftsman does not best illustrate the whence of motion, as that whence is understood by Aristotle. The better example is the counselor or the sower of seeds. That is Aristotle's order, and Heidegger's interpretation is the one that is respectful of that order. To take the maker as the paradigm is to be unfaithful to Aristotle, and to proceed to interpret the maker as an efficient cause is to be doubly violent to Aristotle. Thus we find that the evidence points in the direction of Heidegger's position that both the name and the concept of efficient cause are foreign to Aristotle. It perhaps remains to be seen whether Heidegger can fully work out the alternative notion of causality, but at least we can appreciate the justice of his attempting to do so.

Before returning to Heidegger, let us now summarize the ancient view of causality as expressed in the doctrine of the four causes. First of all, we reject the efficient cause as one of the four. That name is not appropriate to what Aristotle himself understands as the source of motion, namely an arousing or a releasing. Then if I were to propose a new name, guided by what is hopefully a more adequate grasp of Aristotle's sense of this cause, I would call it the "rousing cause," the "nurturing cause," or, at the limit, the "nudging cause."[2] And with regard to causality in general, the one single concept by which all four causes are causes in the same sense, it could be called abetting or (active) releasing. Heidegger's term "obligation" is meant to express the same sense of providing favorable conditions, assisting at birth, midwifery, ob-stetrics. The antithesis is imposition.

Let us raise one final question within the framework of the ancient doctrine of the four causes: when and why did it happen that the paradigm instance of causality became efficient causality and causality in general came to be understood as imposition? It occurred not long after Aristotle's death. Surely, by the medieval era the notion of rousing causality is completely overshadowed by efficient causality. (And the latter is then reinterpreted back into Aristotle. The "whence" of Aristotle is, from medieval times down to our own, translated as "efficient cause," a perfect example of digging up merely what one has already buried. In fact, until Heidegger, the notion of efficient causality as an authentically Aristotelian notion is never even questioned.) In the medieval age, efficient causality indeed plays a central role in philosophy. For example, the notion of efficient causality, rather than releasing causality, is the basis of one of Thomas Aquinas' famous five ways of proof for the existence of God. In fact, this way of proof amounts to an extension of the notion of efficient causality to God, who becomes the ultimate efficient cause; and Being, to be in general, is understood as meaning to participate in some way in efficient causality. Nevertheless, medieval philosophy is not totally divorced from Aristotle's conception of causality, and the doctrine of the four causes remains intact there (although causality is not understood in the original Aristotelian sense). Indeed, the final cause is the basis of another of Thomas' five ways of proof. In the modern age, however, the final cause, the material cause, and the formal cause are laughed out of court, and so is the notion that matter may be pregnant with a form and thereby deserving of respect. Only the efficient cause is allowed, and the notion of causality in general as imposition is solidly entrenched. It is true that some modern philosophers were skeptical about our knowledge of any causal connections among things. What these thinkers rejected, however, was not the sense of causality as imposition, as efficient causality, but the possibility of our human intellect ever knowing the causal connections among things. These philosophers were precisely skeptics, not reinterpreters of causality. Thus in the modern age, the sense of causality as imposition, a sense slowly brewing since the death of Aristotle, holds complete sway.

What does this change in the understanding of causality amount to in terms of Heidegger's history of Being, the domain of the original, motivating events? It is a reflection of the withdrawal of Being; or, more precisely, it is a response to that withdrawal. It is what the gods leave behind in their flight. When Being veils itself, when the gods abscond, then humans are left with a distorted sense of what it means to be in general, and in particular a distorted sense of nature. They might then see nature as what is there to be imposed upon and might view causality as imposition. Impositional technology is thus motivated by the flight of the gods and is accordingly, for Heidegger, not a matter of human failure but, instead, a fate.

Having exposed the sense of causality in Aristotle, we can now understand better the sense of this fate. That is, the causality in play here, by which the withdrawal of Being "causes" modern technology, must be the Aristotelian sense of causality, namely abetting or releasement. Therefore, the fate is not one imposed on human beings, as if they were passive and bore no responsibility for their fate. Heidegger is not exempting humans from responsibility for their fate. He is in no way a "fatalist"; he is not suggesting that humans simply wait and hope for the best. Human beings are not passive matter to be imposed upon by Being. The history of Being, the approach or retreat of the gods, does not impose anything on humans. The gods are indeed the prime movers, but all movers must take direction from the possibilities latent in the ones to be moved.

That is why Heidegger is entirely consistent to call the modern age a fate and to claim that only a fate will overcome it, while, at the same time, urging greater human resoluteness and watchfulness. Heidegger does not absolve humans from responsibility; he heightens human responsibility in the sense of moral responsibility. What he deflates are the pretensions of humans in the power of their own efficacy. If humans think they are the only ones responsible for their accomplishments, if humans think they are efficient causes, if humans think their productions are their creations, then Heidegger's philosophy is ready to expose those claims as pretensions. The concept of responsibility may involve either blame or credit; Heidegger heightens human responsibility insofar as humans can be blamed, and he diminishes responsibility insofar as humans deserve credit. The blame (the moral responsibility) is humanity's own, the credit (the claim to be personally responsible for some accomplishment, to have accomplished something by one's own efficacy) must be shared (with Being or nature). Heidegger's philosophy is, therefore, just as Sartre characterizes existentialism in general, a most austere philosophy and has nothing in common with inaction or moral laxity.[3]

Abetting causality as a reading of Heidegger

We arrive now at the second of the two general questions we raised concerning Heidegger's view of causality as understood by the ancients. We have shown a textual basis in Aristotle for Heidegger's interpretation; i.e., what we asserted as Heidegger's view is borne out through a close reading of Aristotle. The task is now to return to Heidegger's essay on technology in order to see how Heidegger himself presents and develops his interpretation. Causality, as understood in the doctrine of the four causes, means, most fundamentally, for Heidegger, abetting or nurturing. Its antithesis is imposition—i.e., force, compulsion. Yet it is by no means apparent on the surface of Heidegger's text that this is indeed his understanding. Rather than express himself with an immediate, facile intelligibility, his strategy is to introduce a whole series of terms, each of them highly nuanced, in order to clarify his position by their cumulative effect. Yet the nuances are easily overlooked or mistaken, even by a reader of the original German, and they are very difficult to bring out in a translation. Nevertheless, if we approach Heidegger's text as deserving of the same care required to read Aristotle, these nuances will yield themselves up.

In the published English translation of "Die Frage nach der Technik," the series of terms in question is the following: "being indebted," "being responsible," *hypokeisthai*, "starting something on its way," "occasioning," "inducing," *poiesis*, "bringing-forth," *physis*, "revealing," and *aletheuein*. These are the terms in which Heidegger couches his understanding of ancient causality and ancient technology. At first sight, a very mixed bag.

Let us begin with Heidegger's most general sense of causality, as understood within the context of the four causes. We said that Heidegger takes causality there as obligation, in the specific sense that the causality amounts to something in between the extremes of compelling and doing nothing. The four causes are not ways of imposing or forcing change, and neither do they play a merely passive role. The four causes *let* the change come about—in the active sense of letting, namely: nurturing, releasing, abetting, providing the proper conditions, encouraging, nudging, rousing.

The four causes are not "responsible" for the change, in the sense of taking all the credit for it. Conversely, the change does not owe everything to the causes. The obligation in question is the specific one of indebtedness for assistance in coming to one's own self-emergence or in achieving one's own accomplishment. This sort of obligation, I take it, is what is meant in colloquial English by saying we are "much obliged" to someone.

This term, "obligation," Heidegger's *Verschulden*, is rendered in the published translation variously as follows: "being indebted," "being responsible," "being responsible and being indebted," and "owing and being responsible." Part of the difficulty is indeed that the reader of these terms will hardly realize that Heidegger has a single unified concept of causality at all. More to the point, however, the term "being responsible" is quite misleading, especially when applied to the four causes taken together. For instance, the translation says on page 9: "According to our example, they [the four causes] are responsible for the silver chalice's lying ready before us as a sacrificial vessel."

This surely gives the impression that the four causes, acting in unison, have brought it about that the chalice is lying there ready before us, i.e., already made and ready for use. It makes the chalice the effect of the causes, ready-made by the four causes, delivered up and ready for use. This impression is unfaithful to Heidegger's intention in two ways: in the first place, Heidegger does not maintain that the effect of the four causes is to produce something ready-made; nor, secondly, is the activity of the four causes to be understood as an effectuating at all.

The phrase "lying ready before us" and, in the next line, the phrase "lying before and lying ready" translate Heidegger's *Vorliegen und Bereitliegen*. These translations are defensible grammatically, but they are not defensible philosophically, especially since Heidegger immediately places in parentheses the Greek term he is attempting to render. That term is ὑποκεῖσθαι (*hypokeisthai*). The sense of this word for Heidegger is "to lie underneath." It means to be the prepared ground for the appearance of something. It does not refer to what is ready-made but to the making ready of something; it does not refer to something appearing but to the condition of an appearance of something. Specifically, the word "ready" in "lying ready" does not mean ready for use; it means ready to come to appearance, ready to come forth as a chalice, and only then be ready to be used. In other words, the four causes have prepared the chalice for its own coming-forth, they have prepared the ground for the chalice; they are the chalice's ὑποκείμενον (*hypokeimenon*, "substratum"). What the four causes accomplish is what lies underneath the chalice, its ground. But the causes do not effect the chalice, do not bring it about, do not compel it to come forth on its ground. The causes cannot go so far.

That is why Heidegger, in the previous paragraph, explicitly rejects the notion of the causes as effecting. His term *Verschulden*, he says, is not to be construed in terms of effecting, as the published translation rightly puts it. The question remains, however, as to whether, by translating *Verschulden* as "being responsible," the translator did construe it in the wrong way.

To return now to the passage under consideration, its meaning is as follows: "According to our example, the silver chalice is obliged to the four causes for making ready the ground upon which it might come forth as a sacrificial vessel" (FT, 12). Compare that to the published translation, already cited, which speaks of the four causes as "responsible for the silver chalice's lying ready before us as a sacrificial vessel." This latter is a possibly correct translation, as far as grammar is concerned, and a casual reader of the original German might well take the passage in that sense. But a Heideggerian text, just like an Aristotelian one, does not yield up its treasures to a casual reading. Indeed, in terms of philosophical sense, the published version entirely misses the point. It fails to capture the essential nuance, for, as the contrast with our own version makes clear, it expresses a notion of causality as effecting, precisely that which Heidegger warned against.

The essential nuance, to put it as simply as possible, is that causality is nurturing, not effecting. That is what Heidegger expresses by saying the chalice is obliged to the four causes for its *hypokeisthai*, for that which "lies underneath," for that upon which it might come forth. The four causes are not responsible for the thing made in the sense of bringing about the existence of the thing, compelling it into existence, delivering it up ready-made. The four causes offer nurture; they lie underneath the thing in the sense of making ready the ground, preparing the conditions, for the potentiality in the matter to actualize itself. That is how, according to Heidegger, the ancients conceived of causality: not as imposition, but as nurture.

Thus the term *hypokeisthai*, "to lie beneath," confirms the choice of the word "obligation" (instead of "being responsible") to render *Verschulden*. The four causes place the proper ground underneath the thing, they provide the support or nourishment the thing needs to come forth. The thing is, then, in the precise sense, much obliged to the four causes; but it does not owe everything to them, they are not by themselves responsible for the thing. Consequently, "to oblige" and "to lie beneath," the first two terms Heidegger employs to characterize ancient causality, bear out the view that he interprets it in the sense of abetting or nurture. As we proceed through the list, we will find the same interpretation expressed again and again, and the cumulative effect ought to be convincing.

Letting, active letting, letting all the way to the end

The next step Heidegger takes in characterizing the causality of the four causes occurs immediately following the proposal of the notion of *hypokeisthai*. In fact, it is to clarify this notion that Heidegger launches a new discussion, introducing a new central term. As *hypokeisthai*, as "lying under," the four causes prepare the ground upon which the thing might come forth. This accomplishment of the four causes is now described in a disarmingly simple way: the four causes "let the thing come forth" (FT, 12/9). That is the published translation, and it is unexceptionable. It remains to be seen, however, whether the translation will remain faithful to the spirit of this simple assertion.

The most important word in the statement, the new central term on which the discussion will turn, is the word "let." That most precisely describes the accomplishment of the four causes: not to effect or compel but to let. Of course, this "letting" must be understood in the proper sense, i.e., in the active sense, which we have called rousing, nurturing, abetting. It must still be understood as a type of letting or allowing, though not as a passive laissez-faire. To ensure that the letting be understood in the proper way, Heidegger introduces three derivative terms intended to specify the sense of letting. The word for "let" in German is *lassen*, and the new terms are compounds formed by adding prefixes to it: *los-lassen*, *an-lassen*, and *ver-an-lassen*. Heidegger writes them just that way, with hyphens to call attention to the root word, *lassen*, i.e., to show that they are derived from *lassen*, that they are forms of letting.

What do the terms mean? That can be determined by examining the respective prefixes; *los* means "loose," *an* means "on" or "to," and *ver-an* means "all the way to" or "all the way to the end." Thus the prefixes set the words in order from a more passive to an emphatically active sense of letting. The order is this: from letting loose, to guiding onto the proper path to some end, to being in attendance all the way to that end. As applied to the four causes, the sense of the terms is as follows. *Los-lassen*: the four causes let something loose or release it. *An-lassen*: they then let it go on to its path of development. *Ver-an-lassen*: their letting escorts the thing all the way to the end of its development.

It could not be clearer that these terms describe very precisely the process of nurturing. First the daughter (or son) must be given her freedom, then she must be urged onto the right path, and then she must have a shoulder to lean on throughout her journey to adulthood. Or, first the seed must be released, then it must be nourished, and then it must be tended all the way to its end. As Heidegger's terms suggest (in view of the common root, *lassen*), each step is indeed a matter of letting; to nurture is not to compel. But as the prefixes also indicate, this is an active letting; to nurture is to let with full diligence. And so we see that here again Heidegger is characterizing the causality of the four causes, the sense in which they make ready the ground for the thing, and let it come forth, as the active letting connoted by the terms "abetting" or "nurturing."

Heidegger proceeds to summarize his view by stating very succinctly that the *An-lassen* which makes something obliged (to the four causes) is a *Ver-an-lassen*. It would perhaps be quite difficult to translate this statement elegantly and briefly, but the meaning that would need to be brought out is this: something is obliged to the four causes not merely for letting it enter onto the path by which it will fully come forth but for caring for it all the way to the end of its full coming forth. Thus the sentence confirms our view that Heidegger's interpretation of ancient causality is abetting or nurture, i.e., letting in the active sense, letting all the way to the end.

The published English translation, on page 9, renders the sentence in question as follows: "It is in the sense of such a starting something on its way into arrival that being responsible is an occasioning or an inducing to go forward." The crucial idea of "letting" has here been almost entirely covered over. *An-lassen* has become "starting," and *Ver-an-lassen* "occasioning or inducing." Thus, instead of "letting, active letting, and letting all the way to the end," the published translation of this central series of terms is "letting, starting, and occasioning or inducing." Surely this translation does not remain faithful to the idea of letting but, instead, proceeds in the direction of effecting, which is exactly what must be avoided.

The proper translation of *Ver-an-lassen* becomes even more critical in the next lines of Heidegger's text, for there he explicitly proposes the term as the name of the essence of causality in the Greek sense. It would indeed be difficult to find a simple English word to use as a translation, since our language does not seem to possess a compound of the verb "let" that would add the nuance of activity, "letting with full diligence," "letting all the way to the end." The word "nurturing" captures the sense but is too free. I cannot do better than propose "active letting" (perhaps "abetting") as the least inadequate rendering in the present context. Heidegger's full statement then comes down (slightly paraphrasing) to this: "Considering what the Greeks experienced when they spoke of something as being caused, namely its being 'much obliged,' we now give the term *Ver-an-lassen* ['active letting'] a further sense, beyond the usual meaning of the common term *Veranlassen* ['occasioning'], and it then names the very essence of causality as thought in the Greek manner" (FT, 12/10).

Thus Heidegger explicitly distinguishes his term *Ver-an-lassen* from an ordinary German word, *Veranlassen* (the same spelling, without the hyphens). The latter is indeed well translated by "occasioning," and it names the typical modern notion of causality. Consequently, the published translation, which renders both terms, Heidegger's highly nuanced one and the ordinary one, by the same word, "occasioning," must be misleading, since it makes no distinction here where a distinction is explicit and crucial. The published translation merely says that the one occasioning is more inclusive in meaning than the other. Let us examine the distinction as Heidegger expressly draws it, in order to see why the distinction is not one of mere greater inclusiveness; on the contrary, the term "occasioning" is appropriate only in the one case and not at all in the other.

Heidegger characterizes the ordinary word, without the hyphens, as follows: "In its ordinary sense, the term *Veranlassen* means nothing more than collision and setting off" (FT, 12/10). Therefore his special word is not to be understood in terms of collision and setting off. Heidegger is surely alluding here to the favorite example of causality in modern thought, namely the colliding of one billiard ball into another and the subsequent "setting off" of the motion of the second one. This was the example invoked by those skeptical modern philosophers who maintained that there is not any humanly knowable causal connection between the two events, the collision and the starting of the movement of the second ball. All we know is that on the *occasion* of event A (the collision of one ball into another), event B (the motion of the second ball) regularly follows. There is no communication of the motion of the one ball to the other, the one ball does not *give* motion to the other, and so the second ball's motion is simply, and inexplicably, *set off*. We cannot have insight into the intrinsic connection, if any, between the two events. All we have is the extrinsic connection of temporal succession: on the *occasion* of the one event, the other is *started* or *set off*. "Occasioning" is thus the appropriate word for this understanding of causality, but it is as foreign to the ancients as can possibly be imagined. Thus it is misleading to translate *Ver-an-lassen*, Heidegger's proper name for causality in Greek thought, as "occasioning," and the same applies to the translation of *An-lassen* as "starting." Both these English words are appropriate only to our own ordinary, modern, understanding of causality.

Nor does it matter whether occasioning is taken in the skeptical sense or not. Heidegger does seem to be invoking the skeptical theory of occasionalism. Yet he realizes that the common (nonphilosophical) understanding of causality today is not skeptical. For the everyday understanding, causality means efficient causality, and examples of efficient causality are obvious. From the everyday standpoint, it is self-evident that collisions *cause* motion, so much so that the skeptical view would be taken as the typical reversal of the clear and the obscure which philosophy is notorious for. (Anyone still innocent of modern philosophy will surely find it difficult even to imagine what the skeptical arguments could be.) Except to some philosophers and theoretical scientists, the collision is seen today not merely as a temporal predecessor but as *responsible* for the motion of the second ball, as *imposing* that motion.

While the commonsense view might be slightly closer to the ancient understanding, Heidegger's point is that it actually has much more in common with the skeptical outlook than with Greek thinking. In fact, the skeptical view and today's commonsense understanding are identical in essentials. For both, the paradigm case of causality is still, as Heidegger says, collision. For both, what counts as causality is efficient causality. The only difference is that the skeptical view denies to human beings the possibility of ever coming to know the causal connections among things, while for common sense the causal connection is, at least sometimes, obvious to us. Yet what is meant by "causal connection" is the same for both; it means collision: that is, violence, force, overpowering, the imposing of motion from one thing to another, or, in short, efficient causality. For skepticism, only God could have insight into the working of this causality, only God could see the motion being imposed by one billiard ball onto the other, but for both views the meaning of causality is the same: imposition.

It is that sense of imposition that rules out the term *occasioning* as a translation of *Ver-an-lassen*, the term Heidegger proposes as the proper name for the essence of causality as thought in the Greek manner. What is distinctive about the Greek understanding is that there causality does not mean violence, forcing, effecting. It means, basically, *Lassen*, letting. This letting is to be understood in as active a sense as possible; yet it does not ever mean to impose instead of abet. Thus Heidegger's term *Ver-an-lassen* is not "more inclusive" than the ordinary word *Veranlassen*; on the contrary, these terms are incompatible, and only the former could apply to the ancient sense of causality.

Producing, bringing-forth, nature

We have now worked through the first half of the long series of terms by which Heidegger characterizes the causality of the four causes. Causing is "obliging," "making ready the ground," "letting," "active letting," and "letting all the way to the end." All these terms point in the same direction, toward an interpretation of the causality of the four causes as nurturing rather than imposing. The next two terms in the series, however, at first appear to revoke that interpretation, for they assert that the causality of the four causes is a matter of "producing."

Heidegger introduces the new terms by asking about the unity of the four causes, the unity of the four modes of active letting. He begins his account of the unity by placing the letting in a new light: the four causes let what is not yet present come into presence. The idea, in more traditional terms, is that the four causes let what does not yet exist come into existence. Here we encounter a kind of contradiction, for is it possible to *let* something that does not exist come into existence? Is it possible to nurture something so that it comes to be? At first view, that is not possible: only what already exists can be nurtured, and so nothing can be nurtured from nonbeing to being. One thing can be nurtured to give birth to another, such as seeds can be nurtured to bear crops, but nothing can be nurtured to give birth to itself. A thing can be nurtured so as to develop to a more perfect stage, but then it must already exist in some less perfect way. In other words, letting presupposes something already there to be let; and so existence is *presupposed* by letting and cannot follow from it. Thus if "letting" means to let into being, then the letting must be reinterpreted away from nurturing and toward producing. That is precisely the course Heidegger seems to pursue when he says, "Accordingly, the four causes are ruled over, through and through, and in an integral way, by a bringing, one which brings about the presence of something" (FT, 12/10). The last phrase, if taken in its more colloquial sense, could also be translated as follows: "one which produces the existence of something." Thus Heidegger is here interpreting the "letting" of the four causes as a bringing, a bringing about, a producing. Indeed, Heidegger says explicitly that this bringing is the dominant character; it holds sway over the four causes and integrates them into a single causal nexus. The character of "bringing something about" thus has an ascendancy over the "letting" and determines it. The letting is to be understood as a bringing about or a producing, rather than vice versa.

The sense of the bringing as a producing is reinforced by Heidegger's appeal to Plato in this context. Heidegger cites a passage from the *Symposium* in which Plato gives the name ποίησις (*poiesis*) to any causal action by which something comes into being from nonbeing. That is to say, the bringing now at issue, the dominant character of the causality of the four causes, is *poiesis*. And *poiesis* precisely means making or producing; *poiesis* is the bringing into being of what was previously not in being. Heidegger's own rendering of the word *poiesis* here is *Her-vor-bringen*. Translated quite literally, Heidegger's term simply means "bringing-forth." Yet, in the context, it is clear that what is meant here is "bringing forth *into being*," causing to pass from nonbeing to being, or, in other words, "making," "producing." In fact, Heidegger's term *Her-vor-bringen*, "bringing-forth," in its more colloquial sense, does mean simply "producing." And, in another place, Heidegger himself asserts this sense to be the predominant one: "Bringing-forth today means the making and fabricating of an individual object" (*GP*, 85/76).

The two new terms that characterize the causality of the four causes, "bringing" (or, more specifically, "bringing forth") and *poiesis*, thus seem to go back on what was said about the four causes as modes of nurturing. Instead of assisting something to give birth or to develop, it now seems that the four causes produce the existence of something out of its previous nonexistence. The four causes bring it about that what they cause exists in the first place, and they do not merely nurture something along by gearing into it, by going with the thing's own flow. The four causes apparently cause the existence of the thing and first produce its "flow." Thus the causality of the four causes cannot be a matter of "gearing into," since there is nothing to gear into until the four causes have brought it forth. It seems that the thing "owes everything" to the four causes, is produced by them, and is not merely abetted or encouraged. In other words, Heidegger's current discussion implies an understanding of causality as imposing, as bringing about or effecting the existence of the caused thing.

On account of this impression, i.e., the implication that the causality of the four causes is a producing, a bringing about, an imposing, Heidegger immediately goes on to say that "everything depends" on our thinking of *poiesis* in its full breadth and in the Greek sense. Everything depends on this, for otherwise we would indeed be misled into thinking of ancient causality as effecting and imposing. What then is the proper sense of *poiesis*? According to Heidegger, it does not merely refer to handcraft manufacture or to the artistic and poetic production of appearances and images. On the contrary, nature, too, is *poiesis*; in fact, nature is even the paradigm case of *poiesis*: "*Φύσις* [*physis*, 'nature'], too, self-emergence, is a bringing-forth, *poiesis*. *Physis* is even *poiesis* in the highest sense" (FT, 12/10).

How can nature be *poiesis* in the highest sense, the paradigm of bringing-forth or production? It can be the paradigm only if production does in fact primarily mean nurture. Production is then not equivalent to effecting, and so the terms "bringing-forth" and *poiesis* do not retract the notion of causality as nurturing or rousing. Let us try to make that clear.

We begin with the way Heidegger distinguishes nature from manufacture: "For what comes to be *φύσει* [*physei*, 'naturally'] has the source of the bringing-forth, e.g., the source of the blooming of the blossom, in itself" (FT, 12/10). On the other hand, what is brought forth by craft has the source of the bringing forth not in itself but in another, in the artisan.

Heidegger's term I have rendered in a preliminary and neutral way as "source" is *der Aufbruch*. This German term is an excellent candidate to translate κινῆσαν, Aristotle's word for the cause that is the source of the motion, the cause that sets the motion going, the cause that was later named—and understood as—the efficient cause. Heidegger's term has a wide range of meanings, but two basic senses are relevant here: "setting out on one's way" and "blossoming out." It refers then to a kind of setting out that is precisely a blossoming out. The term thus names not only the source—the setting out—but also the way that is set out upon, namely the process of blossoming or, more generally, growth. Thus the term specifies what sort of cause this source is and how it stands at the head of the motion.

In the first place, if the motion is a blossoming, then the source is certainly not an efficient cause, since blossoming cannot be imposed upon anything by an outside agent, cannot be forced upon a passive matter by an efficient cause. Nothing can *make* a bud blossom if it does not have it in itself to blossom. A bud can only blossom out naturally, which is to say that the source of the blossoming must lie within the bud; the blossoming has to be a *self*-emergence. The cause that is the source of a natural motion is then nature itself, the natural tendency of the bud to blossom out, its own directedness to a certain end, its own pregnancy, its own "flow" in a certain direction. What sort of cause is this? A directedness or a tendency is not an imposition; this cause has rather to be understood in the context of nurture. That is to say, this source is a participant in a process of nurture.

To make that explicit, let us look more closely at what does the nurturing in a natural process and what gets nurtured. Let us think of a bud as pregnant with a blossom, as naturally directed to that end. The potential of the bud is not an efficient cause; on the contrary, the potential is a *de*ficient cause. That is, it requires certain conditions in order to come to fruition. The bud will not blossom by itself. Nor can it be forced; it must be *allowed* to grow, it must be "actively let." To let a bud grow is to provide it with the required nourishment, the favorable conditions; it is then up to the bud to take advantage of these conditions. Now, these conditions and nutrients are also nature; they are, let us say, material nature, such as earth, light, water, and warmth. These conditions are precisely nutrients, i.e., nurturers, and not imposers; they cannot force growth. Natural conditions cannot make an artificial bud grow. The conditions merely gear into the thing's own flow, into its own nature, its inborn propensity toward motion in a certain direction. Conversely, to grow, to be nurtured, is to take up these conditions in an active way; to grow is to allow the conditions of growth to be effective as nutrients. Accordingly, the process of growth and the process of nurturing are mutually founding and are intertwined: they each let the other be.

Thus the source of a blossoming movement is nature, and the conditions that let the movement occur are also nature. In the process of growing or blossoming there is an interplay between the source and the conditions, a cooperation or joining together of the forces of nature. If we call the source the cause that was later understood as the efficient cause, then the conditions, taken in a broad sense to include not only material nature but the natural end as well, coincide with the other three causes. Thus all four causes are nature, and all four causes cooperate in producing the blossom. In other words, in bringing forth the blossom, in letting it come forth, the four causes are unified. They are unified as nature, as aspects of the one nature, and unified as cooperating forces, as joining together in a common project. In bringing forth a blossom, the four causes form a single causal nexus, and the forces of nature are unified. That is to say, as *poiesis*, as bringing something forth, *physis* manifests the unity of the four causes. The four causes play together, i.e., get unified, in a special way when it is a case of something coming forth naturally.

Thus the question of the unity of the four causes, the question with which Heidegger had initiated the present discussion, leads to *physis* as *poiesis*. The four causes are most one, their forces are most joined together into a single combined force, their forces are most concentrated, in the case of something produced naturally in the manner indicated: i.e., when the production is growth, when the source of the movement is natural (internal to the thing moved) and the external conditions that nurture it are also natural. Presumably, it is this concentration of forces that makes natural *poiesis* "*poiesis* in the highest sense," as Heidegger claims. Indeed Heidegger does say that *physis* is the highest form of *poiesis* "since" what comes forth by nature has the source of the coming-forth in itself. But Heidegger leaves us on our own to draw out this "since." *How* does that make *physis poiesis* in the highest sense? In other words, what sort of productive forces are being marshalled together here? In what sense is nature the most forceful form of production?

Nature is certainly not the most forceful, if force is taken in the usual sense, i.e., as imposition. A laser beam can impose the form of a flower, by, let us say, etching it into a piece of glass, more forcefully than nature can bring forth a blossom from a bud. The darling buds of May are liable to be shaken, which is to say that they are tender and, in Shakespeare's sonnet, easily "untrimmed," denuded. Nature is not a concentration of the forces of imposition; what is brought forth by nature is not imposed at all. On the contrary, nature's way of bringing forth is to nurture. The causal nexus in the case of nature is a nurturing nexus. Nature is a concentration of nurturing forces. So then we see how *physis* can be *poiesis* in the highest sense, how nature can be the highest form of production: only if production means nurture.

That is of course precisely what we have been trying to show: for Heidegger ancient causality is nurture, and the paradigm of production

[handwritten: land enclosure]

is growth, not imposition. Heidegger employed two further terms to characterize the causality of the four causes, the terms "bringing-forth" (or "production") and *poiesis* ("making" or "production"), and these seemed to imply a notion of imposition. But, according to Heidegger, "everything depends" on thinking of *poiesis* in its full breadth and in the Greek sense. We see now that that sense is *physis*, and this term in the list of characterizations restores the notion of nurture. If bringing-forth and *poiesis* are thought as *physis*, as nature, then production does indeed mean nurture. To bring forth does therefore not mean to bring into being, to impose existence; it means to produce the way nature produces, namely by helping along, by gearing into an already existing tendency in a certain direction. To bring forth thus means to abet, not to create ex nihilo. That is the conclusion we reach if we think of *poiesis* in its full breadth and in the Greek sense. That is to say, all of the terms—without exception—in Heidegger's list of characterizations of ancient causality do point in the same direction, the direction of nurture rather than imposition.

Manufacture and contemplation

We now need to see how this paradigm of nurture applies to production in the usual sense, i.e., to manufacture, to artificial as well as to natural production. Thereby we will begin to join the ancient theory of causality (= the essence of ancient technology) to the practice of ancient technology.

The essential difference between natural production and manufacture by craft amounts to the fact that, in the former, the source (the setting in motion) resides within what is to be produced, and in the latter case the source resides in another, in the artisan. What this signifies is that handcraft does not display the unity of the four causes as plainly as nature does. The causal nexus, in handcraft, does not entirely exemplify a marshaling of causal forces. In handcraft, therefore, the essential character of causality as nurture is less easily visible. Yet, for Heidegger, the same paradigm applies, and handcraft is not to be understood in terms of a new type of causality. The same type of causality holds sway in handcraft, but in a more hidden way.

Heidegger proceeds by offering three instances of handcraft production—i.e., three instances of ancient technology in practice—and shows how the paradigm of nurture applies. The three examples are the farmer, the waterwheel, and the artisan, such as the house builder or the silversmith. The first two can be disposed of rather easily, and we will concentrate on the third.

It is clear that the farmer is a nurturer. Heidegger's account of the traditional farmer implies nurture at every turn: "The field the farmer of old used to cultivate appeared differently, i.e., when to cultivate still meant to tend and to nurture. . . . In sowing the grain, the farmer consigns the seed to the forces of growth, and then he tends to its increase" (FT, 15–16/14–15). The notion of consigning to a higher force is at the heart of the attitude of the traditional farmer. It marks this farmer as a midwife, one who respects an already given pregnancy and who understands himself as being in service to it, submitting to it, gearing into it, rather than imposing on it.

The same attitude of respect is evident in the making of a waterwheel as compared to a hydroelectric dam. The waterwheel in an obvious sense gears into the natural forces of the river rather than imposing on them by direct opposition. Heidegger expresses it this way: the waterwheel is built (*baut*) into the river, but the river itself is mis-built (*verbaut*) into the hydroelectric plant. The word *verbaut* commonly means "blocked" or "obstructed," but it also connotes a wrongful building or a building that misuses or exhausts the building materials. The word is rendered in the published translation as "dammed up." That translation indeed captures part of Heidegger's sense, but it misses the central point, namely that the river is *used up* to make the power plant. The river is itself built into—i.e., made into—a power plant: the river is transformed into something else, into the power plant, and the river now takes its essence from the power plant. Thus the difference is clear: the waterwheel is built into the river, it gears into the flow, and the river remains what it was. But the power plant imposes on the river to such an extent that now the river itself is made into something else; it has been exhausted in favor of the hydroelectric plant. The river has been commandeered by the power plant and is now in essence nothing but a supplier of hydraulic pressure to the plant. The distinction between the respectful attitude of nurture and the hubristic attitude of imposition could not be more striking.

For Heidegger, the hydroelectric plant exhausts the river; i.e., a new essence is forced on the river, and the river is no longer a natural thing. Yet, as Heidegger himself admits, the river can surely still be enjoyed as a part of nature. Even if the Rhine is dammed up, it remains a beautiful river. Nevertheless, for Heidegger, the modern attitude of imposition extends all the way to the natural beauty of the river. For, now, as Heidegger notes in a rare expression of mockery, the natural beauty of the Rhine has been commandeered by tourism, and the beautiful Rhine actually exists "in no other way than as an object on call for inspection by a tour group ordered there by the vacation industry" (FT, 17/16).

Let us now turn to the third example of ancient technological practice, the activity of the maker in the usual sense, the artisan, such as the silversmith. Even she does not make or produce as ordinarily understood; that is, her work is not that of imposing form onto matter. According to Heidegger, the essential work of the silversmith is contemplation! What does the smith contemplate, and how is her contemplation related to the bringing forth of the chalice or piece of jewelry?

Heidegger's statement regarding the contemplation of the artisan is as follows: the silversmith contemplates, and from her contemplation the other three causes are gathered into unity. The published English translation (page 8) says: "The silversmith considers carefully and gathers together the three aforementioned ways of being responsible and indebted." This makes it seem that the silversmith is presented with certain preexisting objects, and her task is to take them up into a careful consideration and then unify them. But that misses the point. On the contrary, for Heidegger the contemplation of the silversmith brings forth its own object, in the precise sense that this object would not exist without the contemplation. On the other hand, the contemplation does not *create* the object, either. The contemplation uncovers something that would remain hidden were it not for the silversmith. The contemplation of the silversmith is, as it were, semicreative. That is what we need to understand.

Heidegger provides two clues indicating how we should grasp the contemplation of the silversmith. Heidegger says that contemplation is based on ἀποφαίνεσθαι (*apophainesthai*, "letting be seen"), and that for the Greeks to contemplate (*sich überlegen*) means λέγειν, λόγος (*legein*, "to gather together"; *logos*, "discourse"). We could say, then, that, for Heidegger, what the silversmith contemplates is what discourse allows to be seen, what is gathered together in the word. But what is gathered together in words? Words gather together in virtue of the fact that they are universals; in the word "chalice" all actual and possible chalices are included. The word touches what unites all the particular instances, what gathers them together, what they all have in common. That is to say, the word names that which makes any chalice one with all other chalices, that which makes the chalice be what it is as a chalice. That which makes something be what it is is called the essence. So, in gathering together, the word expresses the essence.

That is precisely what, according to Heidegger, the contemplation of the artisan aims at, what the artisan sees in contemplation, namely, the essence. In contemplation, the essence of the chalice is revealed to the silversmith. The fundamental task of the silversmith is to uncover the essence of the chalice before that essence actually exists in the silver. The smith does not create this essence, nor does the essence simply lie there as a preexisting object for her careful consideration. The essence is at first hidden; it is latent in the silver, and the primary task of the silversmith is to uncover, in contemplation, the potential chalice buried in the material.

The primary task of the craftsman is therefore to see in advance. That is to say, the craftsman is one for whom something is visible (*apophainesthai*) in a privileged way, and what appears to her is precisely what will be named in discourse (*logos*): namely, the essence. Differently expressed, in seeing the potential chalice in the silver, the smith sees what the silver is pregnant with. The smith does not impose this latent essence on the silver; it is indeed something already there in an inchoate way. The smith must contemplate until the potential chalice is revealed to her. On the other hand, neither is this disclosure of the essence imposed onto the smith; it is revealed to her, but not without her cooperation. She must be open to receive this disclosure, and this openness requires the practiced eye, the creative hands, and, in general, the genius that precisely marks the skilled artisan as such. Thus the smith is semicreative: the buried chalice does not uncover itself to just anyone (and so the smith must be skilled and creative), nor does the smith impose the form of the chalice without regard to the matter (and so the smith must be passive and accept the self-revelation of the already latent essence). In short, the smith must *actively let* the essence be revealed to her in advance. That is how she is semicreative: the appearing of the chalice in advance is a joint product of the silversmith's uncovering efforts and the thing's own self-revelation.

Thus the artisan's primary task, that which makes her be an artisan, is more a matter of theory than practice; it is a matter of insight, disclosive looking, rather than practical skill. The artisan's task is to disclose the essence, to see, in contemplation, the latent chalice interred in the matter. This marks the genuine *poiesis*, the proper bringing forth: *what the artisan brings forth is primarily not that which is visible to all but that which is visible only to her*, the essence she sees with her mind's eye. She does not create this essence, yet she is not uncreative, either. The artisan is semicreative: through her the essence comes to birth; without her, the essence would never be disinterred. In other words, the artisan abets the essence into revealing itself, the artisan nurtures the essence forth. The *poiesis* of the artisan is, accordingly, for the Greeks, nurture rather than production in the usual sense.

Yet what about the bringing forth of the actual chalice, the bringing of the essence into concrete existence, the fashioning of the chalice that all can see? Is that not more of a making than is the mere contemplation of the essence? And is that not a matter of production rather than nurture? For the Greeks, according to Heidegger, the answer to both these two latter questions is no. The fashioning of the chalice is indeed a matter of nurture, and this fashioning is actually less of a *poiesis* than the bringing forth of the essence in contemplation.

The Greek understanding of the bringing forth of the visible chalice would be expressed perfectly, for Heidegger, in the already cited testimony of Michelangelo to the effect that the sculptor merely chisels away the extraneous bits of marble so as to release the latent statue within. The artisan does not impose form onto a passive matter but instead sees what the matter is already pregnant with and nurtures that into actual existence. The artisan is a nurturer both as regards the essence visible in contemplation and as regards the artifact wherein the essence will be visible to all. The artisan is constantly in service to the essence and abets it to become more and more visible; the artisan submits herself to the essence and sees herself as the servitor of the essence, its handmaiden or midwife or way-paver. This is how Heidegger express it, directly in terms of the Greek understanding of *techne*, which here refers to the human, versus the natural, way of *poiesis*:

> For that is what *techne* means: to grasp beings . . . in their outward look, *eidos*, *idea*, and, in accord with this, to care for beings themselves and to let them grow, i.e., to order oneself within beings as a whole through productions and institutions. *Techne* is a mode of proceeding *against physis*, though not yet so as to overpower it or exploit it, and above all not to turn use and calculation into principles, but, on the contrary, to retain the holding sway of *physis* in unconcealedness. (*GP*, 179–180/155)

This says that *techne* is primarily a matter of insight or understanding: it is a grasping of beings or, more properly, a perceiving, in advance, of their outward look, their *eidos*, their essence. Then, in accord with this perceived essence, *techne* involves "caring for beings and letting them grow." In other words, it involves letting beings come into their essence, letting their essence come forth in them, letting the essence come to actual existence in beings. The bringing forth of the actual things is thus a matter of care, of letting or abetting the essence. That is why Heidegger said that, on the Greek understanding, *techne* is a matter of ordering *oneself*. *Techne* does not amount to ordering things, making them submit to human will; on the contrary, it is a submitting of oneself to the essence of things, putting oneself in service to that essence. *Techne* in a certain sense is against nature. It is indeed an interfering in nature, but precisely in order "to retain the holding sway of nature in unconcealedness." This is, no doubt, a difficult phrase, but it surely means that *techne* interferes in nature precisely for the purpose of allowing what is unconcealed in things to come into its own, to hold sway as visible for all. Ancient technology is therefore not an overpowering, an imposition of an arbitrary essence, but instead amounts to allowing what is self-emergent to be self-emergent more fully, to become visible, unconcealed, for everyone. The "interference" of ancient technology in nature is a "gearing into" nature; it is not an imposition upon nature but only an abetting or fostering of nature.

The ancients, then, understand human craftsmanship—i.e., techno-logical practice—as a process of nurture. The artisan does not impose her will onto matter but instead abets what reveals itself to her, abets it to be revealed to everyone. It is a matter of nurture, since the artisan stands in service to a pregnancy, to something incipiently self-emergent, which she respects and abets. The artisan, on this understanding, does not impose her will onto a passive matter; on the contrary, the artisan is the one "im-posed on": her activity is a response to an appeal. The appeal is made upon her by the hidden essence, an appeal to abet its coming forth into visibility. That decisively marks technological practice, in the ancient understanding, as nurture.

The second question we raised above (Which is more of a bringing-forth: the contemplation of the essence or the actual fashioning of the product?) can be formulated in terms of the distinction between *techne* and *empeiria* (ἐμπειρία). The one who sees the essence in advance is not always the one who brings the essence into concrete existence. For exam-ple, the architect has *techne*, he knows what is to be done, but he might not be skilled in the actual doing, in the actual building of the house. The laborer, however, is skilled in construction, although she needs the blue-print provided by the architect. The architect has the *logos*, the *eidos*, the essence; whereas the laborer has experience (*empeiria*), i.e., the practical skill to produce the actual house. Another example would be the physiol-ogist (in our sense) versus the medical practitioner. The former has knowledge of the proper function of the body, while the latter may lack theoretical knowledge but does have the practical skill to be of service in restoring that function when it is disrupted. The question is: which of these has the priority? Which is more properly called the maker of the house: the architect or the construction worker? Which is more properly the begetter of health, the one who knows health in essence or the one who has practical experience in restoring health in particular cases? Ac-cording to Heidegger, the former has the priority in the Greek way of thinking and is more highly honored. Even though the one who possesses *techne* may fail in practice, she is the genuine maker, since she is au-tonomous, and the persons with practical skill rely on her for their end. The one who grasps the essence is therefore more genuinely the source of the motion or change; she more genuinely brings forth the motion.

More precisely, for Aristotle, it is the essence itself that is the source of the motion. This is how he expresses it in his *Metaphysics* (1032b21), according to Heidegger's translation: "The genuine producer [in the case of something brought forth by *techne*], and that which initiates the move-ment, is the *eidos* in the soul" (*PS*, 43/30). The *eidos* is the producer, be-cause it rules the entire process of production: everything else (the work of the architect and that of the construction tradesman) is in service to its becoming visible. Accordingly, the one whose soul is the place of this *eidos* is more of a producer—since she is closer to the *eidos*—than the one who has practical skill but relies on the other for the *eidos*. The one who sees the *eidos* in advance is the genuine producer, and so the architect is more of a producer of the house, more of a cause of the house, than the mason. In other words, it is *techne* that, in the more proper sense, produces the house, not *empeiria*.

In fact, for Aristotle, this distinction between the one who sees the *eidos* in advance and the one who manually fashions the artifact amounts to the difference between the master and the slave: "For, the one who has the power—of mind—to see in advance is by nature the ruler and by nature the master, whereas the one who has the power—of body—to fashion those same things is subject to the ruler and is by nature a slave" (*Politics*, 1252a32).

For Aristotle and the Greeks, a master has to be considered more of a cause than a slave, and so *techne*, seeing the *eidos* in advance, the work of the soul, theory, is more of a cause than is manual labor. Thus, on the Greek understanding, the genuine *poiesis* or production is the bringing forth of the *eidos*; the fashioning of the concrete artifact is a *derived* form of making, just as it is a derived form of nurture. The paradigm case of *poiesis* is not an affair of practice, of manual labor, but is a work of the soul, a work of theory, namely the artisan's contemplation or seeing in advance or disclosure of the essence still buried in the matter and invisible to ordinary eyes. The artisan brings forth this essence first of all in her soul, and that bringing-forth, the paradigm of bringing-forth, is understood by the Greeks as a kind of midwifery or nurture. The artisan who has already contemplated, or some other person—some slave—with the required skill, will subsequently—with his body—bring forth this essence in matter; and that too is understood by the Greeks as a kind of midwifery, abetting the essence to achieve full visibility. The bringing-forth in matter is less highly honored than the bringing-forth in the soul; the former is less of an accomplishment, less of a causing, less of a bringing something about, less of a *poiesis*. If it is also less manifestly an instance of nurture, that fact changes nothing regarding the paradigm. The paradigm that rules throughout the entire process of *poiesis* is nurture: actively letting some essence come into full visibility. Its first, and more important, visibility is in the soul of the one who is able to bring it forth there in advance. Its second, common visibility is its subsequent visibility to all eyes. Throughout the process, as Aristotle says, the *eidos*, the essence, is, in the strict sense, the genuine producer, since the contemplating artisan as well as the manual laborer merely serve it and are both, in a manner of speaking, slaves to it. Yet the artisan is less of a slave than is the manual laborer, since the artisan is closer to the *eidos*. And so, the artisan, the one who possesses *techne*, is more of a producer than is the laborer who puts his hand to the actual fashioning of the thing. The contemplative artisan's mode of causality, her mode of production or bringing forth, namely nurture, is the paradigm of production and the paradigm of technological practice, as understood by the ancients.

Bringing-forth as disconcealment

What then, ultimately, is ancient technology? Heidegger answers by offering two final characterizations of bringing-forth or producing, as the Greeks understood it. Heidegger's concluding question, and his preparatory response to it, are as follows:

> But how does bringing-forth or producing happen, whether that be in nature or in handcraft and art? What actually is this bringing-forth or producing in which the four modes of active letting play out? The active letting concerns the presence of that which in each case is brought to show itself in the bringing-forth. The bringing-forth brings something forth out of concealment into unconcealment. Bringing-forth occurs only insofar as something concealed comes into unconcealment. (FT, 13/11)

The sense of producing or bringing-forth invoked here by Heidegger, namely, the bringing of something out of concealment, bringing it to show itself in unconcealment, is exactly the one we mean when we speak of producing witnesses in court. To produce witnesses does not mean to create them, to fabricate them for the occasion, to bring them into being out of nonbeing. It means, rather, merely to lead them forth, which is indeed the etymological sense of "pro-duce," namely: "draw forth," "lead forth." It means to bring the witnesses (who already exist) out of an invisibility into visibility. It means to bring them out of concealment into presence, into view. To produce witnesses is, then, to put it colloquially, to dig them up. It does not mean to *make* them but merely to find them out, discover them, uncover them, take the wraps off them.

This notion of producing as leading forth into visibility for all to see (rather than making ex nihilo) perfectly summarizes Heidegger's view of ancient causality and ancient technology as he has presented it all along. To bring into visibility is nothing else than to abet, to encourage, to nurture. To produce means to take by the hand and lead along a path that ends with full visibility. It means to let things show themselves—in the active sense of letting, i.e., precisely, digging them up. To let witnesses show themselves does not mean merely to do nothing to prevent their becoming visible. On the contrary, it means to lend an active hand, without which they would remain concealed. To produce witnesses, to dig them up, is, therefore, semicreative. The effort at digging is essential for the witnesses to show themselves, but it is not pure creation, ex nihilo, and instead only gears into an already existent potentiality of the witnesses to show themselves, namely, their preexistence in a state of hiddenness.

It is this sense of abetting that has been in play all along, in the entire list of terms Heidegger has offered to expose the sense of ancient causality and ancient technology: obliging, making ready the ground, letting, active letting, letting all the way to the end, bringing-forth, pro-ducing (as I would now translate *poiesis*), and nurturing (to express the processes of nature and thereby translate *physis*). The new term that Heidegger now introduces, one of a pair that expresses the ultimate sense of ancient causality and ancient technology, should then come as no surprise, especially in view of our discussion of the production of witnesses in court. Heidegger's penultimate term that means to cause or produce in the ancient sense is this: to dig up.

The German term is *Entbergen*; a less colloquial translation would be "to disinter" or "to unearth." The published translation renders it as "to reveal." The word *Entbergen* is coined by Heidegger, but the German language lends itself to coining in exactly this way, namely by the novel combination of two familiar words or, in this case, a prefix and a verb. Heidegger's word is quite clear on the basis of its linguistic constituents. Still, the sense might have been somewhat ambiguous, except for the fact that Heidegger dispels all the ambiguity by providing the Greek equivalent of *Entbergen*. We will come in a moment to that Greek term, which is the last one on Heidegger's list of characterizations of ancient causality and technology. It is one of the most important terms in all of Heidegger's philosophy, and Heidegger has spilled an untold amount of ink over it. What he has taken so much pain to show, and to interpret, is the fact that, as he sees it, this Greek word is constructed upon an alpha privative. Thus it is an essentially negative word that is meant to be expressed by *Entbergen*. Accordingly, the prefix, the *ent-*, is intended in its privative sense. It then means to "deprive of" or "undo" the *Bergen*. Now *bergen* can mean to salvage or harbor, but that would make no sense in this context. *Bergen* must correspond to the remainder of the Greek term at issue, which it can do very well, if it means what it does in many other German compounds. This is its root sense, which derives from its etymological source, *Berg*, "mountain." This root sense implies being concealed or deeply covered over, as with a whole mountain. The privative prefix then adds the idea of digging something out from under a mountain, unearthing it, disinterring it. The word "revealing," used in the published translation, while not obviously a privative expression, does contain the idea of removing veils, and so "revealing" is very close to the mark. "Disinterring" and "unearthing" express better the negative sense and also coincide with the basic meaning of Heidegger's German term. Nevertheless, these two English words, as well as "digging up," while forceful and concrete, are perhaps actually too concrete to be used in the contexts in which Heidegger will eventually employ *Entbergen*. Let us for the moment be content with the general idea of *Entbergen* as an unveiling or uncovering; we shall be in a more favorable position to settle on a definite translation after we have grasped the meaning of the Greek word that corresponds to it.

This Greek word, which, according to Heidegger, expresses what he calls *Entbergen*, is ἀλήθεια (*aletheia*): "Bringing-forth occurs only insofar as something concealed comes into unconcealment. This coming is founded on and transpires within what we are calling *Entbergen*. The Greek word for it is ἀλήθεια, which the Romans translate as *veritas*. We say in German *die Wahrheit*, and we ordinarily understand that to refer to the correctness of a representation" (FT, 13/11–12).

In Heidegger's eyes, something has been lost in the translation of the Greek term *aletheia* by the Latin *veritas* or the German *Wahrheit*. In English, *veritas* and *Wahrheit* both mean "truth," a word that would also have to count as an impoverished rendering of what the Greeks express in speaking of *aletheia*. For Heidegger, there is the original Greek language, especially in its pre-Socratic state, and then there are all the other more recent Western languages. The transition (or translation) from the Greek to the others happens as a falling away from the greatness of the origin. This transition is a mark of essential history; i.e., the transition is motivated by *the* event in the history of Being and is a sign that, after a more wholehearted self-showing, the essence of beings has been withdrawing its countenance from mankind. Let us attempt to see how all this is so.

On the most superficial level, the occurrence of the event in question is reflected in the difference between the negative sense of the Greek term and the positive modern words. The Greeks express with a negative expression (*a-letheia*: "dis-concealedness," "un-hiddenness") what modern Western languages express without any negative connotation ("truth"). This is no mere linguistic accident for Heidegger but in fact has the strongest possible motivation: the one term arises out of an experience of the self-showing of the gods, while the other is motivated by their reticence to show themselves. The negative term accords a priority to Being, while the positive one is oblivious of Being and instead gives precedence to human subjectivity. The negative term corresponds to an age that still felt the presence of Being, an age in which Being still made its presence felt, whereas the positive terms reflect an age that has forgotten Being, an age in which Being offers itself so reticently that human subjectivity could supplant it.

We now think of truth as a human affair: it is the correspondence of our intellect to the things. For us, truth resides in a judgment, and there is no truth without a judgment. Truth exists when some human subject forms a judgment that corresponds to some objective state of affairs. For the Greeks, however, there is something more original about truth than the human powers of forming judgments in correspondence with the things. What the Greeks experience as more original, as the foundation for truth in our sense, is something that does not rely on us but on the things: namely, their coming out of hiddenness and showing themselves at all. The Greeks, according to Heidegger, experience things as stepping forth out of an original concealment. For the Greeks, a disconcealment has come to pass in regard to things, and that is why humans can now form correct judgments. That original disconcealment, however, is not our own doing; on the contrary, it is precisely the condition of the possibility of our doing anything whatsoever. In order for us to do anything, to act upon anything, to stand in any relation to any being, it must have been disclosed to us in advance what a being is in general. Otherwise, action (if it could be called that) would be totally blind, since we would then have no sense of ourselves or of the beings other than us. Consequently, for us to investigate or reveal anything about beings, Being must have already disclosed itself; truth, in the sense of the disconcealment of Being, must have come to pass for there to be a human relation to beings and, thereby, judgmental truth. Our human, judgmental truth therefore lacks autonomy; it depends on the disconcealment of Being.

We can see now, perhaps, something of what Parmenides means by calling truth a goddess. According to Heidegger, the word "goddess" in Greek, θεά (*theá*), is intrinsically related to the word for the look, θέα (*théa*). A goddess is one who in a special way looks at us. Parmenides is then saying that truth is the looking at us of a goddess. Truth occurs when something special looks at us. The Greek gods for Heidegger are not particular beings but are guises for Being in general, for the essence of beings, and so the special look is the look of Being. Thus, in Heideggerian terms, truth occurs when Being looks at us. The notion of the "look of Being" (subjective genitive) is a characteristically enigmatic phrase of Heidegger's later philosophy. But it actually means something very simple, as long as we understand it in the appropriate Heideggerian sense. Heidegger recognizes two forms of looking: the one familiar to us all is the grasping look, the scrutinizing or inspecting of something. But this sort of look rests, for Heidegger, on a more primordial form of looking that does not involve gazing upon but instead amounts almost to the opposite: showing oneself, stepping into the light, offering oneself *to be* gazed upon. This is the particular sense in which Heidegger speaks of the "look of Being." Thus, what Heidegger means here is exactly what Parmenides is expressing by calling truth a goddess. Whether it is Being or a goddess that looks upon us, the meaning is the same: truth occurs when we are looked at in a special way, i.e., when the essence of beings in general steps out of hiddenness, when Being disconceals itself and offers itself to our human gaze. Thus Heidegger and Parmenides are expressing nothing other than the Greek understanding of truth, the truth that is more foundational than human, judgmental truth. They are expressing the unveiling on Being's part, the original disconcealment that is presupposed by the human disclosure of things and is thus a condition of human, judgmental truth.

For Heidegger, the Greek experience of a more primordial truth is expressed perfectly in the negative word *a-letheia*. By speaking of truth as "dis-concealment," the Greeks give voice to their experience of beings in general as having stepped forth out of a more original concealment. Accordingly, the negativity of their word expresses the Greeks' understanding that things were in need of an uncovering and that something or someone has uncovered them. It could not be humans that accomplished this uncovering, since humans can act only in regard to what is already uncovered. If there was an *original* concealment, it must have been surmounted—primarily, at least—by that which was concealed, not by humans. Humans could not wrest or force this original disconcealment, since forcing or wresting requires the possession of something unconcealed to contend against.

The disconcealment that has come to pass with regard to things—i.e., truth—is, then, for the Greeks, primarily an affair of Being and not a human affair. The Greeks understand truth to be the *self*-disclosure of Being; they place Being in the lead as regards disconcealment. That is why, for Parmenides, the goddess *leads the philosopher by the right hand* and why, for Heidegger, we can look at things only because Being has first *looked at us*. That is, the leader in the disconcealment is Being; Being takes the initiative in the original disconcealment, Being gives itself to us, Being offers itself to us as a gift. Our human looking is a response to this gift.

We today, however, have no sense of being led by the hand or of being looked at or of being offered gifts, and so we are oblivious to any more original sense of truth than judgmental truth. We now recognize no goddesses, which is to say that goddesses have withdrawn their look from us, goddesses no longer make their presence felt. In other words, we no longer feel looked at by Being, and consequently we know of only one look—our own scrutinizing gaze—and only one disconcealment—the one we perform by our piercing inspection of beings. All initiative is human initiative. All disconcealing is the work of human beings, which is to say that truth is now judgmental truth: it is on *our* side, it is *our* affair, *we* institute it. That is why we have a positive word for it; we are master over it. Certainly there must also be something to correspond to our true judgments, there must be Being and beings. But these play the secondary role of the follower: they offer resistance. Moreover, even this role is degraded, for we understand it as sheer passivity.

Thus, the transition from the ancient age to our own has been a reversal: the leader and the follower in the partnership of disconcealment have traded places. The Greeks experienced an ascendancy of Being over human subjectivity, and we experience no such thing. For us, the way to truth is research. We must "go around" (= "re-search") and seek, not sit idly by, waiting. Waiting in fact has for us no active sense; it is merely to be idle and so has fallen into complete disrepute. Today no respectable philosopher or scientist waits for Being or for nature to reveal itself. Philosophers do not wait to be led by the hand, they do not wait for an unveiling; on the contrary, they take matters into their own hands and seek to part the veils by their own effort. This applies all the more to the scientist. One who abandoned the laboratory in favor of waiting would be so out of tune with the times that her erstwhile colleagues would not know whether to laugh at her or cry.

Recalling that the transition between the two ages has also been a translation, let us return to the two words at issue, *a-letheia* and "truth." From a Heideggerian perspective, how is it understandable that a positive term corresponds to the modern attitude and a negative term to the ancient? If truth is now a human affair, why do we have a positive term for it? The Heideggerian answer is that our word lacks negativity for the simple reason that we recognize nothing more positive than our human subjectivity, nothing that our subjectivity would stand toward in a relation of lack or deprivation. Our concept lacks privation because we are *unaware* of our deprivation. We see ourselves as self-sufficient in our pursuit of truth, in our uncovering of things. We do not recognize things as needing a more original uncovering than the uncovering we ourselves are able to carry out. Nor do we recognize that such an uncovering has taken place or even could take place. Our term is positive, since we sense ourselves to be in the lead, in control, autonomous. Thus, our term actually is positive for a negative reason: we experience ourselves as autonomous because something is hidden to us, namely the self-disclosure of Being, the look of Being. What is hidden to us is the self-disclosure or disconcealment we ourselves did not carry out. We are oblivious to that disconcealment and do not recognize it as having a priority over judgmental truth. We do not see beyond what we call truth to that which it depends on and lacks. On the other hand, the Greek term is negative because the Greeks experienced their own lack of autonomy as regards truth. Thus their term is negative for a positive reason: i.e., the Greeks did experience what is more positive than humans, what has an ascendancy over the human powers of research into beings (beings that have always already been uncovered in general). The Greek term is negative because the Greeks were aware of a work of un-concealment in the most proper sense, an un-concealment that is more original than human research and that is there-fore out of human hands. The Greeks glimpsed a concealment only Being itself could undo. Their word *a-letheia* names this concealment and the undoing of it by the gods. *A-letheia* names Being itself in its work of dis-closing itself in advance: in advance of—and making possible—a human relation to beings and a human disclosure of beings. In short, the Greeks saw beyond human truth, and the word *a-letheia* names that which they saw there: Being in its un-concealment, the self-disclosure of Being, the look of Being. Their word is negative because they understood humans to play a secondary role and regarded Being as in the lead.

From a Heideggerian perspective, the crucial question concerns the motivation of these two visions or attitudes, the Greek attitude of ac-cording a priority to Being, and the modern one of giving precedence to human subjectivity. How are we to account for the transition between the Greek sight of Being and the modern blindness to Being and thus for the translation of the negative Greek word into the positive modern one? What is it about the modern era that makes the positive word arise? Why does the modern age give the priority to subjectivity rather than to Being? What allowed the Greeks to see beyond human truth; did the Greeks have a more developed eyesight, were they more perspicuous, did they have a greater power of looking? Why did the original Greek vision and word not fare better in history? For Heidegger, to put it as concisely as possi-ble, the transition and the translation were fated. That is, they were not caused by human error or human weakness; the primary responsibility lies on the side of Being, on the side of the gods. It is most emphatically not that in the modern era the presumptuous attitude of humans has caused Being to flee out of *lèse majesté*. It is not human beings but Being itself that has changed.

This change in Being is the transition from approach to withdrawal. Being has changed by offering itself more reticently, by drawing more veils over itself, by looking at mankind less directly. That is the prime motivat-ing factor; Being is the prime mover. If the Greeks could see beyond, be-yond human truth, it is not because they were more insightful or wiser than we are today. It is not that the Greeks developed their powers of vi-sion, while we let ours atrophy or go astray. The Greeks cannot take the credit for what they saw and experienced; the credit goes to Being. For Heidegger, the primary reason the Greeks could see more is that Being showed itself to them more wholeheartedly. If the Greeks sensed the pres-ence of the gods, whereas we do not, that is primarily because the gods of-fered themselves more fully. The Greeks did not surpass us in sensitivity or intelligence, they did not have greater merits; on the contrary, they were favored. The archaic meaning of "favor" is "face" or "countenance." To favor someone is to show him one's face, to regard him, to look at him. That is precisely how, for Heidegger, the Greeks were a favored people; Being freely showed its countenance to them, Being looked at them. Thus the Greeks did not have special powers of looking; on the contrary, something looked *at them* in a special way.

Heidegger often suggests a connection between the history of Being and that of language. Being may approach and withdraw through the vicissitudes of words. From this perspective, the Greeks were favored with the word *a-letheia*; i.e., the favor of the gods came to the Greeks through that word. To possess that word is, ipso facto, to be looked upon with favor. *Aletheia* is the name precisely of that which could be seen and named only if Being showed its countenance, since it is the name of the look or self-disclosure of Being. To experience this self-disclosure is to possess a name for it. Accordingly, the presence of the word *aletheia* marks the Greek age as the first epoch in the history of Being, the epoch in which Being showed itself.

What motivated the transition to the modern age and the translation into the positive word "truth"? In a certain sense, it was simply the withdrawal of the word *aletheia*. Language has withheld that word, and language now speaks to us in terms of "truth." It is not that human translators were careless or that users of modern languages are less wise than were the speakers of ancient Greek. It is that language itself now addresses humans in words that conceal the genuine face of Being. For Heidegger, then, our positive word "truth" indicates we live in an age that corresponds to the second epoch in the history of Being. That word could arise only in an age in which the gods have fled; indeed, that is the word the gods leave behind in their flight.

Disclosive looking

For Heidegger, the two ages of human chronology can be characterized essentially as the age of *aletheia* and the age of "truth," and these eras are motivated by the autonomous events in the history of Being. The two eras are motivated by, respectively, the more full self-disclosure of Being and the more reticent self-showing of Being. Yet, for Heidegger, disclosure always involves a partnership, a genuine partnership in which both partners contribute. The primary responsibility for the disclosure rests with Being, but there is no self-disclosure of Being without the active response of humans. They must meet the look of Being with a disclosive look of their own. Otherwise, an understanding of what it means to be will never arise, no matter how wholeheartedly Being offers itself. This disclosive looking on the part of humans, the active reception of the self-offering of Being, is what Heidegger calls *Entbergen*.

Heidegger's final terms in his characterization of ancient technology, *aletheia* and *Entbergen*, are therefore correlative. *Aletheia* means disconcealment, and since there is always some disconcealment, even in the second epoch, the term *aletheia* can refer to whatever way Being offers itself, whether wholeheartedly or reticently. *Entbergen* then names the corresponding human reception of the self-disclosure of Being. *Entbergen* is the appropriate human looking; the looking that appropriates what is offered by Being. According to our understanding of *Entbergen*, then, let us translate it as "disclosive looking." It is a *looking* (a grasping look) that plays an essential role in the *disclosure* of Being. Thus *Entbergen* is both passive and active: it is a looking, and, as such, it is receptive, not creative. Yet it is not a mere gaping but an active, disclosive looking that must, as it were, meet the look of Being, the self-showing of Being, halfway. Humans must go out halfway toward Being; their looking must stem from an effort at disclosure, from alertness, from sensitivity. Disclosive looking is thus indeed a reception, but an active reception.

For Heidegger, this disclosive looking on the part of humans varies in an essential way according to what is offered. The disclosive looking of the ancient age differs from that of the modern era. It is as if the self-disclosure of Being always calls up the disclosive looking appropriate to it. The more vigorous is the self-disclosure of Being, the less active is the looking on the part of humans, and the more receptive it can be. That is true in a sense. The Greeks were accepting, whereas we in the modern age distrust appearances and instead construct, in science, our own substitute for the apparent world. From a Heideggerian perspective, however, it in fact requires more disclosive power to look at things acceptingly and humbly, and so the more forceful self-unconcealing of Being actually calls up a more forceful, more active, looking on the part of humans. The withdrawal of Being takes this forceful looking from us, and so the scientific construction of reality, characteristic of the modern age, is actually less active than the Greek sensitivity to what is simple. The truly disclosive eyes are the ones attuned to what is simple and naive; the modern construction of scientific reality is, by comparison, feeble in its attempt to compensate for the lack of those eyes.

Technology and truth

Where have we strayed? Here we are, speaking of gods and goddesses, of Being in general, of truth, of the look of Being, of the understanding of

Being that requires a disclosive looking on the part of humans. What has all this to do with technology? Technology is a matter of making things, doing things, is it not? Technology is, as Heidegger says, a matter of ends and means, i.e., instrumentality. What has instrumentality to do with the understanding of Being in general; what has instrumentality to do with truth? According to Heidegger, it has *everything* to do with truth:

> Where have we strayed? We are asking about technology and have now arrived at *aletheia* and disclosive looking. What has the essence of technology to do with disclosive looking? Answer: everything. For all producing is based on disclosive looking. . . . Technology is therefore no mere means. Technology is a mode [Heidegger's marginal note: "or, rather, *the*, decisive, mode"] of disclosive looking. If we pay heed to this, then an entirely different realm of the essence of technology will open itself to us. It is the realm of disclosive looking, i.e., the realm of truth. (FT, 13/12)

For Heidegger, technology is in essence nothing other than an understanding of what it means to be. Technology has to do with the way we understand Being in general. Technology is the way we think Being, i.e., the way we understand what it takes for something—anything—to be. Technology is thus an affair of first philosophy, ontology; and so technology is what makes Dasein be Dasein: i.e., technology makes Dasein a place where Being is understood.

More specifically, technology is our way of disclosive looking in response to the looking upon us of Being. Technology is the way we play our role of partner with Being in the disconcealment of what it means to be. Technology names the way we look back at Being and confirm what Being offers to us in its own look, in its self-disclosure. That is why Heidegger says the realm of technology is the realm of truth: i.e., technology concerns the most universal and basic of all truths, namely the disconcealment of Being in general, the disconcealment that is the prerequisite for all other human relations to particular beings.

Thus technology is a theoretical—not a practical—affair. Technology is not directed toward making things, doing things, finding means to ends, instrumentality. More precisely, technology is *primarily* a theoretical affair. There is a practical side to technology, but that is secondary; it *follows* upon the theoretical understanding. Technology is, of course, related to making things and doing things, but it is so related only because technology first of all is an understanding of what things are in general. Technology does determine our doing and making, but only because it determines what we take to be a thing in general in the first place. Technology is not practical directly, but only indirectly: by disclosing to us what constitutes beings, it provides us with a guideline that governs all our relations to beings, including our practical relations. It is in virtue of the truth disclosed in technology, i.e., in virtue of its theoretical significance, that technology is practical. Technology can do things only on account of what it sees, and what it sees is that which makes a being be a being at all.

Technology is the disclosure of the essence of things; technology is the seeing of the *eidos* in advance. Technology concerns the understanding of Being that is required in advance for any human relation to beings, for any human activity directed to beings. Thus technology is comparable to the seeing in advance of the *eidos* on the part of an individual artisan. Just as the artisan fashions a thing in conformity to the essence he beholds in advance, so technology in general is the beholding of the essence of all things in advance, in light of which humans fashion things and can take any stance at all toward things. Therefore instrumentality or making things is a secondary phenomenon of technology, just as the actual fashioning of the house or chalice is a secondary and inferior affair in relation to the seeing of the *eidos*. What Heidegger means by technology is the primary and superior affair, namely, the theoretical understanding of Being in general that guides all practical dealings with individual beings; so for him technology is primarily a way of looking or understanding, a disclosure of truth, not a way of doing, not instrumentality.

The Greek concept of techne

Indeed this is, as Heidegger admits, a strange prospect, but for him the same prospect opens up if we proceed not from an analysis of instrumentality, from what is required for making and doing things, but from an analysis of the word "technology" itself or, rather, from the Greek word from which it is derived, *techne*. From this standpoint as well, we will see that technology is primarily a matter of our understanding of Being, a matter of our sense of what it takes to be a being at all. What then does *techne* mean for the Greeks?

The main paragraph on this issue in "Die Frage nach der Technik" is an extremely compact one. Heidegger has also treated the exact same issue elsewhere, in a full commentary on the passage he cites here from Book VI of Aristotle's *Nicomachean Ethics*. The full commentary (*PS*, 21–188/15–129) takes 168 pages! Let us first examine what Heidegger has compressed into this one paragraph and then turn briefly to his fuller exposition. The main point of both expositions is the same: as the ancients understood it, *techne* is primarily theoretical, not practical. *Techne* is essentially a matter of seeing or knowing, not doing or making, and what *techne* sees is Being, the essence of beings.

Here in the essay on technology, Heidegger makes this point by referring *techne* to two other Greek words: ἐπιστήμη (*episteme*, "knowledge") and ἀληθεύειν (*aletheuein,* "to disclose the truth"). First of all, Heidegger asserts that, for the ancients, even up to the time of Plato, the word *techne* "goes together" with the word *episteme.* Heidegger means this "going together," of course, in the sense of a convergence of meaning. It is especially Plato that Heidegger has in mind; Aristotle will eventually contrast *techne* and *episteme,* but in Plato the two terms are nearly interchangeable. In particular, Plato does certainly not contrast *techne* and *episteme* in the sense of the distinction between making and knowing, the practical and the theoretical. For Plato and the earlier Greeks, both *techne* and *episteme* simply mean knowing: "Both words are names for knowledge in the broadest sense" (FT, 14/13).

In another place, Heidegger expresses his understanding of the Platonic sense of the word *techne* when he associates that sense of *techne* with wonder, as we have already mentioned. For the Greeks, wonder is an attitude rooted in the knowledge of Being in general; what is wondrous is that Being is disclosed to us. According to Heidegger, the source of wonder can also be called *techne,* for *techne* is our grasp of Being in general; and so *techne* is an affair, not of practice, but of *episteme.* Indeed it follows that *techne* must then go together with the highest *episteme,* the highest theoretical knowledge:

> We only have to be mindful that *techne* still, precisely with Plato, at times assumes the role of denoting knowledge pure and simple, and that means the perceptual relation to beings as such. Now it is clear that this perceiving of beings in their unconcealedness is not a mere gaping, that *techne* is carried out rather in a procedure against beings, but in such a way that these themselves precisely show themselves . . . in their essence, *eidos, idea.* . . . (GP, 179/154–155)

Techne, as a disclosure of beings as such, is not a mere gaping; it is carried out "against" beings. That means that it goes out to meet beings halfway; it is the appropriation of the self-disclosure of beings as such. *Techne* takes effort; it is not a passive receiving. Heidegger even calls the looking that characterizes the *techne* of the Greeks a kind of violence (*EM,* 159ff/126ff). It is a violent looking in the sense that it involves a struggle and an overcoming: namely, with regard to the pervasive, superficial way things ordinarily appear. *Techne* is carried out against the everyday appearance of things; the person with *techne* has made the effort to see the essence that is hidden to perfunctory sight. On the other hand, *techne* is also a submissive looking; it is not against, but precisely in service to, the hidden essence.[4] Thus *techne* is the active appropriation we have called disclosive looking, the seeing in advance of the essence of things. And that is why *techne* is the seeing of the Ideas in the Platonic sense. For Plato, Being, the essence of things in general, is called *eidos* or *idea.* Accordingly, *techne* is central to the Platonic doctrine of Ideas, since *techne* is precisely our grasping of the Ideas, of beings as such, of Being itself:

> Without wishing to preempt a discussion of the doctrine of Ideas, let us merely remark that we will understand the genesis, the primary sense, and what is opaque in Plato's Ideas only if we remain oriented toward the place where the *eidos* first steps forth quite naturally, i.e., in which mode of disclosure it explicitly emerges. . . . It is precisely *techne* that is the ground upon which something like the *eidos* becomes visible in the first place. (*PS*, 63/33)

The point is that the grasp of the Ideas, of Being, of what is wondrous, is the highest *episteme*, the highest theoretical knowledge, and so *techne*, as the prime grasp of the Ideas, is *episteme*. That is what Heidegger means by saying that *techne* and *episteme* "go together" for Plato and the earlier Greeks. To put it more fully, we could say that for Plato all these words go together: *techne*, *episteme*, wonder, Being, essence, Idea, knowledge. *Techne* is then not simply knowledge, as opposed to practice; it is even the highest knowledge. Thus the first connection Heidegger makes, between *techne* and *episteme*, signifies that *techne* is the Greek name for knowledge in the most proper sense, i.e., the name for our understanding of Being in general. This then confirms what Heidegger determined in regard to *techne* when he approached it from the viewpoint of causality and production: the domain of *techne* is the realm of truth, of knowledge, of theoretical looking. *Techne* is not the mere practical manipulation of things.

Heidegger goes on to say, in the paragraph we are discussing from "Die Frage nach der Technik," that Aristotle does distinguish *techne* from *episteme*. But the distinction is still not that between practice and theoretical knowledge. On the contrary, for Aristotle the distinction lies entirely *within* the realm of theoretical knowledge; it is a distinction between two modes of knowledge, two modes of disclosive looking. That is what Heidegger expresses by connecting *techne* to the other Greek word we cited above, *aletheuein*. That is, *techne* and *episteme* are both modes of *aletheuein*: "In a most remarkable passage (*Nicomachean Ethics*, Book 6, chapters 3-4), Aristotle indeed distinguishes between *episteme* and *techne*; but he does so specifically with respect to what they disclose and how they disclose. *Techne* is a mode of *aletheuein*" (FT, 14/13).

What is *aletheuein*? The word is a verb derived from *aletheia* and so means to get at the truth, to see the truth, to look disclosively upon things. In the cited passage from the *Nicomachean Ethics*, Aristotle lists five modes of *aletheuein*, i.e., five ways of access to the truth. What is so significant for Heidegger is simply that *techne* is one of those five. *Techne* is a way of looking disclosively upon beings. Thus *techne* is not divorced from disclosive looking, the way practice might be distinct from theoretical knowledge; on the contrary, *techne is* a matter of knowledge. What then, for Aristotle, is the difference between *techne* and *episteme*, between *techne* and knowledge pure and simple? As Heidegger says, they differ with respect to what they disclose and how they disclose. *Episteme* discloses what is unchangeable, *techne* what is changeable. And *episteme* is disclosure for its own sake, while *techne* has an ulterior motive beyond mere disclosure. Thus *episteme* is literally knowledge pure and simple: it is knowledge of what is simple (the eternal and unchangeable), and it is pure knowledge (for its own sake). Let us delve a little more deeply into this basic characterization of *episteme* in order to understand how *techne* differs from it.

For Aristotle, knowledge does not change. What most properly deserves the name knowledge is constant and permanent. But such a knowledge is possible only of unchanging objects. For Aristotle it is primarily the object that determines the character of the knowledge, not vice versa. There can be genuine knowledge, then, only of what is changeless, and what is changeless is eternal, never having come into being and never going out of being. Hence, there is no genuine knowledge of individual things; knowledge is possible only of the principles of things, the essences of beings (in Plato's terms, the Ideas), and the ultimate principle of beings is Being. The most genuine knowledge is then ontological knowledge, and this more than anything else deserves to be called knowledge, *episteme*. Accordingly, there is only one genuine *episteme*, and that is philosophy or the understanding of Being as such. This knowledge has no ulterior motive, since the object of the knowledge, Being, cannot be influenced or manipulated or changed in any way. This knowledge is disclosive looking for the mere sake of disclosure; it is purely thea-horetical.

Techne, in contrast to *episteme*, is knowledge of changeable things; its objects come and go and change in various ways, and so *techne* cannot be considered knowledge in the most proper sense. In particular, its objects are not the changeable things of nature, which come and go of themselves, but the things that come and go due to a role played by the one who possesses the *techne*. This person discloses what does not yet exist concretely; and that disclosure is subject to change, since the thing may turn out differently than it was envisioned. This is how Heidegger expresses the object of *techne*, to continue the quotation above: "*Techne* is a mode of *aletheuein*. Its object is not that which produces itself [= natural things]; but instead it looks disclosively upon that which does not yet exist before us and which may for that reason turn out to look one way or another" (FT, 14/13).

Moreover, *techne* discloses this object with an ulterior motive, to produce it. *Techne* does have a practical goal. Thus *techne* is not knowledge pure and simple: it is not simple, because its objects are connected to coming and going; and it is not pure, because it is for the sake of producing here before us that which it sees in advance. Nevertheless, it does partake of knowledge, since what is primary in *techne* is the seeing in advance of the essence. The actual construction of the thing, for Aristotle, can be left to slaves. Their masters contemplate and see. They see not the concrete thing but the essence of the thing in advance, and this object to a certain extent does escape from change. The essence is not an individual thing but a principle or an Idea; it is something ideal and so shares, at least to some extent, in eternity and unchangeableness. Essences do not come and go as do individual things; the essence is the unchanging Being of the changing being. Thus, according to Heidegger, Aristotle lists *techne* among the modes of *aletheuein* because *techne*, in what is decisive about it, does disclose something akin to an eternal truth, not the most universal of truths, perhaps, and not purely for the sake of disclosure, but nevertheless an object of stable knowledge: an ideal essence, the Being of some particular being. *Techne* is indeed more practical than *episteme*, but the practical aspect of *techne*, its practical role, is not manipulation but is merely the guiding or ordering of the process of manipulation, just as the master orders the slave about. *Techne* can play this role precisely because it has looked upon something disclosively, because the master has seen an essence in advance, because the master has theoretical knowledge. It is as a disclosive looking that *techne* plays a practical role. The quotation above from "Die Frage nach der Technik" then continues with Heidegger repeating the familiar analysis of *techne*:

> Whoever builds a house or a boat . . . looks disclosively—in advance—upon the essence and the matter of the boat or house and gathers them into a view of the finished thing. Then from this view in advance of the finished thing he determines the manner of construction. Consequently, what is decisive in *techne* does not at all reside in making and manipulating, nor in utilizing means, but in the aforementioned disclosive looking. It is as a disclosive looking, and not as a manufacturing, that *techne* is a producing. (FT, 14/13)

That is the end of the compressed paragraph in which Heidegger connects *techne* to *episteme* and *aletheuein* and in so doing explicates the Greek sense of the word from which our term "technology" is derived. This examination of what the Greeks themselves mean by *techne* is intended to confirm the strange prospect that opened up when we thought through the notion of technology as production or instrumentality. That prospect is the view that technology is only secondarily practical and is primarily theoretical. *Techne* does have a practical or instrumental application, yet what the Greeks mean by *techne* is not the application but the theoretical knowledge that makes the practical application possible. And that is also what Heidegger means by technology. In the proper sense, technology is seeing rather than doing; and its proper realm is truth rather than instrumentality, knowledge of Being rather than manufacture of artifacts. And so, having linked *techne* to *episteme* and *aletheuein*, Heidegger concludes:

> In this way, therefore, our investigation into the meaning of the word *techne*, as determined in the Greek manner, has led us to the same context that opened up when we pursued the question of what instrumentality as such is in truth.
> Technology is a mode of disclosive looking. Technology resides in the domain of disclosive looking and disconcealment, i.e., where *aletheia*, truth, occurs. (FT, 14–15/13)

With regard to Aristotle and his assertion that *techne* is a mode of *aletheuein*, Heidegger's exposition here in the essay on technology is content to show that and how *techne* involves a disclosive looking at all. Heidegger here demonstrates merely a minimum sense in which *techne* is theoretical knowledge: *techne* is the disclosure in advance of the essence of some being, the Being of some being. Yet *techne* is still tied to the particular and the practical. It does not appear to disclose Being in general, truth in general, which it cannot do as long as it is governed by an ultimate intention to fabricate. For Aristotle, then, it would seem, the connection between *techne* and *aletheia* is a tenuous one. *Techne* just barely escapes the realm of the particular and changeable and so just barely qualifies as knowledge.

Actually, for Heidegger, the view of *techne* just expressed is merely Aristotle's initial position. Aristotle developed and deepened his view, steering *techne* away from the particular and the practical, toward the general and theoretical, until, finally, *techne* appears to coincide with philosophy itself, with the understanding of Being in its universality. Heidegger exposes this development and deepening in his full, 168-page commentary on the passage in question from the *Nicomachean Ethics*. Heidegger's commentary is intricate, and this is not the place to enter into the intricacies. Yet we need to see the overall thrust of Heidegger's argument, and we can delineate the main points briefly, provided we paint with broad enough strokes.

At the beginning of Aristotle's account of the modes of *aletheuein*, he makes a division into two. In Aristotle's own terms, it is a division into the modes that contribute to knowledge and those that contribute to deliberation. We deliberate about that which we can change in practice, and so Aristotle's distinction is between the theoretical and the practical. Initially, Aristotle does indeed consider *techne* one of the practical modes of disclosure. He places *techne* on the practical side, along with φρόνησις (*phronesis*), which is prudence or practical judgment regarding what is properly human. On the other hand, the main theoretical ways of access to truth are *episteme* and σοφία (*sophia*, "wisdom").

Aristotle focuses on the common modes of disclosure within each division. These are *episteme* for the theoretical and *techne* for the practical. In Heidegger's eyes, the most significant question Aristotle poses to these two modes is his first question: what is the paradigm of each? Aristotle expresses this question in various ways; he asks about the highest state (βελτίστη ἕξις, *beltiste hexis*), the consummation (τελείωσις, *teleiosis*), or the excellence (ἀρετή, *arete*) of each. That is, what is each tending toward; in what is each fulfilled; what would each look like, if completely developed?

On the theoretical side, Aristotle has little difficulty in finding the paradigm of *episteme* in wisdom. Wisdom is for Aristotle the highest form of knowledge, and it amounts to theory, pure gazing upon or contemplating the "most honorable" of all things, namely Being in its universality. Wisdom (*sophia*) is thus equivalent to philosophy (*philo-sophia*), the knowledge of what it takes for something to be.

What is the paradigm of *techne*? Aristotle denies that it is *phronesis*; *techne* does not tend toward practical judgment regarding the human good. For Heidegger, Aristotle rejects *phronesis* as the highest form of *techne* because the Stagirite recognizes in *techne* a tendency away from practice and toward an "autonomous *episteme*." According to Heidegger, Aristotle is in this regard merely basing himself on the common everyday way of according honor to the one who has *techne*. In Heidegger's paraphrase, this is how Aristotle expresses the respect everyday Dasein pays to *techne*:

> One who possesses *techne* is not honored primarily for the role he plays in making things, the practical things which fulfill the necessities of life or which serve recreation and pleasure. He is honored simply because he advances our knowledge of beings, simply because he *discloses* something or other, beyond what just anyone can see, whether this is useful or not, whether it is great or small. Such a one is then credited with wisdom. (*PS*, 93/64)

Heidegger finds Aristotle confirming this same sentiment when the Stagirite gives precedence to the one who has *techne* over and against the one who has experience:

> The one who has *techne* is admired, even if he lacks the practical skill of the hand-laborers, precisely because he sees the essence. He may thereby fail in practice, for practice concerns the particular, whereas

techne concerns the universal. Despite this shortcoming with regard
to practice, the one who has *techne* is still respected more and considered wiser: in virtue of his privileged way of looking disclosively.
(*PS*, 76/52)

The tendency toward an autonomous *episteme* is expressed most
explicitly by Aristotle in his determination of the paradigm of *techne*. In
Book VI of the *Nicomachean Ethics*, Aristotle finally decides on wisdom,
sophia, as the consummation of *techne*. Thus *techne*, which Aristotle initially placed on the practical side, among the practical modes of disclosure, attains its highest state on the theoretical side. That is of the utmost
importance for Heidegger. *Episteme* and *techne* have the same highest
state. They both tend toward *sophia*, toward knowledge in its purest and
simplest form, i.e., toward the most universal and theoretical form of
knowledge, which is knowledge of the highest or "most honorable" object, namely Being. Thus *techne* is ordered toward an understanding of
what it means to be in general. As Heidegger formulates it, *techne* in Aristotle tends to be conflated with "philosophical reflection," "genuine
understanding," "the most rigorous of all sciences":

> What is most striking now is that Aristotle designates *sophia*
> as the *arete*, "excellence," of *techne* (*Nic. Eth.* VI, 7; 1141a12). The
> highest mode of *aletheuein*, philosophical reflection, which according
> to Aristotle is the highest mode of human existence, is at the same
> time the *arete* of *techne*. (*PS*, 56–57/39–40)

> Aristotle remarks explicitly (*Nic. Eth.* VI, 7; 1141a11f.): "Genuine
> understanding, *sophia*, is the consummation, *arete*, *teleiosis*, of
> *techne*, of the know-how employed to construct something." (*PS*,
> 68/47)

By calling *sophia* the consummation (*teleiosis*) of *techne*, Aristotle is
designating it as the *telos* ("final cause") of *techne*. Furthermore, as Heidegger remarks, for Aristotle the *telos* is not extrinsic. It is not *outside* of
the thing whose *telos* it is; it is not merely an exterior goal. On the contrary, it most properly belongs to the thing; the *telos* defines the thing. It
is in virtue of its *telos* that the thing is most properly what it is. Accordingly, *sophia*, the consummation of *techne*, designates what *techne* most
properly is. *Techne* is most properly *sophia*, the purest and highest theory, the understanding of Being in general.

That is the full significance of Aristotle's statement in the *Nicomachean Ethics* that *techne* is a mode of *aletheuein*. Heidegger's long exposition of it is meant to establish, in their most radical form, the
conclusions asserted in the essay on technology: as the Greeks understood

it, *techne*, technology, is a disclosive looking; it is primarily theoretical; it aims at the universal; its domain is the realm of truth; it has to do with the way we understand Being in general. The strange prospect is thus confirmed, the one that opened up when we thought through the notion of technology as production or instrumentality, the prospect that the instrumental or practical aspect of *techne* is not its most proper determination. Most properly, *techne* concerns the understanding of Being, the understanding that guides the production. Our sense of Being, of what it means to be, determines how we make and do things, and that sense of Being is what the Greeks mean by *techne* and what Heidegger means by technology. Technology is *Entbergen*, i.e., the way we look back disclosively in response to *aletheia*, in response to the looking upon us (or self-showing) of Being. Technology is thus the same as theory, thea-hory; it is constitutive of Da-sein as such. What results from this partnership in disclosure (i.e., the resulting understanding of Being in general) will determine how we humans make things and how we understand the making of things. Technology is not practice; technology is the theory that determines the practice.

Ancient technological practice as poiesis

What then, to conclude our examination of ancient technology, is the specifically ancient sense of Being? What is disclosed in the disclosive looking that comprises ancient technology? What is the ancient understanding of Being, and what sort of making or production follows from that understanding?

To put it as succinctly as possible, for Heidegger the ancient understanding is that Being in general is nature; all things that have come to be have been self-emergent, self-disconcealing. Thus the ancient names for Being are *physis* ("nature," "self-emergence") and *aletheia* ("truth," "disconcealment"). And the ancient understanding of producing things is nurture, respect for nature and gearing into nature, i.e., abetting what is self-emergent to be fully self-emergent, fully visible. The Greek word for making, understood in this way as a pro-ducing or leading forth by the hand, as an abetting, is *poiesis*. Ancient technology in practice is *poiesis*.

Accordingly, for the ancients, the distinction between the natural and the man-made is blurred. All making, all production, is natural, is self-emergence. There is, for the ancients, no strict distinction between growing and producing: humanly produced things merely require more assistance to grow, to come into the light, and that is all; they still are in essence self-emergent. For the ancients, in a sense all things are alive, since all things are natural, all things are self-emergent. The prime mover in every being that has come forth is within that being; i.e., the prime mover is nature, the inner impetus to self-emerge. Some things indeed require human assistance, but then the human artisan is understood simply as a midwife; he merely abets or releases an already extant urge toward self-emergence, even if that urge is imbedded in a block of marble. The human artisan is not the prime mover but is only an ob-stetrician, someone who "stands there" in an abetting way. That is why the paradigm of the maker is the counselor, the farmer, or the doctor, and why there is no strict distinction between the farmer and the sculptor: neither imposes existence. They both pro-duce in the strict sense; they both take something by the hand and lead it forth into visibility, they both release it, set it free, uncover it. The crops in the field, the witness in court, and the statue in the atelier are all produced in the same sense. They all require a human hand, but there is a hidden artisan which is the *prime* mover; that hidden artisan is Being, nature, the inner urge to self-emergence. The human hand is merely the midwife's hand.

Indeed, in the modern age as well, the distinction between the artificial and the natural is blurred. In the sharpest opposition to the first epoch, however, now everything tends to be understood as man-made. Natural growth has given way to human imposition. Nature is no longer the prime mover; humans understand *themselves* as the prime responsible agents everywhere. What used to come about by nature, such as birth and death, the course of rivers, the powers of human memory, the emotions, the crops, the amount of white meat on a turkey, the strength of the odor of a rose, and so on and on, are now imposed by humans. For Heidegger, this modern situation is most dangerous and yet not without promise, and to his analysis of it we now turn.

Part II
Modern Technology

Heidegger begins his characterization of modern technology in "Die Frage nach der Technik" by speaking of the "essential domain" of technology. He does not say explicitly what the term "essential domain" (*der Wesensbereich*) means, but it is readily intelligible. Technology has been determined in its essence as a disclosive looking. Presumably, then, the domain of the essence is the domain gazed at in the disclosive looking. This domain has come to light as the realm of Being, the essence, truth, disconcealment, *aletheia*. The "essential domain" of technology is then precisely the essence, the essence of things in general. Thus Heidegger's term *Wesensbereich* should perhaps be translated very literally as "essence-domain." What it expresses is that technology has the essence *as* its domain, technology is fundamentally the disclosive looking at the essence of things in general. What has just been determined is precisely that technology is this sort of theoretical disclosure, a matter of truth, and not primarily a way of doing and making things.

Heidegger proceeds to raise the hypothetical objection that this determination of the essential domain applies only to ancient and not to modern technology: "In opposition to this determination of the essential domain of technology, one could object that it might indeed hold for Greek thinking and, at best, might apply to handcraft technology, but it does not at all appertain to modern, power-machine technology" (FT, 15/13). Let us look a little more closely at this possible objection. What is supposed not to appertain to modern technology, and why?

Ancient versus modern technology

The objection denies that modern technology is an affair of looking disclosively upon Being or upon the essence of things. Ancient technology

67

might conceivably be understood in those terms, but not modern technology. Why? What is the difference between the two technologies? As expressed here, the difference is between handcraft technology and power-machine technology. That is, the difference is between the hand, or the hand machine, and the power machine. What is this difference? What is the difference between, say, a chisel in the hands of Michelangelo and a laser knife (which is a "high-tech" power tool)? From one point of view, the former is at times more violent than the latter. A chisel would be infinitely more "invasive" than a laser if it had to be used in surgery. But there is a more fundamental sense in which to be gentle means to let come forth, no matter how much noise and brute strength it takes, and to be violent is to impose upon, no matter how little material damage is done. In this sense, the hand tool is gentle, and Michelangelo's sculpting is gentle work, whereas modern surgery, even laser surgery on the eye, is violent and forceful, if it stems from the usual imperious attitude of today's medicine. The difference between the gentleness of hand tools and the force of power machines is doubtlessly in play in the formulation of the hypothetical objection just stated. Handcraft technology can be understood as an affair of looking, for the precise reason that it is gentle. Handcraft does not, so to speak, overpower the matter but only gears into the matter's own flow in a certain direction. Handcraft is not the master of the form buried in the matter, it is the servant of that form. Recall Aristotle's thesis that the *eidos* is the genuine producer and that everything else is subservient to it. That is exactly why ancient technology might be determined in its essence as a disclosive looking. If handcraft is subservient to something already implicit in the matter, then indeed the prime work of the handcraftsman can be understood as the gentle occupation of contemplation, of looking disclosively upon that to which it is subservient, upon that whence it receives guidance, namely the Being of some being, or, speaking generally, Being as such. Because handcraft is gentle,[1] because it desires to nurture Being, it can be understood as primarily theoretical, as the disclosive looking upon Being.

Power-machine technology is precisely powerful; it enforces its will upon matter, imposes a form onto matter, rather than merely nurturing a form from latency to visibility. Power-machine technology is pragmatic; it desires results and cannot be bothered with theory. Through power machines, human will is *inflicted* on matter; the man running a power machine is a dictator. He forces his will onto matter. That is why modern technology does not seem to be an affair of looking disclosively upon Being; such a gentle, theoretical occupation is of no concern to a dictator or pragmatist. Modern technology, we say, is interested only in results; it is practical and precisely not theoretical.

While this distinction is no doubt in the background of the hypothetical objection, Heidegger places a different phenomenon in the foreground. He sees something else as the origin of the objection, something we can grasp by comparing the products of the two technologies. What is the difference between, for example, common pins made by hand, as they used to be made, and those made by modern pin-machines? The most striking difference is that the handmade pins were all individual, whereas machine-made pins are completely uniform. Modern pins have no individuating characteristics; they all look exactly alike. They are all exact, they are precise, and they deviate only within very close tolerances. Whence does this exactitude derive? How is the power machine able to impose this precision and close tolerance? The ultimate source of the exactitude is that upon which the power machine is based, namely exact science. It is the exactitude of modern natural science that is the source of the precision in the products of modern technology. The difference between the two technologies then resides in exact modern science. So it is modern science that lies behind the objection. "It is said that, because modern technology rests on modern, exact natural science, it is incomparably different from all previous technologies" (FT, 15/14).

A few lines down, Heidegger again uses the epithet "exact" to characterize natural science. We ourselves say that modern technology is scientific, that it "has things down to a science," and we mean that modern technology is exact, that it has dispelled all guesswork and chance. On the other hand, we call handcraft technology an art (the Greek word *techne* is even translated very often as "art," understood in opposition to science or knowledge), and we mean that it is hit or miss, that it depends on the skill of some particular person. Thus, if modern technology does rest on science, it cannot be characterized as a disclosive looking at Being, and its essential domain is not the essence of things in general. Modern technology looks to science, to scientific, empirical, practical, proven facts, and is not guided by a murky theory about what it means to be in general. A murky foundation leads to an inexact, "artsy" technology. Modern technology is based on exact, objective science, not upon an obscure disclosure of Being; that is what makes it absolutely novel and incomparably different from the previous technology.

Heidegger proceeds, in this first, introductory paragraph on modern technology, to pose a most penetrating question, one that contains, in germ, a radical undermining of the hypothetical objection. For Heidegger, all technologies have the same essential domain, and modern technology, no less than the ancient, is fundamentally a disclosive looking upon Being. That is why Heidegger now asks: "The decisive question is still: of what essence is modern technology that it can occur to it to employ exact natural science?"(FT, 15/14).

This question, when thought through, will completely undermine the hypothetical objection. For Heidegger, it is not so much that modern technology is *based* on modern science as it is that modern technology *employs* modern science. In other words, Heidegger's question announces a certain priority of technology over science. Let us agree that modern technology does put science to use. What Heidegger's question implies is that, in order to put science to use, there must have previously occurred the *idea* of putting science to use. Someone must have had this idea, which is to say that someone must have seen something, there must have been disclosed to someone the possibility of putting science to use. Someone must have looked disclosively upon this essential possibility. Now the seeing of this essential possibility is what Heidegger means by modern technology. Modern technology is the seeing, the idea, that employs science. Science is then not the source of technology. The seeing (= technology) is not based on science, since the seeing lies outside of the purview of factual, empirical, science. To put a thing to use is, ipso facto, to occupy a vantage point outside of it and above it. To employ science is not a scientific idea; it is not one of the discoveries of the experimental method. To employ science is, quite to the contrary, an *essential* idea; i.e., it rests on an insight concerning essential possibilities, an insight concerning what the essence of things might be. This insight is what constitutes modern technology (or any technology). Thus, for Heidegger, *all* technology is fundamentally an understanding of what it means to be, an understanding of the essence of things merely insofar as they are things; all technology is a disclosive looking upon Being in general.

The preceding is obviously abstract. Heidegger has up to this point merely hinted at the eventual direction of his account of modern technology. In fact, he has done little more than pose a peculiar question. We now possess, however, a thread of Ariadne to guide us through Heidegger's concrete analyses. This guiding thread is the notion that modern technology is an understanding of Being in general, an understanding that takes Being to be such that modern natural science can be applied to beings.

Heidegger concludes his preparatory remarks by stating this guiding thread directly: "What is modern technology? It, too, is a disclosive looking. Only if we allow our gaze to rest on this fundamental characteristic will what is novel in modern technology show itself to us"(FT, 15/14).

Heidegger's task is now to describe the sort of looking he understands to be characteristic of modern technology, and then he needs to justify his claim that modern technology is indeed a disclosive looking and not merely applied science. If modern technology is an understanding of Being in general, then it has a priority over science; thus Heidegger has to show that science is applied technology, instead of modern technology being applied science.

Modern technology as a challenging: The gear and the capacitor

Heidegger's description of modern technology is couched in a long list of unmistakably pejorative, violent, imperious terms: modern technology is a challenging, forcing, ravishing, attacking, throttling, dominating, exploiting, imposing, disposing, exposing, and deposing. Heidegger does not quite use a word that would be literally translated as "rape," but his terms unquestionably describe a violation of nature equivalent to rape. Let us examine these terms in the order Heidegger proposes them.

Heidegger begins by characterizing the attitude of modern technology as a "challenging" (*Herausfordern*), meant in the sense of a challenging to a duel. Duelling stems from an imperious and adolescent-minded bravado, and to challenge someone to a duel is to say: "I demand that you come out here and give me satisfaction." What is to be satisfied, of course, is the person's claim that he has a right to take the life of the other. Now, duelling is done honorably. That is, the challenger exposes himself to the danger of being killed himself. The other man is given a chance to defend himself. For Heidegger, not only is modern technology a challenging, it is a dishonorable one; nature is given no chance to defend itself and is instead *forced* to give satisfaction.

What demand does modern technology place upon nature, what is the satisfaction claimed in the challenge? It is the demand that nature yield up its energies and resources so that they might be on call, i.e., readily available for human use. The claim is made that nature's treasures are merely there to satisfy, as efficiently as possible, human needs and whims. This attitude is diametrically opposed to the one of respect. That is why, for Heidegger, the making or producing that issues from the outlook of modern technology is not a *poiesis*: "The particular disclosive looking that prevails in modern technology does not unfold into a bringing-forth in the sense of *poiesis*. The disclosive looking that holds sway in modern technology is a challenging, one that imposes upon nature the presumptuous demand to hand over energy, energy *as such*, energy which, once it has been ravished out from nature, can then be hoarded" (FT, 15/14).

Poiesis is the way of production that embodies the attitude of respect. *Poiesis* "goes with the flow"; i.e., it defers to the natural ends, the ends with which nature is already pregnant. Ancient technology is primarily a disclosive looking at those ends, those natural possibilities, and *poiesis* is the midwifery that assists those ends to come forth into full visibility. Modern technology, as well, is a disclosive looking at possibilities, but these possibilities are *imposed* on nature, and that, for Heidegger, is what is novel about modern technology. Modern technology is not a deferential looking but a presumptuous one. Modern technology makes an excessive, hubristic, unnatural demand upon nature. How so? It might at first seem that the demands placed upon nature by modern technology are not in the least excessive, since, after all, nature does fulfill those demands. Modern technology works, which is to say that nature lives up to expectations. What then is disrespectful or, so to speak, unnatural about the modern attitude toward nature?

Heidegger does not answer this question directly; instead, he provides examples that are meant to make obvious the presumptuousness of the demands placed upon nature by modern technology. The first example continues the passage just cited above. Heidegger asks whether the old-fashioned windmill did not make the same demand upon the energies of nature: "But does this not also apply to the old windmill? No. Its vanes indeed turn in the wind; they are in fact immediately dependent on the blowing of the wind. But that windmill does not *exploit* the energy of the air currents, with the aim of hoarding it" (FT, 15/14).

The idea of exploiting here is that of making accessible or opening up, as a developer exploits or opens up new markets. Heidegger's word could also be translated as "working," in the sense of working a mine, opening it up for all it is worth. Heidegger is saying that the old windmill does not work the wind for all it is worth; on the contrary, the wind works *it*. Furthermore, not only does the wind work it, but the wind works it "immediately" (*unmittelbar*). The latter is perhaps the most telling word in the passage.

The old windmill is precisely a mill; i.e., it mills grain. It indeed prevails upon the winds for its own purposes, for human purposes, since, left to itself, a wind would never mill grain. Yet the mill merely gears into the wind, which is true in the literal sense that the connection between the millstones and the wind is accomplished through gears. The modern windmill, however, is not designed to mill anything; it is not a mill but a dynamo. It generates electricity, which is stockpiled and distributed to remote places for remote uses. The connection between the wind and these remote uses is an indirect one; it is not accomplished through rude gears but through exact capacitors. The difference between the old windmill and the modern one, between an immediate connection to the wind and a mediate one, thus comes down to the difference between the gear and the capacitor. What is this latter difference, from a Heideggerian standpoint?

The gear of the old windmill is "immediately dependent on [or immediately submissive to] the blowing of the wind." The gear works only while the wind is actually blowing and only while it is blowing in a certain manner: the wind must blow above the threshold force needed to overcome the resistance of the gears, and the wind must blow from a certain direction. Furthermore, the energy of the wind channeled by the windmill is not stored but is immediately exhausted in turning the gears.

On the other hand, the capacitor (one charged by a wind-driven generator) is also *entirely* dependent on the blowing of the wind, but it is not *immediately* dependent on the wind. The capacitor will still work after the wind has stopped, and the capacitor offers no resistance the wind must overcome. Furthermore, the charge of a capacitor can be built up to the full by increments of infinitesimal amounts. Gearing, on the other hand, obeys the law of all or none: below the threshold, the wind has no effect on the gears. Practically speaking, there is no threshold for a modern windmill; the slightest movement of the air can be put to use. That is to say, the modern windmill works the wind for all it is worth. Finally, the capacitor does not exhaust the energy that has been expended to charge it; quite to the contrary, the whole purpose of the modern windmill is to amass that energy and keep it on call. Briefly, then, in Heidegger's eyes, the modern windmill wrings out energy from the wind, ravishes the wind for its energy, and then hoards that energy.

What is disrespectful or excessive about the modern windmill? Why does Heidegger find it necessary to describe it with such pejorative terms as "ravish" and "hoard"? We can begin to respond to these questions by asking what must be seen in advance in order to construct a windmill. What must be seen in the wind—i.e., under what aspect must the wind be disclosed—in order to conceive the possibility of a windmill? From a Heideggerian standpoint, there is an essential difference between the seeing in advance that gives rise to the old windmill versus the seeing that lies at the basis of the modern one. What did our predecessors see in the wind, and what do we now see in it? It could be said that, in general, both the ancients and the moderns see force or energy in the wind. But there is an essential difference. The ancients do not see in the wind *energy as such*. Perhaps we could call what they do see in the wind the *natural* blowing of the air. They see the wind entirely in its natural context, and they respect its natural context. That is why the old windmill has to wait for a "windy" day. To a modern windmill, every day is a windy day, since the air is always in motion and always contains some exploitable energy.

The ancients do not see the wind as a source of energy as such, energy that could be put to any sort of use, but instead they see the wind as a force in a certain direction. The ancients see a directedness in the wind, i.e., they see the wind as already pregnant with something. The old windmill is designed to bring that pregnancy to fruition. With what is the wind naturally pregnant? That can be answered by taking a walk on a windy way and feeling the wind blowing in your face or at your back. The wind is naturally connected to movement: it helps or hinders things in their movement. The old windmill taps into this potential of the wind; the old windmill puts this potential to good use. It does so by harnessing the wind to a turning apparatus. The old windmill does nothing but turn, and turning is nothing but a natural motion the wind may or may not assist. The gears of a windmill merely serve to transfer the turning motion from the vanes to the millstone. The entire windmill then merely taps into and transfers the natural directedness of the wind toward motion.

A modern windmill, composed of vanes, generator, and capacitor, does not simply tap into and transfer, but instead exploits, transforms, and stores. The vanes do indeed turn, but, since they offer practically no resistance, it does not require wind, a windy day, to turn them but any sort of air current; that is how the modern windmill *exploits* the wind. Secondly, a modern windmill needs no gears, and the generator does not transfer motion but instead *transforms* it into electrical potential. The capacitor, finally, does not use or use up that new form of energy but instead *hoards* it, so that it may be discharged when and where humans see fit. Heidegger describes this process as follows:

> The disclosive looking that holds sway in modern technology has the character of a . . . challenging. The challenging amounts to this, namely that the energy latent in nature is exploited, the exploited is transformed, the transformed is stored, the stored is, in turn, distributed, and the distributed is converted anew. Exploiting, transforming, storing, distributing, and converting are characteristic modes of this disclosive looking. (FT, 17/16)

What sort of disclosive looking makes possible these modes? That is, more specifically, what must be seen in advance in order to conceive of the possibility of an exploiting, transforming, and storing modern windmill? The answer is that what must be seen in the wind is not merely that with which the wind is naturally pregnant, namely movement, but energy as such. The wind must be seen out of its natural context, where it assists or hinders some thing's own movement. The wind must be seen not so much as wind, as that which we feel *in concreto* when we walk outdoors, but rather as mere anemo-pressure. This anemo-pressure or anemo-energy is not Boreas, nor the West Wind, nor any wind with which we are familiar. It is something we do not experience at all, for it is the result of an abstract way of looking at the wind. Anemo-pressure is the wind viewed only in terms of the energy that may be extracted from it, and anemo-pressure is no more the wind than H_2O is water.

What does it take to view the wind in this artificial way as anemo-energy? From a Heideggerian standpoint, it takes hubris. It takes disrespect for nature; it requires an imposition of a foreign standpoint, one that sees in nature only what can be extracted out of it for human needs and whims. That, for Heidegger, is what is excessive or unnatural about modern technology. It reduces nature to something at the beck and call of humans, rather than respecting nature and nature's own ends. Modern technology is a reductionistic looking upon nature; what is disclosed in such a looking is a reduced face of nature, reduced from the concrete to the abstract, reduced from nature as it presents itself in our experience to nature in the form that allows us to exploit it. We can exploit water, understood as H_2O; we can exploit it for its hydrogen and oxygen. But no one swims in H_2O; no one baptizes with H_2O. To see in water H_2O is equivalent to looking upon a woman as a mere sexual object: in both cases, we have the same reductionism, the same violation, the same exploitation. For Heidegger, it is indeed science that teaches us water is composed of hydrogen and oxygen, but it is technology that actually performs the reduction, since the technological outlook is what motivates science to see in water a chemical compound in the first place.

Likewise, it is science that teaches us how to build a modern windmill, but it is modern technology that supplies science with its motivating idea, namely the idea that the wind is a source of energy as such. The modern windmill certainly arises as the application of scientific discoveries; but it is modern technology that motivates that application in the first place. Modern technology supplies the idea of nature as something exploitable; that is what motivates the actual exploitation by science.

In this first example we also see, in a preliminary way, that for Heidegger the antidote to the danger of modern technology is not conservation, or, at least, it is not *merely* conservation. A modern windmill is "environmentally friendly"; it exploits a renewable energy source and does not pollute. For Heidegger, however, such a windmill is not the solution but is part of the problem. The solution must go deeper than conservation, must go all the way to the root of the problem, which is the attitude toward nature at the heart of modern technology. Conservationism may actually include the exact same attitude that nature is merely there to be exploited, only now it is recognized that nature's treasures are finite and we must make them last. For Heidegger, such an attitude is essentially the same as the one of rampant exploitation of nature; they both embody the same view of nature, and it is that view that holds the danger. Thus for Heidegger, as we already hinted and will take up more fully in Part III, the danger is not that technology might get out of hand and make the world uninhabitable; the danger is not merely to human life but to something even more precious, to something even more worthy of defending, namely, human freedom and dignity.

Modern technology as an imposition

The second of the main terms by which Heidegger characterizes the attitude of modern technology is "imposition." Modern technology *imposes* upon nature, precisely in the sense that one person can be an imposition on another, namely by taking unwarranted advantage of the other. The idea is that through modern technology humans inflict themselves on the resources of nature, abduct them, carry them off by force.

The German word is *stellen*, and its basic meaning is "to pose" in the sense of placing into position. Many compounds are formed out of *stellen*, and Heidegger is about to take full advantage of them. (I shall try to render all those terms as forms of the English word "pose": oppose, impose, dispose, depose, etc.) *Stellen* can mean simply "to put" or "to place," in a neutral sense, but the word often bears the connotation of *forceful* putting. Most colloquially, *stellen* means to "corner" or "buttonhole" someone, i.e., to press upon or importune. In hunting, it means "to bring to bay." It can also mean "to set upon" someone, in the sense of "having at" someone, attacking, besieging. And it is said of conditions, when they are dictated upon the vanquished.

It is this sense of forceful posing that is in play here. Heidegger had in fact already used the word in a forceful sense, when he claimed that modern technology, *precisely as a challenging*, "imposes on nature a presumptuous demand." Later, Heidegger will even say explicitly that *stellen* is to be taken in the sense of challenging. In order to retain something of Heidegger's word play, while also capturing the crucial sense of forceful infliction, I render *Stellen* as "imposition." The published English translation is "setting upon." I have no quarrel with this term, and it even has this advantage, as would "pressing upon," namely that it connotes a kind of sexual self-infliction. And Heidegger is going to come very close to calling modern technology a rape of nature.

The introduction of the notion of imposition occurs in the passage immediately following the mention of the old windmill:

> In contrast, today the land is challenged; i.e., it is ravished for its coal and ore. The earth is now looked upon precisely as a coal lode, the soil as an ore depository. The field the farmer of old used to cultivate appeared differently, i.e., when to cultivate still meant to tend and to nurture. The farmer of old did not challenge the soil of the field. In sowing the grain, the farmer consigned the seed to the forces of growth, and then he tended to its increase. In the meantime, the ordering of the field has been sucked into the maelstrom of a different sort of ordering, one that *imposes* on nature. It imposes on it in the sense of challenging it. Agriculture is now mechanized foodstuffs industry. The air is imposed upon to relinquish nitrogen, the soil to relinquish ore, the ore to relinquish, among other things, uranium, and the latter is imposed upon to disgorge atomic energy, which can be unleashed for destructive or peaceful ends. (FT, 15–16/14–15)

This is a clear and vigorous paragraph that scarcely needs commentary. The main point is unmistakable, as illustrated in the example of traditional farming versus modern agriculture. The farmer of old submitted, tended, and nurtured. These are the quintessential activities of *poiesis*; the old way of farming is midwifery, and what it brings forth is that with which nature is already pregnant. Modern agriculture, on the other hand, hardly brings forth *crops*; it produces "foodstuffs" or, perhaps we should rather say, ingesta. Modern agriculture does not submit seeds to the forces of growth; on the contrary, it interferes with the seeds, genetically manipulating them. The forces of growth are now in the farmer's own hands, which is to say that she *imposes* the conditions that determine growth. The end product, in the extreme case, to which we may be heading inexorably, is astronauts' food. It would be a travesty to say grace before "eating" a "meal" of such "foods." They are not gifts; they are human creations. They are not grown; they are synthesized. They are created by someone *playing God*, and it would make no sense to *pray to God* before ingesting them.

What Heidegger means by "imposing" is "playing God." To play God is to place oneself above nature, to look upon nature as subservient to one's own bidding. For Heidegger, this is an imperious, adolescent, violent attitude. Modern technology violates nature; it *forces* nature to hand over its treasures, it throttles them out of nature, and nature then must precisely "disgorge."

According to Heidegger, the earth, the air, and the fields now look different. We see the earth as an enormous mineral lode, we see the air as anemo-energy, we see the river as hydraulic power. There is an obvious sense in which this is true, but the correct order of motivation is not so obvious. It is not *because* the earth is ravished that it now looks like a store of minerals; on the contrary, the earth comes to be ravished precisely because of the way we now *see* it. The disclosive looking comes first; the possibilities come before the actualities. We must first look upon the earth, upon nature in general, in a certain way; then we can exploit what we see. And that way of looking is the way of modern technology; i.e., it is the disrespectful way that sees in nature something there merely to satisfy, as efficiently as possible, human needs and whims. That is the most basic outlook of modern technology; concretely, it amounts to seeing in nature energy as such, minable, hoardable, exploitable energy. Nature is exploited because it is disclosed as something exploitable; the disclosure of the exploitable possibilities precedes the actual exploiting. It requires scientific advancements to exploit nature; but the precedent seeing of nature as exploitable is not a matter of science. It is a theoretical and not a practical or experimental affair; it is a way of disclosive looking that expresses, for Heidegger, the essence of modern technology.

Thus far, Heidegger has characterized this disclosive looking of modern technology as a challenging and an imposing. He next offers an even more violent and pejorative characterization.

Modern technology as a ravishment

The new term is *Fördern*. It can have various meanings, depending on the context, and Heidegger does play here on those different senses. Thus it is not possible to translate the term with the same English word each time, and, indeed, it is a false ideal to set up a one-to-one correspondence between terms in a philosophical translation. In the published English version of Heidegger's essay on technology, *fördern* is rendered as "expedite," when Heidegger proposes it as an essential characterization of modern technology. But the word is also translated in these few pages as "extract," "put out," "further," "haul out," "dispatch," and "exploit."

There are two main connotations of the word *fördern*. The first is a neutral one, where the meaning is simply to convey or move along or promote. A *Förderband* is what we call a conveyor belt. But *fördern* can also suggest the use of brute force, and then it means not simply to transport but to drag out (against resistance), to hoist up (as dead weight), to extract (with effort). *Fördern* is a term used in mining, and perhaps it is that context, in play ever since Heidegger began speaking of coal and ore, which suggested the word to him. In mining, the term has a strong, violent sense: it characterizes the way coal is brought to the surface of the earth, not by being gently "promoted" but by being "lugged out."

In addition, the term *fördern* (Heidegger also uses *herausfördern*) is closely related to the word for "challenge," *herausfordern*. There is no doubt that Heidegger intends these two words to be heard together. Indeed he uses them as synonyms twice. Thus the connection with *herausfordern* corroborates the view that *fördern* is meant in its forceful sense. In fact, everything leads us to take *fördern* in the strongest possible sense, when the term is used as a characterization of the essence of modern technology. Accordingly, the published translation as "expedite" is too weak. That is a neutral term which covers over the pejorative connotation. That connotation is even made explicit by Heidegger, who stipulates the sense in which he means *Fördern*, namely: exposing and exploiting.

To expose and exploit is to rape. It is to force something (or someone) to relinquish its (or her) treasures. It is to take the other as merely there for one's own satisfaction. To challenge is to demand satisfaction, and to rape is to obtain that satisfaction by force, by imposition, by pressing upon. What Heidegger is saying is that modern technology *rapes* nature for its energies and resources. Modern technology does not "expedite" these from nature; it is a matter of abducting them. In the context, "abduction"—not as a neutral "drawing-out," but as a forcible carrying off for illicit purposes—would be a defensible translation of *Fördern*. To abduct, to expose and exploit, to rape—these describe a typically imperious violation of something or someone, and in Heidegger's eyes, modern technology, like any rape, is a violent, immature, self-infliction or self-imposition.

I then propose "ravish" as the translation of *fördern*. To ravish is to rape with special violence, so as to leave wasted, and that is precisely what is at issue here. The word had already been introduced in the previous paragraph ("today the land is challenged; i.e., it is ravished for its coal and ore"), and now Heidegger elaborates by showing a *double* violation of nature on the part of modern technology. That is what the term "ravishment" now adds to the previous characterization of modern technology as a challenging and an imposition:

> The imposition that challenges nature to relinquish energy is a ravishment and is so in a two-fold sense. It ravishes in that it exposes and exploits. This ravishing, however, is in advance subordinated to the ravishing of something else, i.e., to the impelling forward of something to its maximum utility at the minimum expense. The coal obtained by ravishing a coal lode has not been extracted so that it might simply be present at hand somewhere or other. The coal is stockpiled; i.e., it is placed on call to fulfill an order for the sun's warmth stored in it. The warmth of the sun is challenged to relinquish thermal energy, which is then ordered to supply steam, whose pressure drives the works that keep a factory running. (FT, 16/15)

The double violation is this: nature is ravished to extract coal, and the coal is then ravished for its energy. There is first of all a forcible carrying off for illicit purposes and then an actual execution of those illicit purposes. These two acts are precisely what we mean by abduction, rape, or ravishment. *Fördern* cannot mean here "expediting" and "furthering." It is true that Heidegger does play on the etymological meaning of *Fördern*: the prefix "*för-*" means "forward," and that is why Heidegger describes it as an "impelling forward" (*vorwärts*). But this does not make it a furthering in the sense of promoting or benefitting. The earth is not benefited by being stripmined; the coal is not benefited by being forced to disgorge its thermal energy. Heidegger's point is that the earth and the coal are "wasted" by modern technology in its challenging of them; i.e., modern technology lays them to waste, ravages them, exhausts them. The earth and the coal are not benefited, humans are. What is promoted is the fulfillment of *human* needs and whims. It is something of a joke to say that the coal is impelled "forward" or "upward and onward." It would be like giving a man a raise—by hanging him—or like driving him forth—in a tumbrel. The very fact that the forward motion is "impelled" indicates that the *Fördern* is not a furthering of the coal in a beneficial or even in a neutral sense. Human interests are indeed furthered, but the coal is simply drained more and more, depleted ever more thoroughly and with ever more efficiency. In short, then, what Heidegger is saying is that the ravishment of the coal lode is for the sake of the ravishment of the coal, which is for the sake of the unbridled satisfaction of human desires.

Thus the term *Fördern*, understood as ravishment, develops the same basic characterization of modern technology expressed in the terms "challenging" and "imposition." The result is a view of modern technology as a violation of nature akin to the immature and violent acts of duelling, pressing upon, and rape.

Modern technology as a disposing

The fourth, and final, term Heidegger offers as an essential characterization of the attitude of modern technology is *Bestellen*. We are already familiar with its root word, *Stellen*, which means "imposition." *Stellen* and various of its derivatives rule over these central pages of Heidegger's essay, the pages devoted to the essential characterization of modern technology. Indeed, one or another form of *stellen* occurs, on the average, twice in every sentence here. It would be impossible in an English translation to capture the nuances of meaning and at the same time connect all the relevant English words etymologically. The published English version does gamely attempt it, in certain passages, by employing phrases grouped around the word "set": set upon, set up, set in order, set into, set going, set to. I myself shall employ, as much as possible, English compounds of "pose." Yet Heidegger has recourse to too many German terms, all sharing the common root *stellen*; the correct response on the part of a translator is nightmares.

The most important of the *stellen* compounds, in the essay on technology, is *bestellen*. In ordinary German, the word has two principal senses. First of all, it means to place an order, in the sense of ordering goods, reserving a table, commissioning a work of art. As applied to people, it means to summon (to order into one's presence) or to appoint someone. Secondly, the word means to place *in* order, to arrange, to cultivate or till. In the published English translation of Heidegger's essay on technology, *Bestellen* is for the most part rendered as "ordering." But it is also translated there as "commanding," "setting in order," "cultivating," "setting up," and "subordinating." The term *bestellbar* is rendered mostly as "orderable," but is also translated as "available," "available on demand," "at one's command," "on call," and "on call for duty."

Heidegger invokes, in his use of the term *Bestellen*, the two senses of placing *an* order and placing *in* order. Heidegger purposely plays on this ambiguity in the German word. The English word "order" contains the same ambiguity, and so the published English translation is, to that extent, unexceptionable. Nevertheless, the term "order" conceals the etymological connection between *bestellen* and *stellen*, and so it fails to express the important ideas of posing (by a subject) and imposing (forceful posing by a subject). I intend to translate *bestellen* as "dispose." This word also contains an ambiguity: it means to use at will, the way we speak of disposable income or of some resource as at our disposal. It also means to arrange, such as we speak of the final disposition of cases in court, or to put in order, in the sense of the disposal or deployment of troops. To dispose then means both to "order about" in the sense of using at will and to "order up" in the sense of placing in order. The advantage of the word "dis-pose," compared to "order," lies in its connection to the posing and imposing activity of the subject, a connection that, as we shall see, must be brought out. Furthermore, to dispose can also mean to get rid of, to discard, and Heidegger will eventually invoke that sense as well.

I will concentrate on a single characterization of modern technology that Heidegger repeats three times (FT, 18/18, 20/19, 23/22). He says that modern technology is, in the published translation, an "ordering revealing." The German phrase is *das bestellende Entbergen*. I would render it as "a disclosive looking that disposes." In what sense or senses is modern technology a disposing?

In the first place, "disposing" here means using at will or ordering about and is a synonym for "challenging." Indeed Heidegger explicitly places these two terms together on numerous occasions and even speaks of a "challenging disposing" (FT, 22/21), i.e., a disposing that exemplifies the challenging carried out by modern technology. Heidegger also explicitly joins "disposing" in this sense to "imposition" and "ravishment." Thus "disposing" expresses the attitude of modern technology we have already seen, namely that the resources and energies of nature are merely at our disposal, there to satisfy human desires. All the characteristic terms of modern technology join forces in the following passage:

> The hydroelectric plant is imposed on the flowing Rhine. It imposes on it for its hydraulic pressure, which forces turbines to turn, and this turning drives the machines whose works produce the electric current. The relay station and the power grid are then put at the disposal of the further ravishment of the river. In the domain of this interconnected sequence in the disposition of electrical energy, even the flowing Rhine now appears as something at our disposal. (FT, 16/16)

Thus the characterization of modern technology as a disclosive looking that disposes is meant to indicate, first of all, that modern technology regards nature as something to be imposed on, something to be ordered about at will. The resources and energies of nature appear to be entirely at our disposal, merely there to satisfy human wants and desires, merely there to be ravished and wasted. Accordingly, "disposing," in the sense of using at will, is here just another name for the imperious attitude Heidegger has already ascribed to modern technology.

But there is another sense of disposing at play here in the phrase "disclosive looking that disposes." The phrase also means that modern technology arranges things in a certain way, sees things in a certain way, assigns things to a certain order. Modern technology discloses things as belonging to a certain order. Modern technology is precisely the looking which corresponds to the self-disclosure of things as belonging to a certain order. That is the second sense in which modern technology disposes: it sees in things a certain disposition, it sees things as belonging to a certain order, it sees a certain order as appropriate to things. For Heidegger, to see things in this way is precisely what constitutes modern technology. Modern technology does not simply come onto the scene after things have been investigated insofar as they pertain to this order; on the contrary, modern technology is that which sees this order as pertaining to things in the first place and so gives the investigations their initial impetus.

What is this order? What is this way of disclosing things? It is the scientific way. The order is the scientific order, which means the mathematical order, the calculable order. What Heidegger is saying is that modern technology is the disclosure of things in general as subject to calculation. Modern technology reveals things as possible objects of science. Modern technology is the outlook which sees that things may profitably be subject to scientific investigation. For Heidegger, then, to put it in a still preliminary way, it is modern technology that starts science going; modern technology is not a subsequent application of science and mathematics. Modern technology is the outlook on things that science needs to get started. Science is driven by the conviction that nature is calculable; that conviction, that outlook, is precisely what Heidegger attributes to modern technology. Modern technology is an insight into the essence of things in general, namely that things in general are coherently calculable. That is an insight into the essence of things, an insight into the Being of beings. As an insight, it is a disclosive looking, and as an assigning of things to a certain order, it is a disclosive looking that disposes.

The relation between science and modern technology will be explored in full presently. For now, we merely need to note that modern technology disposes of things in two senses: it avails itself of things, i.e., it imposes on them at will, and it assigns things to a certain order, it sees them in a certain way. Which of these two sorts of disposing has the primacy? Does the way of seeing follow from the imposition, or does the way of seeing make possible the imposition? For Heidegger, the latter is the case. It is not because things are ordered about that they come to be seen as merely there for our satisfaction; it is because things are unconcealed in a certain way, under a certain aspect, that we can impose on them and ravish them. The disclosure of the possibility, i.e., the unconcealing of things as ravishable, precedes and makes possible the actual ravishment. Things look ravishable; that motivates the actual ravishment. It is not that our ravishing of them makes them look like mere ravishable material. The look, the unconcealment, has the priority.

How *do* things now look, what sort of unconcealment now holds sway? Moreover, how do things come to be unconcealed in this way? In other words, is it human beings who are ultimately responsible for the way of disclosure? Is the unconcealment of things a human accomplishment? These are the questions Heidegger takes up on his way toward showing the priority of disposing as a way of looking over disposing as an imposition of one's will. These questions also lie on his way toward showing the priority of modern technology over science.

"Disposables"

The first question concerns unconcealment. How are things unconcealed in the age of modern technology? How are they disclosively looked upon by modern, technological mankind? What do things look like today? What essential aspect do they present to us? What is their essence?

Heidegger describes the unconcealment of the things of today's world in one of the most important and difficult passages in the entire essay. The passage is only one short paragraph in length but contains such an intricate wordplay that no English translation could do it full justice, i.e., retain the wordplay and at the same time render all the nuances of meaning. There is one especially crucial term in the passage; it is the word Heidegger offers as a proper name for the unconcealment prevailing today. That term is *der Bestand*.

In ordinary German, *Bestand* means "stock-in-hand" or "inventory." The root of the word is *stehen*, which means "to stand," and Heidegger certainly does play on that root meaning. Indeed, the brief passage includes ten occurrences of the word *stehen* or of one or another of its derivative forms. Interspersed among these are the familiar plays on the word *stellen*. So *Stehen* and *Stellen*, standing and posing, or imposing, are here intertwined or, rather, set off against one another. In general, the *stell-* words apply to the things of modern technology. These things are precisely posed by us—in various senses of the term. As posed, things today lack their own standing; they are not self-standing or autonomous. They have a peculiar standing, and it is that peculiar standing Heidegger attempts to capture in his term *Bestand*.

The published English translation of *Bestand* is "standing-reserve." This term obviously succeeds in displaying an etymological connection between *Bestand* and *stehen*. It also conveys the correct general idea of things as stock-piled resources. But the term "standing-reserve" does not capture the nuances Heidegger explicitly wishes to impart to the word *Bestand*. In the first place, that English translation fails to capture the peculiar, shaky standing of things today. Furthermore, Heidegger explicitly asserts that the things which have the status of *Bestand* are not mere supplies. In addition, according to Heidegger, the things characterized as *Bestand* are not objects. If *Bestand* is translated as "standing-reserve," it is very difficult to make sense of the distinctions Heidegger is here trying to draw. For, "standing-reserves" are precisely supplies, resources on hand. Moreover, an "object" is a "thing" that has been degraded in status. An object is a thing thought of merely as the correlate of some human attitude; for example, H_2O is the "object" of scientific consciousness. But water as such, on the other hand, is a "thing," a real thing that does not merely stand in relation to us but is a thing in its own right, standing on its own footing, independent of us. Therefore the standing-reserve should be composed precisely of objects (since it is composed of things looked upon merely as at our disposal, merely in terms of our challenging attitude), and yet Heidegger says just the opposite, that the *Bestand* is objectless. What then is the proper sense of *Bestand*, and what sort of standing is implied in Heidegger's use of the word, if *Bestand* is to be distinguished from supplies and objects?

Heidegger intends the term *Bestand* to connote, in the first place, something we have already seen, namely that all things are today taken to be at our disposal. Everything exists to serve our needs and our pleasure, and nothing deserves respect as possibly standing outside of the uses we may make of it. Secondly, and more significantly, things are not merely taken to be at our disposal, they are also viewed as disposable in the sense of discardable. Not only can we dispose of things, deploy them, order them about, but we can discard them once we have used them and exhausted their utility. Many consumer products are disposable these days; they are designed to be used once and then cast away. What Heidegger is suggesting in the term *Bestand* is not only that nature as a whole is approached today with a consumer mentality but that this is even the most disrespectful consumer mentality. The things of nature are not only consumables, they are disposables. We need feel no compunction about ravishing them and leaving them wasted.

The point is this: if all things are disposables, then nothing has a permanent footing. Not only are natural things resources, supplies of which we can avail ourselves, but they are not even deserving of respect *as* supplies; they are negligible, since they can be discarded at will. The things of nature have thereby taken on an ephemeral quality; they appear to lack stability and permanence. That is why these things, according to Heidegger, are not simply supplies. They are *disposable* supplies, supplies we can treat with slight regard and even with contempt. It is possible to take things as supplies and still respect them; think of Michelangelo and a block of marble. But no one respects a disposable pen or a disposable coal lode or a disposable river or any disposable natural resource. This then is the sense of Heidegger's distinction between *Bestand* and supplies. The term *Bestand*, according to Heidegger, "says something more" than is said simply by "supplies." *Bestand* says expendable, inconsequential, negligible supplies.

If we understand *Bestand* to mean not simply what stands in reserve for our use but what is disposable and consequently ephemeral, we can then also make sense of Heidegger's distinction between *Bestand* and objects. The word for "object" in German is *der Gegenstand*, that which "stands (*stand*) over and against (*gegen*)" us. As Heidegger uses the term here, the emphasis is on the standing, not on the relation to us. That is, Heidegger means by this term something that has its own autonomous standing. It misses the point, then, to translate *Gegenstand* simply as "object," for our term by itself does not convey the idea of autonomy; in fact, its etymology suggests just the opposite. An "ob-ject" is something that we "throw in the way," i.e., something that stems from our throwing or projecting or constituting. Our word "object" is correlated to "subject." An object is precisely that which a subject has projected; an object is dependent on some subject. We could also say that an object is that which is opposed to a subject. But the word "op-posed" has to be taken in its literal sense: an object is that which has been *posed* by a subject to stand over and against itself. An object has no standing on its own; it is precisely *posed* by a subject, placed in a certain position by a subject. The sense of the word "object" is also captured by the term "proposal." An object is something pro-posed, something the subject poses in front of itself. Now this sense of being op-posed or pro-posed is exactly *not* what Heidegger means by *Gegenstand*. He gives the emphasis to the standing, the self-standing of the *Gegen-stand*. And so he is referring to something that stands on its own, in relative autonomy from human subjectivity. A *Gegenstand* does not have footing or standing merely as something posed. Consequently, it would be misleading to translate *Gegenstand* here as "object" pure and simple. The crucial nuance, the connotation of autonomy, would be lost. The sense of

Heidegger's term can be rendered only by adding a qualification, provided we do retain the English word "object." Here *Gegenstand* must be translated as "autonomous object," "stable object," "self-standing object" (although these terms are indeed self-contradictory if taken literally, since an ob-ject is posed, not self-standing).

It should now be quite clear why a thing of *Bestand* is not a *Gegenstand*. Both terms are related to "standing," but *Bestand* has a negative relation and *Gegenstand* a positive one. Thus in play here is the distinction between posed objects, disposable objects, ephemeral objects, objects viewed entirely in terms of human subjectivity, and permanent objects, objects that must be respected as standing on their own. According to Heidegger, the things of *Bestand* have a "peculiar footing," i.e., a shaky footing, a precarious standing. That is why for Heidegger an airliner is not a *Gegenstand*, not a stable object. It certainly appears to be so; it is massive and sturdy and powerful. Yet as the airliner is disclosed within the attitude of modern technology, it is merely something "that we dispose of [*bestellen*] in order to impose and guarantee [*sicherstellen*] the possibility of transportation." That is to say, the airliner is just another disposable thing. It is there merely for us to order about, to exhaust for our pleasure, and then discard. As such, the airliner is ephemeral, it only stands in relation to our employment of it; and so it is an object only in our English sense. It is not a *Gegenstand*, an autonomous object with its own stable footing. It is only an object that we ourselves pose (oppose, propose, impose on, dispose of), not a self-standing one.

The foregoing interpretation of the distinction between *Bestand* and *Gegenstand*, *viz.*, as a distinction between posed objects and self-standing things, is borne out by Heidegger's parenthetical remark concerning "Hegel's definition of a machine as an autonomous [= 'self-standing,' *selbständig*] tool." What Hegel means is that a machine operates by itself; it does not need a human operator as does a handsaw. A machine such as a pin maker needs only to be fed; for the rest, it stands free of the human operator, who simply watches it. Here Heidegger completely turns the tables on Hegel. According to Heidegger, it is the hand tool that is self-standing, and the modern machine is "utterly non-self-standing." Heidegger's remark is as follows: "As a characterization of the tool of handcraft, Hegel is correct [i.e., such a tool is indeed self-standing]. But to think of a machine in this context is precisely not to think of it in terms of the essence of *that* technology in which it actually belongs. Seen as a piece of modern technology, a machine is utterly non-self-standing, for it stands there solely on the basis of the disposing of the disposable" (FT, 18/17).

In what sense is the tool of handcraft technology self-standing? Obviously a chisel and a file will not work by themselves; they are dependent on a human hand to operate them. In that sense, hand tools are utterly nonautonomous. But it is also a commonplace that the hand-craftsman respected his tools. This does not mean simply that he prized his tools, took care of them, and did not treat them as disposables. Indeed the ancient handcraftsman could doubtlessly not *afford* to keep discarding and replacing his tools. But there is a further sense in which tools used to be respected. It is the same sense in which matter used to be respected. The traditional sculptor respected the marble for what it itself is pregnant with; the modern sculptor, wielding a laser knife, has no respect for the marble. Now, just as the marble gave direction to the handcraft sculptor, so too did the tool with which he worked. The possibilities of sculpture that are imposed by a hand tool are very different from those delineated by a laser. Laser sculpture is basically unrestricted; every possible form, however intricate, is at the disposal of a man wielding a laser. That is not the case for a woman with a hammer, chisel, and file. Such a woman has to take into account the forms her tools put at her disposal. She has to take direction from her tools, and so the tools have a role to play in determining the sculpture. That is the prime sense in which the traditional artisan respects her tools: she looks to see what they are prepared to accomplish.

Thus hand tools do have a certain autonomy. They are not simply at the disposal of the artisan; on the contrary, the artisan must, as it were, put herself at the disposal of her tools. The tools are not simply wielded by the artisan; they do not come into play merely as the agents of her will. The artisan does not dispose of her tools at will. Her will is to a certain extent subservient to her tools. In other words, the tools do not work solely by being wielded by a human operator; they have, we might say, a life of their own. They have their own standing, their own proper determination of the possibilities of the sculpture, and are not defined merely in terms of the will of the sculptor. Therefore the tools are not simply posed; they are not ob-jects, entirely referred back to a subject. Nor is the sculptor entirely a subject, totally free and dominant over her tools. The tools resist domination and to a certain extent exercise their own domination over the sculptor. That is the crucial sense in which tools used to be respected and were not disposables, not *Bestand*, not ob-jects, but autonomous, self-standing things.

What about a modern machine? If autonomy means *not* to be entirely at one's disposal, then the machine is nonautonomous, for it *is* entirely disposable. The machine does not have its own standing but, on the contrary, is something posed by us. Let us consider briefly two examples.

First, pin-making machines. Adam Smith begins his *Wealth of Nations* with a discussion of the manufacture of common pins. A man working by himself, with hand tools, can produce, according to Smith, 20 pins a day. With the division of labor, so dear to Smith, 10 men, each specializing in one of the 10 steps of pin-making, yet still working with hand tools, can make 48,000 pins per 11-hour day, or 4,800 per man. Today there are pin-making machines, which run almost entirely automatically. It requires only one semiskilled worker to operate several pin-making machines simultaneously, and her solitary output per 8-hour day is many millions.

Certainly today's pins are made as disposables; they are nearly worthless. Hand-made pins were neither disposable nor worthless; people saved up "pin money" for the express purpose of buying them. Today no household expressly buys pins; we have all incidentally acquired too many already. Now, what about the machine that produces these disposables? It is as automatic as a machine can be, yet for Heidegger it is utterly nonautonomous, since it has its footing "solely on the basis of the disposing of the disposable."

We can perhaps see what Heidegger means here, if we begin by asking why an automatic machine was ever constructed. To be sure, it is there to supply us with disposable goods, but, more than that, it is there so we can indeed dispose of those goods. In other words, the machine is designed to run automatically so that we need work less and can have the leisure to enjoy disposable goods. We have put the automatic machine at our disposal in order to have at our disposal the time to dispose of disposable things. That perhaps expresses the full sense of what Heidegger means by saying the machine stands on the basis of the "disposing of the disposable." The automatic machine has been ordered up by us in our attempt to make everything disposable, including our time. The machine has its standing entirely within this context of disposability. And so, in a sense, the machine does not make disposable goods; the disposable goods make the machine. That is, the desire for disposability calls up the necessity for automatic machines.

From a Heideggerian point of view, it is not because machines are so efficient that we can treat their output as disposable. On the contrary, it is because we see everything as disposable, because everything is unconcealed to us as disposable, that we are forced to build efficiency into our machines. The disclosive looking motivates the building, not vice versa. And that is why, for Heidegger, the machine is "utterly nonautonomous." The automatic machine is something we pose, something we demand, and something we command. We do not take direction from such a machine; we give it direction. We lord it over such a machine, from its design and purpose to the use of its output. Everything about the automatic machine is at our disposal, and so it has no autonomy.

To consider very briefly another example, let us compare again a laser knife to a sculptor's hand tools. From a Heideggerian standpoint, the latter have an autonomy, and a laser knife is nonautonomous. Yet this is not so because the laser fails to offer us any possibilities of sculp-

disposability as precondition of machine

ture. It is so because the laser offers unrestricted possibilities—i.e., none peculiarly its own. It imposes no limits and so is entirely at our disposal. We can dispose of the laser at will and do not have to respect it. We do not have to look to it, do not have to consider its limitations in making a sculpture—because it has no limits. Any form may be imposed by a laser onto any matter. All forms are put at our disposal by a laser knife. For Heidegger, again, it is the seeing of all forms as disposable that calls forth the necessity of a tool such as a laser knife. It is not the tool that makes the forms look disposable; the disclosive looking comes first. The looking upon things as disposable has a priority over the machine that carries out that disposability. So the laser is ordered up, forced into existence by our disclosive looking at things, by the way things are unconcealed. Consequently, the laser is utterly nonautonomous; it has its standing solely from our posing and disposing.

What is this unconcealment of things that lies behind modern machines? That is, what is the sense of Heidegger's *Bestand*? How are things in general disclosed to us today? I suggest that the sense is best rendered by "disposables." Heidegger's full statement is then as follows:

> What sort of unconcealment characterizes that which stands there to be challenged and imposed upon? Everywhere things are posed to be on hand, to stand at our disposal at every moment, and indeed to stand there in such a way that they can be disposable for a further disposing. Things that are posed in this way have a peculiar [shaky] footing. We call them disposables. This term says something more and something more essential than mere "supplies." The term "disposables" now attains the rank of a title. It designates nothing less than the mode of existence of everything that is disclosed by way of being challenged. Things that have the standing of disposables no longer stand over and against us as self-standing things. (FT, 17/17)

The sense of the word "disposables" should, by now, be clear. It designates things insofar as they are disclosed to be at our disposal and entirely at our disposal. *That* is the unconcealment prevailing today; all things appear to be there solely for what we can get out of them. After we have exhausted them, they are meant to be discarded. The opposite attitude is the one of respect, whereby things are viewed as having their own autonomy, their own standing, and are not merely posed by us in order to be opposed to us, exposed by us, imposed on by us, and disposed of by us.

It is true that by rendering *Bestand* as "disposables," instead of "standing-reserve," the etymological connection with *stehen*, "standing," is lost. But the loss is slight, since *Bestand* actually has a negative connection to standing; the things of *Bestand* have a peculiar standing and are not self-standing. These things are posed instead of being self-standing, and so we actually gain by rendering *Bestand* as "disposables." We gain another connection to the word "pose" (*stell-*), the word that in general characterizes, for Heidegger, the attitude of modern technology toward things.

Therefore, we can say, slightly adapting Heidegger's list of terms: "The fact that now, wherever we try to display modern technology as a disclosive looking that challenges, the words 'pose,' 'oppose,' 'propose,' 'expose,' 'impose,' and 'dispose' obtrude and accumulate—in a dry, monotonous, and therefore oppressive way—is grounded in that which is about to come to utterance" (FT, 18/17).

Ge-stell, *the "all-encompassing imposition"*

What is about to come to utterance is introduced by a telltale question of the later Heidegger. The question is an unmistakable sign that we are moving in the realm of a thought that has been turned back to a premetaphysical outlook, that accords the priority not to the human grasping look but to the "look of Being," that takes the gods to be the prime movers in the disclosure of truth. This question marks a transition. We are about to enter a deeper (i.e., more originary, closer to the origin of things) and more enigmatic level of thought. In fact, the last words from the previous citation already presage the transition. Heidegger did not say "that which we are about to utter" but precisely "that which of itself is coming to language, that which will itself speak to us." It is not our speaking that has the priority over language, but vice versa. Language (or something within language) will address us, and our own speaking must be a response in conformity with what we hear.

The question that marks the transition will immediately strike the reader as an odd one. Yet the oddity does not stem from any apparent profundity or mysteriousness. On the contrary, it is odd because it is too simple; it is odd that anyone would ever raise such a question. The question has an obvious answer, and Heidegger answers his own question with the obvious answer: "Who accomplishes the challenging imposition whereby that which we call reality is disclosed as made up of disposables? Obviously, human beings" (FT, 18/18).

This is the answer that is obvious to a thinking that has not been turned back from metaphysics. Heidegger immediately proceeds to undermine its obviousness: "To what extent are humans capable of such a disclosure?" (FT, 18/18). That is to say, are humans really capable of it? Heidegger proceeds to delimit what humans are and are not capable of:

> Humans can indeed represent [i.e., pose before the mind, *vor-stellen*], mold, or work on this or that in this or that way. But

humans do not control unconcealedness itself; they do not control whether and how reality at any given time will show itself or withdraw. The fact that, ever since Plato, reality has been showing itself in the light of Ideas is not something Plato himself effected. The thinker merely spoke in conformity with that which addressed itself to him. (FT, 18/18)

This is a most characteristic and rich expression of the later Heidegger. The passage touches upon almost every aspect under which he views the priority of Being over human subjectivity.

To begin with, Heidegger is saying here that we humans can attend to beings, can effect changes in beings, can control beings, but we cannot control whether and how those beings are for us beings in the first place. We cannot control what makes a being a being, which is to say that Being is not in our control. Being itself is in control. In order for us to attend to beings, Being must first attend to us. Being must turn toward us, disclose itself to us, if we are to be able to recognize a being *as* a being and then take it up in one way or another. But we cannot take up Being; Being must take us up, must work upon us, offer itself to us. For the later Heidegger, the disclosure of Being is a genuine self-disclosure, an offering, a gift; and we do not control which gifts will be given us.[2]

Secondly, in terms of unconcealedness, we humans can occupy ourselves with unconcealed beings, but that by which beings are unconcealed at all is out of our control. That there is unconcealment at all, and what sort of unconcealment it is, is not primarily a human affair but an affair of that which is unconcealed. It is up to the latter itself, as Heidegger says, to show itself at any given time or withdraw.

Thirdly, the passage speaks of light. We humans can deal with beings that stand in some sort of light. We can deal with beings that are already illuminated in one way or other. But we cannot control the illumination itself. We cannot make the light, nor can we determine what sort of light it is. For example, the light may be a false light, showing things as they basically are not, or it may be a true light, allowing things to show themselves more adequately. But the kind of light is not at our disposal; it is a matter of the light giving itself to us in one way or another.

Lastly, in terms of language and speech, the passage claims that we can speak about beings, we can say what beings are, but we cannot *dictate* what they are. In our speaking, we have to cor-respond (*entsprechen*) with a more originary speaking to (*zu-sprechen*) us, a more originary speaking or more originary language. That originary language (in which, as it were, Being addresses us and discloses itself to us) is not in our control; we need to be subservient to it, shape our speech in correspondence with it.

Thus the terms of the passage in question are beings and Being itself, unconcealed realities and unconcealedness itself, illuminated things and the light itself, our speech and the speaking that addresses itself to us. In each case (indeed these are merely different aspects of one single case), Heidegger's claim is the same: what we are capable of depends on something beyond us. We are not in control; we are subservient. Our disclosive looking upon beings depends primarily on how those beings will disclose themselves. Most generally, our grasp of beings as such, i.e., our understanding of what it means to be, depends primarily on Being. Being may approach or withdraw, show itself more or veil itself more, but that is not in our control. It is out of our control and is primarily in the hands of Being itself.

Of course, Heidegger acknowledges that we humans still have our essential role to play. There is no disclosedness without our cooperation and consent. There is no disclosure without our disclosive looking, no illuminated beings without our opening our eyes to the light, no true speech unless we make the effort to heed that which is addressed to us and then mold our speech in conformity to it. Being may *offer* itself to us in one way or another, but Being cannot force its way in on us. Being may indeed be in the lead, but to lead is not to dictate.

Besides speaking in general, in the passage just cited, Heidegger also presents a particular example, the example of Plato and the Ideas. We can assume that this is not an accidental example, not just one example among others, but *the* example, the quintessential example. If so, then Heidegger is here naming concretely the possibilities he had just mentioned: the possibilities of the approach and withdrawal of Being. The withdrawal of Being corresponds to Plato and his theory of Ideas. The Platonic philosophy marks the transition from an earlier epoch, in which Being showed itself more wholeheartedly, to our present epoch ("ever since Plato") in which Being has withdrawn and shows itself reticently. What does the theory of Ideas have to do with the withdrawal of Being?

Specifically, Heidegger says that reality is now showing itself in the *light* of Ideas. What is inadequate about this light? In what sense is that light still illuminating beings today? And in what—presumably truer— light did Being show itself prior to Plato?

Heidegger does not pursue these issues in the present context, but I will venture a very general interpretation. I venture to say that what Heidegger means by an "idea" here is simply a mental representation. (This is, strictly speaking, more the modern understanding than the genuinely Platonic one.) A representation is something we pose (in German, *vor-stellen*) before our mind. If an idea is a representation, then it is something we pose to ourselves, which means that we are not *given* it but instead must *form* it, abstract it in thought. Therefore, if, according to

Turning concept of Plato

Platonic doctrine, ideas are the really real, the ultimate reality, i.e., if reality shows itself primarily in the light of ideas, then reality is understood as something we pose. It is this basic understanding of Being, as something correlated to our posing activity, that begins with Plato and then continues on consistently, up to the present. The modern period does introduce a modification, however. The modification is to harden the basic doctrine and exaggerate the notion of beings as objects posed by subjects, until beings become objects entirely at the dis-posal of subjects. Yet the roots of this contemporary, technological outlook lie in Plato. Plato inaugurates, with his theory of Ideas, the ascendancy of subjectivity and its posing activity. This is the inauguration of humanism, the ascendancy of humans over Being. Accordingly, Plato marks a turning point.

In Heidegger's eyes, the theory of Ideas also marks the withdrawal of Being; it is a response to that withdrawal. The pre-Socratic sense of Being was radically different; beings were not objects, and humans were not posing subjects. It was quite the reverse: beings were the subjects, beings had their own autonomous standing, beings grew of themselves (= *physis*, "nature"), and human technology was understood as service to the natural growth of beings. For Heidegger, the pre-Socratic outlook could arise only because Being was offering itself more wholeheartedly then. From the time of Socrates and Plato on, Being has been withdrawing, which is why subjectivity has acquired an ascendancy. The elevation of subjectivity is the human response to the withdrawal of Being, to the reticent "look" of Being.

Thus Plato's theory of Ideas is not his own invention. He did not veil Being, or cause Being to withdraw, on account of hubris. He did not elevate subjectivity out of disdain for nature. On the contrary, his theory is a response to the withdrawal of Being. By the same token, the pre-Socratics were not more intelligent or more sensitive; instead, they were privileged to be addressed more directly by Being. They sensed this direct address and so could understand themselves as ones addressed, as recipients, and not as posers.

The passage we are now considering is therefore history proper, not human chronicle. It relates an episode in the history of Being. According to that historical outlook, the real events, the autonomous, genuinely motivating events, lie on the side of Being or the gods. The withdrawal of Being motivated Plato's philosophy; that is what Heidegger means by saying that Plato merely spoke in correspondence with that which spoke to him. The theory of Ideas (the ascendancy of the posing activity of the subject) is not something Plato effected. Plato's personal role was secondary, although his creative genius was indeed necessary; the theory of Ideas was primarily accomplished by Being itself. It was accomplished by the withdrawal of Being; that is the autonomous event which is the genuine

source of the theory of Ideas. Beings now appear in the light of Ideas because that is the light now shining upon them; it is not that Plato by himself placed them in such a light. Plato merely ratified the light—by the
way he looked at beings—just as he ratified what was addressed to him—
by the way he spoke about beings.

With the modern age, things appear in the light of disposability.
Things not only appear to be posed in general (= ideas), but they appear
to be entirely at our disposal (= disposables). This latter appearance, for
Heidegger, also has its motivating event. And so, the disclosive looking of
modern technology, the outlook that challenges, ravishes, and disposes, is
not primarily a human accomplishment; it is not under human control, to
return now to the odd question Heidegger raised at the beginning of this
discussion. It is an accomplishment of Being. Therefore the obvious answer, after the turn to a premetaphysical outlook, is, at most, "correct,"
which is a pejorative word for Heidegger. The correct is superficial. If our
thought is turned closer to the origin of things, then we see that the true
origin of the outlook of modern technology is Being. It is Being's doing; it
is primarily accomplished by the gods. Being's self-withdrawal lies behind
the challenging and imposing that have been brought by humans to such
a height today.

Our age is indeed new, for Heidegger, but it is not radically new.
We are not witnessing a new event in the history of Being but only a modified old event, an exaggerated version of the previous event, i.e., a further withdrawal of Being. How shall we then characterize the current
state of this event in the history of Being? That is to say, what is the
proper name for Being today? What, specifically, has motivated the challenging and imposing outlook of modern technology? What is modern
technology responding to? What motivates the posing, exposing, opposing, and disposing of modern technology?

Heidegger devotes four complete pages to these questions, to the
proper name for Being in our epoch. These pages are the true center and
high point of the "Die Frage nach der Technik." We need to attend to
them with the utmost care.

The main theme is announced at the very beginning: "Only insofar
as humans are, on their own part, already challenged, challenged to ravish nature for its energies, can there occur a disclosive looking upon
things as disposables" (FT, 18/18).

The theme is thus that the challenging accomplished by humans is
encompassed by a more general challenging; humans challenge nature because they are themselves challenged to do so. Humans look upon things
as disposables because humans are themselves at the disposal of a more
general disposing. Humans take up a posing attitude because they are
themselves subjected to a more encompassing imposition. *This more*

encompassing imposition is the current event in the history of Being. The current guise of Being is an *all-encompassing imposition*. In other words, that which is addressed to humans today is of the nature of an imposition; Being imposes on humans, imposes on them to impose in turn. Human posings, opposings, exposings, imposings, and disposings are merely the human responses that conform to the more encompassing imposition that includes humans in it.

Heidegger immediately wonders whether this is not going too far, since it seems to mean that humans are *forced* to comply with the dictates of Being, just as nature is forced to comply with the dictates of modern technology: "If humans are challenged, i.e., if they are at the disposal of a more encompassing imposition, then are not humans, even more originally than the things of nature, disposables?" (FT, 18/18).

There is indeed evidence that humans are looked upon today as disposable material. For example, we speak of people as human "resources," or as graduate school "material," and we talk about the future "supply" of consumers, soldiers, priests. Heidegger mentions the circulating German terms *das Menschenmaterial* ("man-power reservoir") and *das Krankenmaterial* ("patient reservoir"), and then he offers an elaborate example, beginning with the forester:

> The forester who, in the woods, measures the felled timber and, to all appearances, walks the same forest path and in the same way as did his grandfather, is today at the disposal of the lumber-exploitation industry, whether he realizes it or not. He is placed at the disposal of the disposability of cellulose, which for its part is challenged out of wood by the demand for paper, which is in turn put at the disposal of newspapers and illustrated magazines. These then impose on public opinion to swallow what they print. Thereby what they print is at the disposal of the imposition of a pre-arranged common opinion. (FT, 18–19/18)

Despite all this evidence that humans are today being reduced to their functions within a technological society, that they are becoming mere cogs in a machine, or, in more Heideggerian terms, despite the evidence that humans are forcibly imposed on by an all-encompassing imposition, Heidegger, of course, does not believe that humans ever become disposables, the way the things of nature do. Humans never stand toward Being as things stand toward humans. Humans retain their spontaneity and autonomy: "Yet precisely because humans are challenged more originally than are the energies of nature, i.e., challenged into the realm of disposability, humans never become mere disposables. Since it is humans who carry on technology, they participate in disposability by way of a disclosive looking" (FT, 19/18).

This is no doubt a cryptic passage, but the point, which Heidegger will develop more fully later, is evidently that humans retain their autonomy because they retain an awareness (or at least the possibility of an awareness) of the demands that are being placed upon them. Humans retain the ability to look disclosively at the impositions besetting them. Humans can *see* the nexus of disposability in which they are caught up. Since humans "carry on" technology, since they bring it to fruition, they remain agents (although the prime agent is Being) and are never the mere objects of technology. As agents, humans retain their autonomy—or at least the possibility of their autonomy—and their freedom. The opposite of a free agent is a blind slave. To see is to escape from being a slave to technology, a cog in a machine. To look disclosively is to dominate. That is what raises humans above disposable material, and the ability to disclose is going to become, for Heidegger, the very source of human dignity.

At this point, however, Heidegger does no more than hint at what saves humans from being entirely at the disposal of disposability, entirely challenged, entirely reduced to a function within a nexus of efficient productivity. Humans can accomplish a certain disclosive looking upon the nexus of disposability, and that gives them a certain control over it. Heidegger's present focus, however, is on what humans can *not* accomplish, what is not in their control. Humans can participate in disclosedness or unconcealment, but they do not fabricate unconcealment itself; whether and how beings show themselves at all is not in human control: "But unconcealment itself, within which disposability unfolds, is never a human fabrication, no more than is the domain through which humans are already transported, whenever they as subjects relate to objects" (FT, 19/18).

We note here in the first place that Heidegger now correlates subjects and objects. This might seem inconsistent with Heidegger's use of "object" to mean that which has its own standing and is not merely posed by a subject. Heidegger now seems to be using "object" in our English sense of that which is "ob-jected" or "op-posed." But there is no inconsistency, since Heidegger is here using a different German word, not *Gegenstand*. Indeed the German term he now uses is the cognate of our Latinized word "object," namely *das Objekt*. *Gegenstand* and *Objekt* have very different etymologies, and they have very different senses for Heidegger, at least here in the essay on technology. *Objekt* does precisely not signify what is self-standing; an *Objekt* is indeed posed by a subject. An *Objekt* is thus not a *Gegenstand*. That makes perfect sense. But it is then misleading to render them both, as does the published English translation, with the same term "object." We could say that a "mere object" is not an "autonomous object," or an "ob-ject" is not a "self-standing thing," but it would make no sense to say "an object is not an object."

More substantively, what is Heidegger saying here about subjects and ob-jects? (To resolve all ambiguity, I will render *Objekt* as "ob-ject.") He is saying that the appearance of things in general as ob-jects is not a human fabrication, not a human accomplishment. Heidegger speaks of "the domain through which humans are already transported, whenever they as subjects relate to ob-jects." That means humans have to be transported into a certain domain for things to show themselves as ob-jects. This is just another way of saying that a thing has to disclose itself in a certain way, in a certain context, in order for humans to take it as an ob-ject, as correlated to themselves, now taken as subjects. This way of self-showing is the current one of modern technology. The domain of ob-jects is exactly the nexus of disposability. For things to show themselves as ob-jects is equivalent to their showing themselves as disposables.

We could also speak here in terms of light. Humans have to be transported into a domain with a certain illumination in order for things to show themselves as ob-jects. Ob-jects are things that stand in a certain (false) light. Heidegger's point is that the light, or the self-showing, the unconcealment, the transportation into a certain domain, is not a human accomplishment. To see things as ob-jects, humans must have been *already* transported into the proper domain. The passage just cited also states that disposability unfolds within a certain unconcealment. That is to say, things unfold as disposable, things show themselves as disposables, because they already stand within a certain general unconcealment. Humans do not transport themselves into the domain of ob-jects, and humans do not place things within a certain unconcealment or in a certain illuminated domain. The illumination, the unconcealment itself, is out of human control.

Thus far, the characterization of the current event in the history of Being, the characterization of the unconcealment prevalent today, has been entirely negative. Humans do *not* control unconcealment itself, unconcealment is *not* a human accomplishment. The more positive characterization begins with the obvious question: "Where and how does disclosedness then occur, if it is not a mere human accomplishment?" (FT, 19/18). Heidegger's initial response to this question is couched in unmistakably religious terms:

We need not look far. All that is necessary is to apprehend in an unprejudiced way That which has always already claimed humans and has done this so decisively that a human can be a human only as one who is thus claimed. Wherever people open their eyes and ears, unlock their hearts, give themselves over to meditating and striving, forming and working, beseeching and thanking, they always find themselves already brought into the unconcealed. The unconcealment of the unconcealed has already come to pass as often as it calls humans forth into the modes of disclosive looking meted out to them. (FT, 19/18–19)

The religious overtones of this passage, beginning with the capitalized word "That," are plain.[3] The "That" could be God, the God who is not far, who claims humans, in relation to whom we have to stand in order to be ourselves, into whose presence we are brought if we have eyes that see and ears that hear and, above all, hearts that are open, whom we beseech and thank, and who himself metes out to us these modes of disclosing him.

Nevertheless, no sooner does Heidegger (apparently) open this religious dimension than he closes it off. The "That" loses its personal character and is spoken of simply as unconcealedness itself, Being, the all-encompassing imposition. The only claim now made upon humans is to disclose things in accordance with the way these things are already illuminated. This is not God making a claim on the human heart, the proper response to which would involve beseeching and thanking. This claim is one that God would never make; it is a violent claim. What humans are called on to do is to disrespect nature, to violate natural things by taking them as disposables: "Accordingly, when humans, through research and exploration, waylay [*nachstellen*] nature as a sphere they themselves have posed in thought [*vorstellen*], they are already claimed by a mode of disclosedness, one that challenges them to attack nature as an object of research, until all objects disappear into the object-less domain of disposables" (FT, 19/19).

Here, of course, the word for "object" is *Gegenstand*. And here "research" means scientific research. Thus the passage says, first of all, that the pursuit of science is the human response to a certain mode of disclosedness, the response to a certain way Being as such shows itself. Science arises as a response to a claim laid upon humans by Being, by the way beings in general appear. Secondly, in pursuing science, humans "waylay nature as a sphere they themselves have posed in thought." Heidegger's word for "waylay" literally means "to pose after." And his word for "pose in thought" is literally "to pose before." Thus what he is saying is that science first poses or sets up a certain domain and then aggressively sets out after it. What, for example, is the domain of the science of chemistry? That domain is an abstraction; it is the domain of chemical formulas. Nature, for chemistry, is basically a realm of formulas. Scientists pose this realm by way of a reduction; it is an artificial realm that arises only from a very artificial attitude adopted toward things. Water has to be *posed* as H_2O. Once it is so posed, once things in general are reduced to chemical formulas, then this entire domain can be waylaid or exploited for practical ends. One can, for example, make fire out of water, once water is seen as a compound of hydrogen and oxygen. Finally, the passage above says that nature, as conceived by science, is object-less. That is obvious, as long as "object" is taken in the sense of *Gegenstand*. What is missing from nature, as understood in science, is precisely autonomous objects, such as water. For science, nature is composed of formulas, and a formula is not a self-standing object. A formula is posed; it is an ob-ject. Furthermore, a formula is exploitable. And thus science not only turns things into posed ob-jects, it turns them into disposables.

The meaning of the passage under discussion should now be clear, at least as regards the human response to the supposed claim. Yet the claim itself is still unclear. It remains unclear what is the current "mode of disclosedness," from which the claim issues. Heidegger still has not provided a positive characterization of unconcealment. He has argued only that the disclosive looking carried out by humans must be understood as a response to the way beings already present themselves in a certain light. What sort of light is prevalent today? Heidegger takes one last preliminary step before offering his answer to that question. This step amounts to a final characterization of the way human disclosive looking is under the sway of disclosedness itself:

> In this way, then, modern technology, as a disclosive looking which disposes, is not a merely human doing. Therefore we must also take that challenging which imposes on humans to dispose of realities as disposables just as it shows itself. That challenging encompasses the disposing of things on the part of humans. This encompassing concentrates humans on disposing of realities as disposables. (FT, 20/19)

The key word here is "encompassing." The German term is *Versammeln*, and the published English translation is "gathering." *Versammeln* can indeed mean "gathering," in the neutral sense of accumulating or amassing. Gathering in this sense signifies an expansion of volume, an extending outward, an increase of mass. But *Versammeln* can also connote almost the opposite, i.e., not an extending outward but a condensing inward. In this sense the word is in German a synonym for focusing or concentrating. Indeed Heidegger explicitly invokes this sense when he says, "This *Versammeln* concentrates." That is a redundancy in German; *Versammeln* already means "concentration."

Perhaps the best translation of *Versammeln* in this context is "rallying." Indeed, in colloquial German, *die Truppen versammeln* means precisely "to rally the troops." But to rally troops does not mean simply to gather them or summon them together in one place. To rally means to arouse, to move to action, to focus energy in one certain direction. To rally has both an extensive and an intensive sense, as it were. A political rally not only gathers *many* partisans together, it focuses them and incites them to *one* course of action.

Heidegger's use of *Versammeln* incorporates both the extensive sense of gathering and the intensive sense of rallying. When Heidegger speaks of a challenging that is a *Versammeln* of humans, he indeed means a challenging that rallies or incites humans to ravish things, to look upon them as mere disposables. That is to say, the challenging is not a neutral offering of a possibility; it includes a definite incitement to take up that possibility. "Rallying" would indeed be an excellent translation of *Versammeln*, except for the fact that Heidegger also plays on the more neutral sense, which the word "rally" lacks. For instance, Heidegger applies the word to mountains; it would not make sense to say the mountains are rallied into a chain. Thus we need an English term with the same ambiguity as the German: either mere inclusion or definite incitement. I suggest "encompassing."

Commonly, encompassing has the sense of surrounding or enclosing, i.e., bringing together into a closure. In this sense it means the same as "gathering together" and could be applied to mountains. But, less commonly, to encompass something means to accomplish it, bring it about. To encompass a task means to be equal to the task, to besiege the task and carry it out. Heidegger says a "challenging encompasses the disposing of things on the part of humans." If we take "encompassing" in both its senses, Heidegger's meaning will be clear.

To begin with, let us rephrase Heidegger's statement. The disposing of things on the part of humans amounts to the attitude of modern technology. And the challenging that Heidegger is here speaking of is the "That" which claims humans. Another word for it is Being. So what Heidegger is saying in his assertion that "a challenging encompasses the disposing of things on the part of humans" is that Being encompasses modern technology. Let us interpret this form of Heidegger's statement in light of the two senses of "encompass."

In the first place, Heidegger means simply that modern technology is included in a broader context. Modern technology does not stand on its own but is gathered into a more general movement on the part of Being. The sense of encompassing here is that of reaching out and accumulating. Being, so to speak, *annexes* modern technology and gives it a place within its own movement of self-presentation.

But Being, for Heidegger, also encompasses modern technology in the other sense of encompassing. That is, Being itself *accomplishes* modern technology. To be sure, humans are still agents of technology, they are still free, they are only motivated and not coerced, but the motivation issuing from Being is a high-pressure one. The motivation includes incitement and insistence; it is not the simple offering of a possibility. The motivation is a rallying, a summoning up and focusing of energy. For Heidegger, the self-presentation of Being is well-nigh irresistible in its motive force, so that Being itself can be called the prime agent of modern technology. Humans are only the subordinate agents. That is this second sense in which Being encompasses modern technology: Being itself is what primarily carries out modern technology. Being imposes modern technology on humans, who then impose on nature.

The introduction of the notion of "encompassing" is the final preliminary step in determining the proper name for Being in our epoch. It completes the preliminaries, since this notion allows us to characterize the current sense of Being, and then we will only be left the task of finding the name to express that sense. Heidegger articulates this characterization of the current meaning of Being in what amounts practically to a formal definition. He offers three, slightly different variants. They are as follows. Under its current guise, Being is:

> that challenging claim which encompasses humans by imposing on them to take as disposable the things that are disclosing themselves as disposables. (FT, 20/19)

> the encompassing of that imposition which imposes on humans—i.e., challenges them—to impose on reality in turn and thereby to look disclosively upon reality as composed of disposables. (FT, 21/20)

> the encompassing of that imposition which imposes on humans to look disclosively upon reality as composed of disposables, which humans do by way of an imposition. (FT, 24–25/24)

What Heidegger is saying here, in the simplest possible terms, is that Being now possesses the sense of an *all-encompassing imposition*. That is the sense for which we will have to find a proper name. Let us first attempt to explicate this rich characterization very briefly. The richness—or, perhaps, the convolution—stems from the fact that both "imposition" and "encompassing" have here a double meaning.

To begin with, Heidegger is saying that Being is an imposition which imposes on humans to impose in turn. Or, Being is a challenging which challenges humans to challenge in turn. Thus there are two different impositions involved: that of Being (imposing on humans) and that of humans (imposing on natural things, which is equivalent to looking upon them as disposables). Heidegger maintains that Being encompasses both these impositions, "encompassing" taken in both its senses. That is, Being *includes* both these impositions (Being embraces the imposition of modern technology under a broader imposition), and Being *accomplishes* both these impositions (Being is the primary agent of them both). That is how Being is all-encompassing: it encompasses all the impositions in all the senses of encompassing. We could also express the same by saying that Being is the "original collection" of impositions. As a *collection*, Being encompasses the impositions in the first sense of encompassing, the sense of embracing within a larger whole; as *original*, Being encompasses the impositions in the second sense: Being is the source of the impositions, their springboard, the collected origin from which all individual impositions subsequently spread out.

The foregoing, in Heidegger's view, expresses the sense of Being in our current technological age; i.e., it characterizes the present event in the history of Being. To repeat, Being now possesses the sense of an "all-encompassing imposition" or an "original collection of impositions." Having fixed this sense, Heidegger proceeds to search for the proper name for Being, the name most appropriate to the current sense of Being.

His search takes its directive from a certain grammatical peculiarity of the German language. There are a number of German words that have a collective—and, for Heidegger, originating—sense imparted to them by the prefix *Ge-*.

> That which, as an origin, spreads the mountains out into ranges and draws them together in a single spread or compass is the encompassing we call "the high country" [*das Gebirg*].
> That original encompassing from which are spread out our various moods and tempers is what we call "temperament" [*das Gemüt*]. (FT, 20/19).

Heidegger is invoking here the distinction in German between *der Berg* ("mountain") and *das Gebirg* ("the mountains as a whole," "the high country," "the highlands") and between *der Mut* ("courage," "cheer") and *das Gemüt* ("temperament," "general temper"). Another example would be *die Wolke* ("cloud") versus *das Gewölk* ("clouds," "clouds as a whole," "clouds in general"). Likewise, *das Wasser* is simply "water," whereas *das Gewässer* is "waters," "water as a whole," "all the water." In these terms, and in others, the prefix *Ge-* has a collective force; it gathers into a whole all the instances of that which is named in the root word. Heidegger would say that the resultant sense is that of an original collection. The collection, named in the *Ge-* word, is the origin, the source, of the various single instances; the latter "spread out" from an original whole, just as our various individual tempers are possible only because we are endowed with such a thing as affectivity or temperament in general in the first place. For Heidegger, temperament is not the mere sum or average of our tempers; on the contrary, it is the prior condition of the possibility of any individual temper. We do not have a temperament because we have tempers or moods; for Heidegger, it is just the opposite. It is because we are "temperamental," open in general to beings through affectivity, that we can have specific moods and feelings.

Thus, from a Heideggerian point of view, the *Ge-* words in question are all-encompassing—in the precise sense that they designate "original collections," wholes which stand at the origin of that which they collect rather than merely being subsequent to the collected individuals. These *Ge-* words are therefore encompassing in both senses of encompassing. They are all-encompassing—by embracing all the instances in a wider whole and by accomplishing (as their origin or source) all the individual instances.

Recall that the current sense of Being, according to Heidegger, is that of an all-encompassing imposition or an original collection of impositions. Accordingly, there is no mystery to his recourse to a *Ge-* word in order to call Being by its proper name: "We now name that challenging claim, which encompasses humans by imposing on them to take as disposable the things that are disclosing themselves as disposables, *das Gestell*" (FT, 20/19).

Thus we finally arrive at *Ge-stell*, the word Heidegger offers as the most appropriate name for the current event in the history of Being, i.e., the proper name for Being in our modern technological epoch. If we take *Ge-stell* as a *Ge-* word, in analogy with Heidegger's examples of *Gebirg* and *Gemüt*, then its sense is as clear and simple as can be. The prefix *Ge-* means "all-encompassing," the root word *stell* means "posing" or "imposing," and so *das Ge-stell*, in a very tidy little turn of phrase, signifies "all-encompassing imposition," just the sense that was supposed to be expressed. Now, how to translate *Ge-stell* into English in an equally tidy term?

The published English translation is "Enframing." This might at first cause surprise, since it seems to express nothing of the required sense of "all-encompassing imposition." I hope to show indeed that "Enframing" is not an entirely satisfactory translation, but, if it is an error, it is a motivated one and does not entirely miss the mark.

The motivation stems from the fact that *das Gestell* (without the hyphen) is a common German word and is not a *Ge-* word in the special sense just delineated. *Das Gestell* does mean something like a frame. The word is used for various types of holders or stands: e.g., a pipe rack, a book case, an umbrella stand, a pedestal. It also means "frame" in the sense of the frame of a car (= chassis), bed frame (= bedstead), umbrella frame (= ribs), or eyeglasses frame. It is not used for a picture frame. It means supporting frame or interior framework, rather than mere exterior, surrounding frame.

What is "Enframing" supposed to signify? To put the best possible construction on the term, the sense would be that in the age of modern technology beings are given to us configured in a certain way (as use-objects) and we are ourselves imperiously called to take them under that configuration. The "enframing" amounts to this, that just as the frame of ribs gives an umbrella its shape, and our frame of bones gives us our shape, so things today appear in a certain shape because they are enframed in a certain way, namely as there merely for our use. There is this difference, however: an umbrella is both ribs and material, just as we are bones and flesh, whereas things today are just a frame, there is nothing else to them but the use we make of them. We have the mere skeleton of their Being. Things are then "enframed" in the precise sense of being skeletonized, and that is all there is to them. Things are skeletons of their real selves, just as an ob-ject (say, H_2O) is a mere skeleton of a thing (water).

This way of construing the term makes sense, and indeed it touches on an important aspect of Heidegger's theory. It is one way to link Heidegger's term *Ge-stell* to the ordinary word *Gestell*. But it is not what Heidegger primarily intends in his use of the term *Ge-stell*. Heidegger proposes a much more daring use, and for him the connection between *Ge-stell* and *Gestell* is not that they have something in common but that *Ge-stell* is precisely nothing *Gestell*-like. To grasp this we need to go slowly over Heidegger's own comments on the term *Ge-stell* and examine carefully his employment of it.

Immediately after introducing *Ge-stell* as the name for the all-encompassing imposition, or all-encompassing challenge, Heidegger remarks:

> We are daring to use this word in a totally novel way. . . . In its usual sense, *Gestell* means some sort of gadget, e.g., a bookrack [*Büchergestell*]. A skeleton, too, is called a *Gestell*. And just as a skeleton is something horrid, so the use we are now proposing to make of the word *Gestell* will appear horrible and, it goes without saying, completely arbitrary . . . Can idiosyncrasy be pushed any further? Certainly not. (FT, 20/19–20)

What is idiosyncratic here is simply, I maintain, Heidegger's making a *Ge-* word out of *Gestell*. To draw attention to the two parts of the term, as he understands them, namely the prefix and the root word, Heidegger will always hyphenate. Without exception, he will write the word without a hyphen when he is referring to the word itself or to its ordinary sense, and he will consistently employ the hyphen for his idiosyncratic sense.

This idiosyncratic sense is not far to seek. Heidegger observes that an idiosyncratic use of words is an ancient practice in philosophy, especially where it is a matter of thinking "the highest," and he takes as a paradigm example the Platonic term "Idea." Then Heidegger immediately makes explicit his sense of the term *Ge-stell*: "*Ge-stell* is the name for the collection [or encompassing] of the imposition that imposes upon man, i.e., challenges him, to impose upon reality in turn by looking disclosively upon realities as disposables" (FT, 21/20).

Here we have the primary sense Heidegger attaches to the word *Ge-stell*. It names a collection of *stell*, a *Ge-stell*. "Enframing" expresses neither this primary sense nor the connection, as Heidegger sees it, between *Ge-stell* and things such as frames and other gadgets. We will take up this connection momentarily, but for now let us return to the question that inaugurated our present discussion, the question of how to translate *Ge-stell*.

Ideally, the translation should be a single word that denotes a collection of imposition. Furthermore, to be perfectly analogous to the German, it should have this denotation only if taken in an idiosyncratic, horrid way. We can hardly hope to meet this ideal; my best proposal is to translate *das Ge-stell* as "the com-posing." We will see eventually that "composites" are examples of the things called *Gestell* (without the hyphen), and so the relation between *Ge-stell* and *Gestell* will play out as the relation between the com-posing and composites. (The equivalent English words of Greek derivation would be syn-thesis and synthetics.)

The word "com-posing" is to be taken here very literally. The prefix co- (= col- or com- for euphony) is a collective prefix of modern English; in Old English the collective prefix was actually ge-, as it still is in contemporary German. And "posing" is here to be understood in the forceful sense of "imposing." So "com-posing" means the collection of all the impositions. This is a somewhat idiosyncratic use of the word, since "composing" ordinarily means to pose together, to put together into one, whereas we are now taking it in the sense of the togetherness of all the puttings, the collection of all the posings or imposings. "Composing" also ordinarily has anything but a violent, forceful sense. Composing is what poets and composers (i.e., music composers) do. The work of composing is ordinarily the gentle one of contemplation; composition in this sense is *poiesis*. Thus it is idiosyncratic to use the word to refer to the opposite, forceful, activity of imposition instead of nurture.

For these reasons of etymology and idiosyncrasy, then, I suggest "com-posing" as the fittest word to render Heidegger's *Ge-stell*. Let us now recall what "com-posing" or *Ge-stell* is meant to express. Com-posing is the name for the current event in the history of Being, the guise of Being in our present technological epoch. For Heidegger, this epoch is fundamentally characterized as one of imposition: modern technology is an imposition, but this imposition is only a response to a more originary imposition on the part of Being. Being encompasses all the impositions: that is what "com-posing" means and what Heidegger expresses straightforwardly, in the passage just cited, to the effect that *Ge-stell*/com-posing is the collection of impositions in which is included the imposition upon humans to impose on things in turn, i.e., to look upon things in the spirit of modern technology, to look upon things as disposables.

Heidegger continues the passage as follows: "Com-posing names the mode of disclosure that holds sway in the essence of modern technology and that is itself nothing technological" (FT, 21/20). There are two issues here: first, the relation of com-posing to the essence of modern technology and, secondly, the sense in which com-posing is nothing technological.

As to the first, Heidegger asserts a very close relationship between com-posing and the essence of modern technology. At times, he indeed calls com-posing the name for the essence of modern technology. In other places, Heidegger maintains that the essence of modern technology "rests on" com-posing or "shows itself" in com-posing. The passage just cited states that com-posing "holds sway" in the essence of modern technology. In what is perhaps his fullest formulation of the relationship, Heidegger says: "in com-posing, that unconcealedness comes to pass in conformity with which the work of modern technology looks disclosively upon realities as disposables. Therefore, it [i.e., modern technology] is not merely of human doing, nor is it a mere means to enable humans to do things" (FT, 22/21).

Can com-posing, which, as we have portrayed it hitherto, is the name for Being in its current guise, also be the name of the essence of modern technology? We can appeal to the last passage cited in order to respond to this question. The crucial word in the passage will prove to be "therefore." As usual, it requires a careful reading to understand the premises here and to see how the conclusion "therefore" follows.

Recall that for Heidegger, modern technology is essentially, fundamentally, a certain mode of disclosive looking. Modern technology is only secondarily a doing, or making, of certain practical things. Modern technology makes disposable things, but that is necessarily subsequent to its *looking* upon things as disposables. For Heidegger this looking is itself subsequent to an even prior looking, namely the "look" of Being, the self-disclosure of Being to humans. Currently, according to Heidegger's history of Being, this self-disclosure—or unconcealedness—can be called "com-posing." Being, in its current guise, is an all-embracing imposition; that is what the term "com-posing" expresses. The passage at issue begins by saying that in com-posing an unconcealedness comes to pass. That is simply another way of stating that com-posing is a certain guise of Being, a certain way Being unconceals itself, a certain way Being looks at us. The passage then asserts that *in conformity* with this look—i.e., as the appropriate response to this look—modern technology in turn looks disclosively upon things, in the way, namely, that takes things to be mere dis-posables. That is the main work or essence of modern technology: to look at things in such a way. Precisely as a response, modern technology is primarily accomplished ("encompassed") by that to which it conforms, by Being, by the all-encompassing posing. Accordingly, the word "therefore" in the citation is warranted. If the human role is to conform to the lead of Being, then indeed it follows that modern technology is "not merely of human doing." The way things appear is primarily of Being's doing, a matter of the coming to pass of a certain unconcealment or self-disclosure of Being. That is the simple conclusion drawn in the passage. Furthermore, it follows that modern technology is not primarily a means, i.e., a practical affair. As long as modern technology is understood as essentially a disclosive looking upon things, then it is primarily a theoretical affair and not a mere means for doing things.

And so we can clarify the close relation between com-posing, as the name for Being in its current guise, and the essence of modern technology. To take in order Heidegger's characterizations of the relationship, it is obvious, first, how com-posing, as a certain self-disclosure of Being, can be said to "hold sway" or rule in modern technology: modern technology, by conforming to the look of Being, is, so to speak, in service to that mode of unconcealedness, subservient to it, ruled over by it. Also evident is Heidegger's assertion that the essence of modern technology "rests on" com-posing; it rests on it in the sense of being the appropriate response to it. Furthermore, it could also be said, perhaps speaking somewhat loosely, that com-posing *is* the essence of modern technology. The essence of modern technology amounts to its way of disclosive looking *in conformity to* the look of Being, in conformity to the self-disclosure of things in general as disposables. Being and modern technology can thus be said to partake of the same essence; that essence is the disclosure of beings as disposables. Admittedly, modern technology is not an *all*-embracing imposition; as a response, it cannot be called com-posing in the strictest sense. Yet Heidegger evidently views Being as holding such sway over modern technology—and modern technology as so dominating the current age—that modern technology *embodies* Being; modern technology embodies Being's current look. In other words, modern technology *is* com-posing in its concrete manifestation. That is the very close relationship Heidegger asserts between com-posing and the essence of modern technology.

The essence of modern technology as nothing technological

Let us now turn to the second of the two issues we raised above: in what sense is com-posing, "the mode of disclosure that holds sway in the essence of modern technology, . . . nothing technological"?

What is being asserted here is—as Heidegger also phrases it several times—that the essence of modern technology is nothing technological. What does that mean?

The issue is raised in the very first paragraphs of "Die Frage nach der Technik":

> Technology is not the same as the essence of technology. When we are seeking the essence of a tree, we must become aware that that which holds sway in every tree precisely as a tree is not itself a tree, one that could be encountered among other trees.
> In this way, then, the essence of technology is nothing techno-logical at all. (FT, 7/4)

This is a very clear and simple statement and is preceded by a clear example. Just as the essence of a tree is not tree-like, not a woody thing, so the essence of technology is no technological thing. The same applies to every essence: the essence of a man is not itself a man. If I am by my-self in a room, there are not two human beings there, myself and my essence. My essence possesses no humanity; it is not another me or an-other human thing like me. Everyone knows not to seek for the essence of humanity the way one seeks for individual men or women.

On a first level, Heidegger is making the same simple point with regard to the essence of technology. There are technological things, i.e., high-tech gadgets and gizmos, the products of modern technology. Plexiglass is a technological thing. But the essence of modern technology is not a high-tech gadget; we cannot search for the essence of modern technology the way we would look for a piece of plexiglass. The essence is not one among other technological things. The essence is no techno-logical thing. That is what Heidegger means by saying that the essence of modern technology is nothing technological.

How then are technological things related to the essence of technol-ogy? Heidegger expresses this relation as follows:

> Com-posing names the mode of disclosure which holds sway in the essence of modern technology and which is itself nothing technolog-ical. On the other hand, among technological things can be found all that we call gadgets and gizmos [*Gestänge, Geschiebe, Gerüste*] and that are components of a device. Devices, along with their compo-nent gadgets, are applications of the work of technology. These ap-plications arise only as responses to the challenge of com-posing [*Ge-stell*]; they do not constitute com-posing itself or bring it about. (FT, 21/20–21)

"Gadgets and gizmos" is a free translation of the three German words in brackets. The published English translation is somewhat more literal: "rods, pistons, and chassis." But this translation, too, is a creative one. If Heidegger did intend these particular mechanical parts, he did not choose their usual German names. His terms go together only vaguely; most literally, they mean "shafts, thrusts, frames." His choice of terms would indeed be puzzling, except for one circumstance, namely the fact that the three words all begin with *Ge-*. Heidegger chose the best *Ge-* words he could find to fit the context. That is the clue to the meaning of the passage.

The three words in question begin with *Ge-*, but they are not *Ge-* words in the special, collective sense. Heidegger does not hyphenate them, and he is not taking them in the special sense. These words, then, correspond to *Gestell* (without the hyphen); they name examples of *Gestell*, and so Heidegger is here clarifying the relation between *Gestell* and *Ge-stell*, between technological gadgets and com-posing, between the products of modern technology and its essence, between things that have been imposed on and the all-encompassing imposition, between disposables and the disclosive looking upon things as disposables.

Let us give the name "composites" to the high-tech gadgets Heidegger is referring to. We mean "composites" in the specific sense in which the term is used of high-tech, "space-age" materials, such as plexiglass, polymers, and laminates. These materials do not occur naturally; they are specifically com-posed, artificially compounded in a laboratory. The other name for them is "synthetics." These materials are specifically synthesized: they are "posed together," forcefully and intentionally. They do not come together on their own.

"Composites" in the sense just indicated can easily serve to name all the products of modern technology. All these high-tech devices are synthetic; scientists force them into being artificially, in laboratories. Thus "composites" can serve to translate *Gestell*. The latter could mean "eye-glass frame," but, as a high-tech gadget, what makes a frame *Gestell*, in Heidegger's sense, is that it is composed today of acrylic, and the glass it holds is made, not of glass, but of thermoplastic. It is as an artificial, synthetic, composite frame that a frame is *Gestell*.

To see how the things of *Gestell* are related to *Ge-stell* is to understand the second sense in which Heidegger says that the essence of technology is nothing technological. How are composites related to com-posing? According to Heidegger, as we have just read, composites "arise only as responses to the challenge embodied in com-posing; they do not constitute com-posing itself or bring it about." This expresses a priority of the essence of technology over technological things. The latter come to be only as *responses* to the former. The essence of technology is a certain way of looking, a certain way of disclosing things, namely the way that takes things as disposables, as merely there to be imposed on by humans. Composites are the actual disposables; composites are things that have actually been imposed on, things that have been unnaturally, violently, synthesized. Now

what Heidegger is saying is that com-posing is not itself one of the composites (that is the first sense in which the essence of technology is nothing
technological), and, furthermore, com-posing does not come into being on
account of the composites. The disclosive looking, the com-posing, the
challenging, is not only *other* than the composites, it is *prior* to them. It is
because we take things as merely there to be imposed on that we ever conceive of the idea of synthesizing composites. That is the second sense in
which the essence of technology is nothing technological; the essence does
not derive from technological things. The essence of technology is prior to
technological things—not only logically, as the condition of possibility, but
even temporally or historically, as we are about to see. But if the essence
does not derive from high-tech things, whence does it arise? For Heidegger,
the essence, the disclosive looking, is indeed a response, it has its motives,
and these motives lie in the history of Being. The looking upon things in
general as disposables is the human response to the withdrawal of Being,
the response to a deficient self-showing of Being. That is the source of the
essence of modern technology; the source is Being in its current guise, Being
as an all-encompassing imposition.

Therefore, according to Heidegger, the essence of technology does
not derive from technological things; on the contrary, technological
things derive from the essence of modern technology. How? How does
the essence of technology give rise to high-tech gadgets? That is the historical question Heidegger is about to broach. For Heidegger, the essence
of modern technology and high-tech things are joined by an intermediary.
That intermediary is modern science, and so Heidegger is about to broach
the question of the historical relation between science and modern technology. Before turning to science, however, Heidegger makes one further
remark with regard to *Ge-stell*/com-posing. He relates the essence of
modern technology to its own historical precedent, *poiesis*.

What Heidegger claims is that the imposition on things to yield
composites, the forceful syn-thesizing of high-tech things, does not exist
side by side with *poiesis*. On the contrary, the one has supplanted the
other. Modern technology, as Heidegger will say later, "deposes" *poiesis*.
Not only has modern technology "descended" from ancient technology,
but modern technology has *expelled* the ancient way of doing things.
Thus the two technologies do not exist side by side, but one after the
other. They are indeed both of the same essence; they both are ways or
modes of disclosive looking. Yet they are not concurrent modes; in the
age of modern technology, the ancient mode is present only as an echo:

> The word "*stellen*" in the title *Ge-stell* does not merely signify
> challenging; at the same time, it is supposed to preserve the echo of a
> different "*stellen*," from which it is descended, namely that pro-ducing

[*Her-stellen*] and presenting [*Dar-stellen*] which, in the sense of *poiesis*, is a letting, one that lets the self-emerging come forth into uncon- cealedness. The pro-ducing that brings forth, e.g., the setting up [*Auf- stellen*] of a statue in the temple precinct, and the challenging imposition [*Bestellen*] now under discussion are, to be sure, funda- mentally distinct, and yet they are related in essence. They are both modes of disclosedness, of *aletheia*. (FT, 21–22/21)

We will learn, however, that only in a special sense are they "modes" of the same essence. They are not modes of disclosedness the way oaks and elms are kinds or modes of the same essence, tree. Oaks and elms may exist side by side; but Being does not disclose itself in two "fundamentally distinct" ways simultaneously. The epochs of the history of Being are precisely "epochs," i.e., they perform an *epoché*; they "hold back" one another and do not exist alongside each other, concurrently. In the terms of the passage above, this applies to the self-emergent versus that which is challenged or imposed on. In the first epoch of the history of Being, things in general disclose themselves as self-emergent (= *physis*, nature), and the technological practice of that epoch is a letting, a nur- turing. In the second epoch, things show themselves as there to be im- posed upon, and the respective technological practice is the actual imposing on things, the forcible synthesizing into composites. What Hei- degger is saying is that the appearance of things as nature and the self- showing of things as composites are indeed both modes of disclosure, and so they share a common essence. But nature and composites do not share the same time; they are distinct in time, historically distinct. Composites have descended from nature but have left nature behind. Only an echo of nature is present today.

Heidegger will eventually develop the notion of modern technology as deposing *poiesis*. He will also propose a third sense in which the essence of technology is nothing technological, but that sense must wait upon Heidegger's redetermination of the very concept of "essence" in a subsequent part of the essay. He turns now, finally, to the relation between modern technology and science.

Science as harbinger

The issue is introduced by a discussion of the significance of exper- imentation in modern natural science. The relevant paragraph is an ex- ceptionally dense one; I will cite it in a slightly paraphrased form:

> To be sure, it remains true that humans in the technological age are, in an especially predominating way, challenged into a mode

of disclosedness. This disclosedness concerns, in the first place, nature, which is viewed as the ultimate storehouse of disposables, in the form of energy. Accordingly, the impositional [*be-stellend*] attitude of humans is embodied first in modern, exact, natural science, whose way of representing is a posing in advance [*vor-stellen*] or setting up of nature as a calculable nexus of forces. Nature, as this nexus, can be set out after [*nach-stellen*] and waylaid. But it is not *because* it sets instruments on to the interrogation of nature—i.e., attacks nature with experiments—that modern physics is impositional. Just the reverse is the case. Physics, precisely in advance as pure theory, already constrains nature in its very way of posing nature, constrains nature to present itself as a calculable nexus of forces, and that is the reason experiments are then imposed upon nature, namely for the sake of seeing whether and how nature, already posed in a certain way, will report itself. (FT, 22/21)

The basic point Heidegger is making here is that the idea of nature in modern natural science does not arise as a result of experimentation. The general idea that nature is a calculable nexus of forces does not derive from scientific work, from the work of conducting experiments. On the contrary, that idea of nature is what motivates the work of science in the first place; the idea stands at the head of the experiments and is not the result of experiments. For Heidegger, modern science *presupposes* a view of nature; i.e., modern science must begin as "pure theory," as a view in advance of what things in general are like. Modern science must possess this theory, this conception or disclosive looking, *before* it starts to work, i.e., before it conducts experiments. Subsequently—in light of this view of nature—science devises experiments to discover whether, to what extent, and how nature, as so conceived, reports itself, i.e., how nature, as so conceived in advance, looks in detail. Experimentation can indeed fill in the details, but experimentation cannot discover *what* nature is, what the essence of nature is, since a conception of the essence of nature is presupposed for all experimentation. Without that conception in advance, the scientist would not in the least know what sort of experiments to devise.

Science cannot proceed randomly; experiments must be guided by a general idea of what is there to be found. The practice of science must be guided by a preconceived theory about the nature of nature, about the essence of things in general. In Heidegger's terms above, the general idea of nature in modern science is that of a "calculable nexus of forces." This is the conception of nature as a mathematical manifold. What Heidegger is maintaining is that science cannot discover that nature in general is mathematical, or that nature is lawful, or that it excludes final causes. Science presupposes these ideas and then conducts experiments *especially designed* to determine which mathematical formulas apply and which laws hold for nature. The point is that the mathematical goal has to be designed into the experiment; only mathematical experiments, so to speak, yield mathematical results. In this regard, Heidegger is merely making more specific Kant's famous observation that natural science was set on a secure course only when nature was constrained to answer not random questions but questions stemming from an explicit design of reason. Heidegger is specifying the design of reason in natural science as a design of *mathematical* reason.

Modern science could then never discover that nature is nonmathematical, or unlawful, or that final causes exist in nature, for these results are ruled out in principle. Scientific experiments can do no more than demonstrate how nature *reports* itself if viewed in a certain way and asked certain sorts of questions. Science can indeed prove which specific laws apply to nature, but science must *assume* that nature is what the laws apply to. That is a very large assumption, and in another essay (BH, 324/205) Heidegger remarks that it has as little validity as does the notion that the essence of nature has been discovered in atomic energy. It could even be that nature, in the face it turns toward a scientist's experiments, is simply *concealing* its essence, putting on a false front, showing itself in a deficient way. Science can take great strides within its realm, once it has been given its realm to work on. But science has no power over the adequacy of that realm as a conception of nature. Is the field within which science does its work of experimentation truly nature? Are things in general essentially mathematical? Is nature genuinely a calculable nexus of forces? The answer to these questions depends on how much truth there is in the theoretical outlook that precedes the practice of science. That is to say, in Heideggerian terms, it depends on how wholeheartedly Being is revealing itself in our current preconception of nature. But Being is an autonomous agent; nothing can compel Being to unveil itself, and scientific experiments, in particular, have no power over the self-disclosure of Being.

How is natural science related to modern technology? Recall that Heidegger had just emphasized the essential connection between modern and ancient technology. They share a common essence, and in essence they are not primarily practical or instrumental but theoretical; they are modes of disclosive looking, modes of disclosedness, *aletheia*, truth. Technology is "pure theory," taking "theory" here, as always, in its original sense of "looking back in response to the look of Being." Technology is a way of disclosing things in general, a way of looking disclosively upon things, in correspondence to the way they offer themselves. Technology is essentially correlated to the Being of beings; technology names the role of the human receiver, the role of Da-sein, in the self-disclosure of Being. Technological knowledge is the knowledge of what it means to be at all.

Modern technology discloses things in a specific way, and things currently appear as merely there to be imposed upon, as disposables. How does modern technology then relate to nature? In the words of Heidegger just quoted, modern technology, as a mode of disclosedness, "concerns, in the first place, nature, which is viewed as the ultimate storehouse of disposables." The word "concerns" must be taken here in a specific sense. What Heidegger is saying is that nature is now viewed as a storehouse of disposables precisely *because* modern technology looks upon nature, upon things in general, as merely there to be imposed on. Modern technology, as a mode of disclosedness, *gives rise to* the understanding of nature as a storehouse of disposables. Nature is today a storehouse of disposables precisely because we look upon all things with the impositional eyes of modern technology. That is the reason nature is a storehouse of *energy*; all we see in nature is energy, raw power to be harnessed and put to our uses. The crucial point is that nature presents itself as a storehouse of disposables, a storehouse of energy, only when disclosed in the mode of disclosure characteristic of modern technology. So it is not because nature is *already* a storehouse of disposables that modern technology is concerned with it. On the contrary, nature is a storehouse of disposables only because and precisely because modern technology is concerned with it, precisely because modern technology looks upon nature, upon things in general, in an impositional, domineering, proprietary way. What we term nature, a storehouse of disposable energy, is constituted by our looking at it as such, and modern technology is that looking.

Accordingly, as Heidegger says, it is not because science attacks nature with experiments and instruments that it is impositional. The prime imposition occurs in the preunderstanding of nature that gives direction to the experiments and sets science on the path of its work. Nature must already have been waylaid, already constrained, before the experiments can begin. The "pure theory" that precedes the experimentation is the prime locus of the imposition. Experiments do indeed carry out the work of waylaying nature, but that is only a matter of filling in details, discovering how nature reports itself in details. Experiments presuppose a nature that has already been waylaid, already been disclosed as nothing but a storehouse of disposable energy, nothing but forces to be dominated through the application of mathematics and instruments. The attacking work of *science* presupposes a disclosive looking in advance that is already an impositional look. This particular disclosive looking in advance is precisely what, for Heidegger, characterizes modern technology. *In nuce*, that is how, for Heidegger, science presupposes modern technology rather than vice versa.

Hence, modern technology is the pure theory, the ontological knowledge, the disclosure of what beings are like in general, that stands at the head of science, that opens up for science its realm of work, and that thereby sets science upon its path of experimentation. Modern technology is the theory, the knowledge of nature, and modern science is the practical application. Thus modern technology is not applied science; science is applied technology, applied ontological knowledge.

For Heidegger, to sum up, modern technology precedes science and gives science its start. Science merely furthers the attack on nature inaugurated by the impositional way of disclosing things that is characteristic of modern technology. Science, *from its very start*, is in service to modern technology, in service to the disclosure of things as disposables. Accordingly, modern technology *poses* science, sets science on its way. Therefore modern technology is the basis *of* science and is not based *on* science. That is the conclusion whose paradoxical character is not lost on Heidegger:

> But mathematical natural science arose almost two hundred years prior to modern technology. How then is science supposed to be from the start something posed by modern technology, in service to modern technology? The facts testify to the contrary. Surely modern technology got going only when it could be supported by exact natural science. Calculated chronologically, that is correct. Thought historically, it does not attain the truth. (FT, 22–23/21–22)

Heidegger's resolution of this paradox turns on the distinction between modern technology (or technological things) and the *essence* of modern technology. The essence of modern technology is nothing technological. Com-posing, the essence of modern technology, is not a composite, not a high-tech gadget, not a technological thing, not a thing at all. The essence of modern technology is not a thing but is instead a theory, a way of understanding what makes a thing a thing at all, a way of looking disclosively at things as such, an impositional looking that precedes the manufacture of high-tech things.

It requires history, in Heidegger's sense, to recognize the essence of modern technology. Chronological reckoning, which takes its bearings exclusively from humans, is superficial and does not attain the level of Being or essence. Chronology is oblivious to the essence of modern technology and understands technology merely in terms of its human employment. Accordingly, chronology identifies modern technology with high-tech gadgets. That is why, calculated superficially, science appears to be prior to modern technology. High-tech gadgets indeed arise as the practical application of science, and so science seems to antedate modern technology— by two hundred years. Modern technology, if equated with technological things, is applied science and so requires an already advanced science.

If we do recognize the essence of modern technology, as a disclosive looking at beings as such, then we have three items to place in historical order: the essence of modern technology, science, and high-tech things. How are these related? Heidegger answers as follows:

> Modern physics, as science of nature, is the pioneer sent out not indeed by technology but by the essence of modern technology.[4] For the challenging encompassing into an impositional disclosive looking holds sway already in physics. Yet it is not explicitly manifest in physics. Modern physics is the harbinger of com-posing, yet the origin of this harbinger is still unfamiliar, since the essence of modern technology has been concealed for a long time. (FT, 23/22)

Thus the properly historical order, according to Heidegger, is this: first arises the essence of modern technology, then comes science, and finally there appear technological things. Science mediates between the essence of modern technology and technological things. It does so as a pioneer or harbinger. The word "harbinger" perfectly expresses Heidegger's meaning here, provided it is taken in its original, etymological sense. "Harbinger" derives from the middle English word for "inn" or "lodge," *herberge*. (Compare the current French word *auberge* and the Italian *albergo*.) A harbinger, in its original sense, is a person who is sent ahead to secure lodgings. That is precisely how, for Heidegger, science serves the essence of modern technology. Science is the harbinger sent out by the essence of modern technology. Science goes ahead and secures for that essence a lodging in the visible world, a lodging where the essence can then take up residence. This residence is the end-product of science, namely high-tech things. When the harbinger has produced composites, then the essence of modern technology can come into its own and be fully manifest.

The role of science can also be described as that of a pioneer. A pioneer is the first to settle a territory, so that others may follow. In Heidegger's view, science is a pioneer serving the essence of modern technology. This pioneer settles the territory by advancing so far that it can be applied and thereby produce high-tech things. The essence of modern technology then follows, in the sense of showing itself explicitly in these things. The essence follows—as far as visibility is concerned—but was indeed the invisible source all along.

The essence of modern technology is the beginning, the source, but it is not manifest until the end. That is what Heidegger means by saying, as just quoted, that the essence of modern technology already holds sway in physics but is not explicitly manifest in physics. In other words, science is directed by a "pure theory" (= the disclosure of things as disposable = the essence of modern technology) which sets science on its way. Science follows this theory. Yet the essence of modern technology is not explicitly manifest in science itself. Things do not manifestly appear as disposables until science has advanced far enough to be applied, applied so as to produce actual disposables, composites, high-tech gadgets. These gadgets are the lodging in which the essence of modern technology can show itself in full visibility. When high-tech gadgets appear, it is clear that we are in the age of modern technology. What is not so clear is that this age actually antedates these gadgets and even antedates science.

It antedates them the way any essence holds sway from the start or the way theory antedates practice. Yet the essence does not show itself from the start; the essence remains hidden until the end, until its end-products appear. Even then, it does not become immediately clear that the essence was holding sway from the start. That is why Heidegger says the origin of science, that which sent it forth as a harbinger, is still unfamiliar. The essence of modern technology, as the origin of science, is unfamiliar to anyone who does not penetrate beyond the perspective of human chronology. It is unfamiliar to anyone who is oblivious to the history of Being. Expressed more precisely, it is unfamiliar as long as Being or the essence keeps itself concealed, and the essence is precisely what does conceal itself the longest. While Being or the essence is the first, in the sense of that which holds sway from the start, it is the last to disclose itself: "Modern physics is the harbinger of com-posing, yet the origin of this harbinger is still unfamiliar, since the essence of modern technology has been concealed for a long time, concealed even where power machines have already been devised, electrical technology has been underway, and nuclear technology is in force. Every essence, not only that of modern technology, keeps itself concealed the longest" (FT, 23/22).

While the essence of modern technology is unfamiliar today, i.e., largely unknown (unknown for the most part and to most people), it is not totally unknown. If any philosopher has transcended the superficial attitude of human chronology, then that could be only on account of a new initiative on the part of Being. The credit lies not with any particular philosopher but with Being. If, at long last, Being is reapproaching mankind, then the task of philosophy is, in Heidegger's words, "to be in wonder at the approach of the earliest" (FT, 23/22). Heidegger himself here puts the emphasis on the futural connotation of the word "approach." Thus, for Heidegger, philosophy is future-oriented and not a mere attempt to revive the past, to recapture the ancient era when Being showed itself wholeheartedly. Yet we could also emphasize the "wonder" and thereby understand "approach" in a slightly different sense.

In a lecture course[5] delivered a few years prior to the essay on technology, Heidegger painstakingly distinguished wonder (*das Erstaunen*) from related attitudes, such as admiration (*Bewundern*), marvelling (*Verwundern*), astonishment (*Staunen*), and awe (*Bestaunen*). For Heidegger, the basic difference is that the other attitudes arise in the face of some definite being, whereas wonder is the proper human response to the disclosure of Being. Only Being is wondrous.

From Heidegger's long and intricate analysis, we can focus on two particulars. First, as was already pointed out, Heidegger identifies wonder with *techne* in the Greek sense. *Techne* is the human way of appropriating the self-disclosure of Being; according to Heidegger, "in *techne*, the wondrous, the Being of beings, unfolds and comes into its own." Thus *techne*, as wonder, is here precisely what we have taken it to be: a matter of theory, a matter of ontological knowledge. Secondly, Heidegger characterizes wonder as a "creative tolerance" (*schaffende Ertragsamkeit*). He even calls wonder a suffering, although he is careful to obviate a misunderstanding of it as either passive or active in the usual sense. The term "creative tolerance" is meant to express an active passivity, an active acceptance, an acceptance with the full exercise of one's grasping powers. What is to be accepted (suffered, undergone) is the self-approach of Being. The initiative lies on the part of Being, the credit for *techne*, for the understanding of what it means to be, goes to Being, not to any particular philosopher. That is what Heidegger is expressing in the essay on technology by calling the task of philosophy "wonder at the approach of the earliest." In other words, the task of philosophy, first philosophy, is equivalent to the philosophy of *techne*, which can also be characterized as wonder in the face of Being, active acceptance of the look of Being, diligently playing the role of Da-sein.

Science as mediator

Let us now summarize the central tenets of Heidegger's philosophy with regard to the relation between modern technology and science.

The basic, central point is that modern technology has a precedence over science; i.e., modern technology is not applied science. Specifically, Heidegger draws a distinction between the way science is related to the essence of modern technology and the way science is related to technological things. Science mediates between the essence and the things. The essence of modern technology (= an understanding of Being as such) is the ultimate source of science. The latter merely works out the impositional attitude already at play in the disclosive looking that characterizes the essence of modern technology. The essence of modern technology precedes science and sends science forth—as a pioneer or harbinger to secure lodgings in the visible world. When science has advanced far enough, it can be applied so as to produce technological things, which are indeed subsequent to science. The essence of modern technology will then manifestly inhabit these things, will take up residence in them in a manifest way, but the essence was in force, was holding sway, from the very outset.

Causality; modern physics

Heidegger concludes his characterization of the essence of modern technology the way he began his account of ancient technology, namely by discussing the concomitant understanding of causality:

> If modern physics must increasingly resign itself to the fact that its representations are non-intuitive, this renunciation is not dictated by some commission of scientists. It is demanded by the holding sway of com-posing, which insists on disposability and sees in nature merely disposables. That is why physics, as much as it abandons the claim to represent self-standing objects—although this representation was indeed the scientific ideal until recently—can never renounce this one thing, namely that nature report itself as calculable and thus be disposable as a system of data. This system is thus determined by a causality that has changed once more. Causality now neither manifests the character of the active letting that brings forth, nor is it a type of efficient causality, and a fortiori it has nothing in common with the formal cause. Causality has shrunk, presumably, into a registering of challenged contents that are guaranteed to appear simultaneously or successively. To this would correspond the process of increasing resignation Heisenberg's lecture has just depicted in such an impressive way. (FT, 24/23)

A word of background is necessary here. Heidegger's essay on technology was originally presented as a lecture during a five-day colloquium (November 16–20, 1953) sponsored by the Bavarian Academy of Fine Arts. (Heidegger's essay was originally published the following year in the *acta* of this colloquium.) Six other philosophers and scientists also delivered lectures on the theme, "The arts in the technological age." Heidegger's predecessor to the podium was the physicist Werner Heisenberg, whose chosen topic was, "The picture of nature in contemporary physics." It is to this lecture that Heidegger alludes, and we must turn to it for a moment.

Heisenberg's thesis was that the picture of nature in contemporary science can less and less be called a picture of *nature*. Natural science is no longer *natural* science; science has resigned itself to the fact that its representations are abstractions and do not picture that which we experience as nature. Physics has become a representation of the-physicist-knows-not-what. Furthermore, physicists do not care what the object of their scientific knowledge is, as long as practical results are guaranteed. That is the "growing resignation" Heidegger refers to.

Heisenberg sees mathematization as the first, but only the first, abstraction. Mathematization makes the ob-ject of science nonintuitive. For science, the color red, e.g., is reduced to a formula describing a certain electromagnetic wave. A person can then possess a perfect scientific understanding of color and yet be completely color blind. By the same token, a person who knows red intuitively, by perceiving red things, will fail to recognize the scientific formula as representing her lived experience in the least. That is what it means to say that science is nonintuitive.

At first, physicists maintained that the things of nature, as we experience them (e.g., red things), were still represented by the scientific formulas—only indirectly. Heisenberg, however, shows that a further abstraction—and a further resignation—has occurred in physics. Basically on account of Heisenberg's own principle of indeterminacy, physicists today have no confidence that their formulas apply to autonomous objects, to an independent nature, but only to that which is responding to the scientist's experimental intervention in nature. According to the principle of indeterminacy, what is registered by the experimental apparatus is—in part at least—*produced* by that apparatus. What is registered is thus separate from a supposed nature "in itself," and science has no way of attaining an independent nature. Consequently, scientific formulas are not even *indirectly* applicable to nature; there is no picture of nature in modern physics. Science is not a picture at all, i.e., a representation of some original; there is no original. In other terms, the object of science is precisely an ob-ject; it is something *posed* by science, *created* in the very act of carrying out scientific experiments. Heisenberg therefore acknowledges that the object of "natural" science is, paradoxically, not nature.

According to Heisenberg, physicists have resigned themselves to this situation. It actually does not matter at all, as long as the experiments of science register data that can be relied on and applied in practice. As long as it can be guaranteed that certain phenomena will appear simultaneously or successively, as long as the predictions of science are dependable, as long as science "works," it does not matter whether or not physicists know what—if anything—science is supposed to be a picture of:

> We [physicists] have resigned ourselves to the situation just described, since it turned out that we could represent mathematically and say in every case, dependably and without fear of logical contradiction, what the result of an experiment would be. Thus we resigned ourselves to the new situation the moment we could make dependable predictions. Admittedly, our mathematical formulas no longer picture nature but merely represent our own grasp of nature. To that extent, we have renounced the type of description of nature that was customary for centuries and that had been valid as the self-evident goal of all exact natural science. Even provisionally, we cannot say

more than that in the field of modern atomic physics we have resigned ourselves, and we have done so because our representations
are dependable.[6]

The French phenomenologist Merleau-Ponty, at the beginning of a
small treatise on art, traced this same process of resignation in science:

> Science manipulates things and renounces inhabiting them.
> Science provides itself with its own internal models of things and,
> carrying out upon these indices or variables the transformations
> permitted by their definition, encounters the actual world only
> every now and then. . . .
> Yet classical science retained a feeling for the self-standing of
> the world and understood itself as getting at this world through its
> constructions. . . . Today, however, there holds sway the completely
> novel understanding that these constructions are autonomous. . . .
> Thinking has come down to predicting, manipulating, transforming,
> and the only cross-check is an experimental control where the phe-
> nomena are all already highly "wrought," i.e., where our appara-
> tuses produce these phenomena rather than merely record them.[7]

To return now to Heidegger, in the paragraph in question his starting point is Heisenberg's portrayal of the abstractness of science and the
resignation of the scientist. Heidegger then proceeds to ground these phenomena in the history of Being.

Heidegger begins by noting that physics has renounced intuitiveness. That is exactly what Merleau-Ponty means, when he says science
has renounced inhabiting things. The world of science is not the world in
which we do live or could live. We can inhabit only a meaningful world,
and meaning derives from intuition, i.e., from ordinary perception. That
is why the mathematical formula of red is meaningless to someone who is
color blind; it is the intuitive world that gives meaning to the abstract
mathematical one, not vice versa. No one could live in or walk around in
or see anything at all in a world reduced entirely to mathematical formulas. Such a formula could indeed be used to program a laser and thereby
sculpt very accurately some person's face. But no human being could use
that formula to recognize a particular person in a crowd. A world reduced entirely to mathematical formulas would be schizophrenic: on the
level of abstract thought, everything would be perfectly rational; on the
level of ordinary experience, however, nothing would make sense.

What motivates the renunciation of the lived world on the part of science? According to Heidegger, this renunciation is not of human doing, it
is not dictated by a "commission of scientists." On the contrary, it is
Being's doing, it is "dictated" by Being in its current guise, by the way Being

is currently disclosing itself. The current guise of Being is com-posing, i.e., an all-encompassing imposition, and beings present themselves today as merely there to be imposed on, as disposables. In Heidegger's eyes, science must have recourse to an abstraction, to mathematization, precisely because mathematization serves disposability. Mathematization is the *reculement pour mieux sauter*, the step back from things that makes it possible to impose on them with all the more force. Visible light, for instance, can be manipulated all the more efficiently by first reducing the colors of the spectrum to mathematical formulas of waves. These formulas have no intuitive meaning, but they do have practical applicability. The laser is a case in point; its beam is so intense because its light is "coherent," i.e., one single mathematically determined wavelength is imposed on this light. Examples could be multiplied ad infinitum; the scientist's recourse to mathematical formulas, to calculation and quantification, i.e., the renunciation of things as intuited, makes possible an eventual heightened imposition on those very same things. For Heidegger, science is commanded to be mathematical insofar as "com-posing holds sway," insofar as beings in general disclose themselves as disposables. Accordingly, it is merely *correct* to say that science imposes on things because it is mathematical; it would be closer to the truth to say that science has recourse to mathematics because science is already impositional, already under the sway of disposability in general.

Heidegger goes on to declare, then, in the paragraph quoted above, that there is one thing physics will never renounce. Since the attitude of disposability holds sway over science, physics could never renounce disposability. Science may renounce intuitiveness in its objects, may even renounce determinacy in its objects, but science will never renounce understanding its object as "calculable, and thus disposable as a system of data." In other words, physics may no longer provide a picture of nature, physics may not even care what—if anything—it does picture, but physics can never abandon the goal of providing a *coherent* picture, a calculable, dependable, predictable picture. The reason is that such a picture is required by disposability, and science, as the human response to the current self-disclosure of Being, can never renounce disposability. If a new epoch of Being should arise, i.e., if com-posing should no longer hold sway, then disposability might well be overcome. But this simply means that the human response to the new mode of Being will no longer be science.

Finally, Heidegger draws out the implications (of the current state of science) with regard to the concept of causality. Causality has shrunk into a "registering of challenged contents that are guaranteed to appear simultaneously or successively." First of all, the contents of science are challenged in the sense that, as Kant says, nature has been *constrained* to present itself in a certain way, constrained to respond to questions stemming from a specific design of reason. Or, in Heisenberg's terms, the contents of science are—at least in part—produced by the scientific intervention into nature, produced by the very experimental apparatus that is meant to peer into nature. Or, in Merleau-Ponty's words, the phenomena of science are "wrought." What, for example, does the scientist observe? She observes (or, rather, her instruments record) the path of a humanly induced streak of light in a humanly made cloud. This path is a highly wrought phenomenon. It is not an *observed* phenomenon in the usual sense of something received, something to which we stand in service (*ob-servare*), something to which we are servile; on the contrary, it is something we order up. It is a highly elaborated, constrained, challenged content.

Heidegger remarks, secondly, that causality now refers to the "registering" of these challenged contents in terms of simultaneity and successiveness. That is to say, what is registered is precisely the simultaneity and successiveness of the contents. Science is not a knowledge of the contents as such. Science indeed has abandoned its erstwhile goal of knowing contents as such. Science is merely a knowledge of the *order* of contents. Science registers which contents regularly appear together and which succeed one another. Science is the knowledge of the *occasions* on which particular contents appear. Thus causality has shrunk into occasionalism. Science has learned which contents occasion which others, "occasioning" understood merely in the sense of being the temporal companion or temporal antecedent. Science has become accustomed to the order of simultaneity and succession and can make dependable predictions. Science can guarantee the order of appearances but can claim no insight into the essence of what is appearing. Thus, for science, causality is not a matter of an essential connection; it is merely a customary one. That is why Heidegger says causality is today neither what it was for the ancients, namely the active letting that brings forth, nor is it efficient causality, and a fortiori it is not formal causality. Those older ways of understanding causality all presuppose an insight into the essence: active letting begins with a contemplation of the essence, which it then nurtures and brings forth into visibility; the formal cause is, of course, nothing but the essence; and even the concept of efficient causality implies an insight into an essential connection and is not reducible to a mere registering of temporal succession.

Occasioning is a *blind* causality. It is entirely dependable, completely guaranteed, but its workings are absolutely hidden to us. Science knows only the *results* of this causality, and knows them with certainty, but makes no claim to know *what* is thereby causally connected or what the causal connection actually is. In this regard, scientists perfectly exemplify the prisoners Socrates describes in his famous cave allegory, which is a "likeness of our nature, with regard to learning and ignorance" (*Republic*, 514a).[8] See prisoners, Socrates asks of us, sitting in a cave watching shadows. The shadows are cast by things behind the prisoners, but the prisoners are in chains, unable to turn their heads, and so they see only the shadows in front and not the things behind the shadows. The prisoners have been in this predicament since childhood, and thus they are ignorant of the nature of that which they see; they are unaware that the shadows are shadows. Yet these cave-dwellers are learned, too. They can register very well the order of successiveness and simultaneity in what they see, which enables them to make predictions, and they honor the one who is best at this sort of learning. That is, they honor the prisoner: "who best remembers which of the shadows customarily pass by prior to others, which succeed others, and which appear simultaneously, and who thereby has the greatest power of prophesying which shadows will come next" (516c–d).

The mastery of the shadows, despite the ignorance about their true nature, is all that counts to the cave-dwellers. They are content with their learning, such as it is, and would even do violence to anyone who attempted to release them from their bondage to the shadows (517a). Blind mastery, the power to predict, is more honored than insight into the object of the mastery. For Heidegger, the resignation of today's scientists would correspond to the contentment of the prisoners in the cave. It is the dependability or predictability of scientific knowledge that has made it easy for the scientist to be resigned to the lack of insight into the object of science. That is precisely what is expressed in Heisenberg's words, already quoted: "Thus we resigned ourselves to the new situation the moment we could make dependable predictions." The guaranteed results have compensated for the blindness; better to master I-know-not-what than to know the what without the mastery.

The novelty of modern technology

Let us close by returning to the beginning, i.e., to the "decisive" question Heidegger raised at the start of his characterization of the essence of modern technology. Heidegger expressed a hypothetical objection, to the effect that modern technology is not comparable to the previous technology and so is not a disclosive looking at Being, because modern technology looks to science instead of to Being. Modern technology takes direction from scientific facts and not from a vague theory of Being. To that objection, Heidegger posed this undermining question: "The decisive question is still: of what essence is modern technology that it can occur to it to employ exact natural science?" (FT, 15/14).

What has come to light is that modern technology, in its essence, is indeed a looking upon Being and is, specifically, an impositional or dispositional looking. The essence of modern technology is the disclosive looking upon things as disposables. Precisely on account of this essence, it can occur to modern technology to employ exact natural science. Indeed, this essence *demands* science, demands that things be referred to a domain of calculability. That is one sense in which modern technology is dispositional: it appoints things to science, orders or refers them to science. It sees calculability as appropriate to things, since calculation enhances their disposability. Thus the essence of modern technology does precisely "employ" science. It puts science to use in order to further its own disclosure of things as disposables. Accordingly, in Heidegger's terms, science is a harbinger of the essence of modern technology, sent out by that essence to produce actual disposable things, composites, high-tech gadgets, wherein the essence of modern technology can manifestly lodge.

Immediately upon posing his decisive question, Heidegger answered it, with an equally decisive answer, the decisiveness of which we can now appreciate: "What is modern technology? It, too, is a disclosive looking. Only if we allow our gaze to rest on this fundamental characteristic will what is novel in modern technology show itself to us" (FT, 15/14).

Assuming we have allowed our gaze to rest on the essential characteristic, then what *is* novel about modern technology? Certainly its impositional character is decisively novel, in comparison with the nurturing character of the earlier technology. Ancient technology looked upon things in general as nature in the original Greek sense of what is growing, self-emergent, pregnant. Ancient technology was then a matter of nurturing or midwifery, in service to an already given potentiality or pregnancy. Modern technology, to state the opposition as simply as possible, is disrespectful; it looks upon things as disposable and proceeds to turn them ever more manifestly into disposables. Modern technology disrespects all but its own humanly chosen ends. Modern technology is blind to nature. Modern technology is, *sit venia verbo*, a *blind* disclosive looking. That is perhaps what is most decisively novel about it.

In an obvious sense, of course, namely in terms of the sophistication of the products of the two technologies, anyone would say the blindness resides on the ancient side, not the modern. Ancient ingenuity produced nothing more marvelous than a folding chair, and the technology that has placed humans on the moon and synthesized gore-tex could hardly be called blind. Heidegger would naturally concede all this; the blindness of modern technology is more insidious—and more dangerous. For Heidegger, what is dangerous is self-blindness, blindness to one's own essence. In Heisenberg's portrayal, science is uncertain as to what it is actually a science of, and thus it is blind to itself precisely as science. A knowledge of causality, in its current shrunken state, is likewise blind: blind to itself, blind to what the causal connection actually is. The current knowledge of causes does not know what it knows. For Heidegger, modern technology, too, is self-blind; blind to its own essence as a disclosive looking. Modern technology is unaware of its own role as a looking upon Being in response to the way Being offers itself. For Heidegger, humans of the technological age cannot be authentic receivers if they are blind to their role as receivers in the first place. And therein lies the danger—not to the existence of humans but to their dignity—since, in Heidegger's eyes, the high vocation and essence of a human being lie in playing, with full diligence, the role of the receiver of the self-disclosure of Being. It is that role which is in danger in the age of modern technology. Accordingly, we now turn to the danger, as Heidegger sees it, and to his proposal of that which may possibly save us from it.

Part III

The Danger in Modern Technology

The general rubric under which Heidegger presents his essay on technology is that of a questioning, an asking. Yet the sense of the questioning—and of the possible answering—is by no means unproblematic. What sort of questioning is taking place in this essay, and what kind of answer is being sought?

Asking about and asking for

The title of the essay is "Die Frage nach der Technik." We could say simply, "The question about technology," and it is in this straightforward sense that the published translation renders the title: "The question concerning technology." In this sense, the essay is an inquiry into technology; technology is the theme, which is to say that the aim is to discover something *about* technology. For Heidegger, of course, a philosophical inquiry always asks about the essence, and so what the essay seeks to determine about technology is its essence. The essay attempts to bring to light the essence of technology or, more particularly, the essence of modern technology. To answer the question is then precisely to bring this essence into the light; the question would be answered when we are able to see the essence in an adequate light.

Our commentary has now reached the point in "Die Frage nach der Technik" where the essay is—in this straightforward sense of questioning and answering—complete. Insofar as the question *concerns* technology, insofar as technology itself is the theme, the question has been answered. The essence of modern technology has been brought to light as composing, as an all-encompassing imposition.

On the other hand, the title of Heidegger's essay can also be taken in a different, more subtle sense. The title could be translated to mean not an "asking about" or a "questioning concerning" but instead an "asking for" technology, in the sense in which we ask for some person, ask to see or speak to someone. When a German businesswoman returns to the office from lunch, she might say, "*Hat jemand nach mir gefragt?*" That does not mean, "Has anyone been trying to discover things *about* me?" but rather, "Has anyone asked *for* me?", "Has anyone called wishing to speak to me?" The theme, the concern, that for which this asking would be undertaken, is not at all the person asked for but is instead some interest of the one who does the asking. Presumably the caller is not inquiring into the essence of the businesswoman, and the businesswoman herself will not be the focus of the conversation. Instead, the caller wishes to speak to the businesswoman about his own concerns. The focus of the ensuing interview will be the questioner, some personal affair of the inquirer. The questioner in this sense is actually a petitioner and not a mere theoretical inquirer. He asks the businesswoman to present herself because it is his relation to her, or to her business, that concerns him. He seeks out the businesswoman on account of some interest of his own. That is, he does not merely want to see and meet the businesswoman but precisely to discuss business.

If we take Heidegger's title in this sense of "asking for," then it does not at all mean "the question *concerning* technology." The question does not concern technology; it concerns the questioner, Dasein. To answer the question is then not simply to bring the essence of modern technology into the light but, rather, to resolve thereby some issue of pressing interest to Dasein. Taken in this respect, the essay is now by no means complete. We have merely brought the essence of modern technology into the light, we have let the essence of modern technology show itself, but we have not yet even voiced our concerns. We have not yet broached the question for which, according to Heidegger, we sought to know the essence of modern technology in the first place, namely the question of how we are to relate appropriately to that essence. This ulterior motive was indicated by Heidegger in the very first paragraph of the essay. What the question genuinely concerns is not technology but our freedom: "We are asking for technology—in order to prepare thereby a free relation to it. If the relation is going to be free, our Dasein must be open to the essence of technology. If we then respond appropriately to that essence, we will be able to experience technological things in their proper limits" (FT, 7/3).

After having determined the essence of modern technology and, presumably, opened our Dasein to that essence, Heidegger now returns to the ulterior motive: "We are asking for technology in order to focus light on our relation to its essence. The essence of modern technology shows itself in what we are calling com-posing. But this determination is by no means the answer we are seeking in asking for technology, insofar as to answer means to respond appropriately, i.e., in a way appropriate to the essence we have asked to see" (FT, 24/23).

In order to prepare this response, and to understand exactly what concern Dasein has in the essence of technology, Heidegger says we need to take "one more step" in our meditation, one more step in reflecting on what "com-posing itself as such is" (FT, 24/23). This further step has to do with the way modern technology is our *destiny*.

Sent destiny, history, chronology

In preparation for this further step, Heidegger repeats what he has stressed throughout, namely that technology is in its essence not a technological thing but the way things in general disclose themselves. From the human standpoint, technology is the way we, in response to the self-disclosure of things, look disclosively upon them. What is primarily responsible for technology as an understanding of what it means to be in general is the self-showing of the gods, the self-offering of Being. That is, our current disclosive looking upon things as disposables is encompassed by a more general imposition which disposes of us. Thus, as Heidegger says once more, the disclosure of things as disposables is not something that occurs in a realm somewhere beyond all human activity, yet "neither does it take place exclusively in man nor primarily through man" (FT, 24/24). That is to say, humans, in their disclosive looking, are the followers, and Being is the leader. It is this relation of leading and following that makes modern technology, or any technology, a destiny:

> The essence of modern technology leads humans onto the way of that disclosive looking whereby all realities, more or less perceptibly, become disposables. To lead onto a way—that is what our language calls "to send" [*schicken*]. And so we can name the all-encompassing sending, which leads man onto a way of disclosive looking, destiny [*das Geschick*]. It is in this regard that the essence of history [*die Geschichte*] must be determined. (FT, 25/24)

The words for "destiny" and "history" are related back etymologically in German to the word for "send." An etymological connection, of course, does not prove anything, and Heidegger does not ever base his philosophical claims on etymology. Yet the history of a term can be highly suggestive and often does "represent the sedimentation of general philosophical experience," to modify slightly Erwin Straus' justification of the appeal to word-origins.[1] Heidegger has recourse to etymology only for its suggestive or corroborative value. What Heidegger finds corroborated in the present instance is an understanding of history as a sending and of destiny as what is sent.

For Heidegger, destiny is an ontological affair. What we are destined to do, most fundamentally, is to look upon beings as a whole in a certain way. This—the way we understand what it means to be in general—is the foundation for any further vocation we may have. Our basic destiny is simply our ontology, our understanding of Being. Since ontological knowledge is, for Heidegger, technological knowledge, he can also say that our technology is our destiny. It is destined inasmuch as Being itself is in the lead. The ascendancy of the self-disclosure of Being over our own disclosive looking is precisely what, for Heidegger, makes our destiny, our ontological knowledge, something led onto a way or sent.

History does the sending. That is to say, history refers to the event of the self-disclosure of Being. That self-disclosure may change over time, by reason of the approaching or withdrawing of the gods. Those events are the genuinely autonomous, sending, destining ones and are therefore historical in the highest sense. (They also most properly deserve the name "events.") Thus we see that the etymological connection between the words for "send," "destiny," and "history" is grounded in the matters themselves: the technology that constitutes our destiny is led on its way by the history of Being.

What we ordinarily call history, namely the record of human affairs, is for Heidegger mere "chronology." Human activity is founded on the human understanding of what it means to be, an understanding that is sent and not autonomous; that makes chronology subordinate to history. Human affairs are only mediately historical: "History is not merely the object of chronology, not the mere record of human activity. It is only as something destined that human activity stands in relation to history" (FT, 25/24).

If, currently, the historical is identified with the merely human, then that too must be a matter of destiny. In fact, it is included in the sending of the current guise of Being as an all-encompassing imposition. For com-posing motivates or challenges us to make everything our ob-ject and to elevate our human subjectivity as the poser of ob-jects. The current guise of Being has destined us to represent beings precisely as that which is op-posed by us and to us, i.e., precisely as ob-jects. In our current mode of disclosive looking, things are no longer autonomous objects; they have become posed objects and even scientific ob-jects, since human posing activity reaches its zenith in science. All autonomy is now seen as lying on the side of the human subject. The point is that this attitude amounts precisely to an unawareness of history in Heidegger's sense. Chronology is for us today a record of autonomous events; we are heedless of any more remote events to which human actions would merely be the motivated responses. Therefore, it is on account of our objectifying attitude that we take history to be nothing but chronology. We have been destined to reduce things to ob-jects. As long as we are the subjects, the only subjects, then the chronological is equivalent to the historical. Thus the destiny to reduce things to objects also reduces history to chronology. That is the conclusion Heidegger now draws: "Only the destiny to take up an objectifying mode of representation has reduced the historical to the chronological, i.e., reduced it to an object of science, and thereby made possible the current equating of the historical with the chronological" (FT, 25/24).

Freedom

Recall that Heidegger has been attempting to take "one more step" in determining the essence of modern technology, in order to prepare our response to that essence and to see what concern Dasein has in the essence of technology in the first place. The step was to consist in an understanding of technology as a destiny. We have now taken that step, and we could accordingly say: com-posing, the current guise of Being, dispenses a destiny, and that destiny is modern technology. Com-posing sends us a certain way of looking disclosively upon things, sends us on the path of a certain technology, namely an impositional technology. The earlier guise of Being also dispensed a destiny, a technology, though a much different one, namely *poiesis*. That is what we learn by taking one more step in reflecting on what "com-posing itself as such is": "As challenging us into an impositional outlook on things, com-posing sends us on the path of a disclosive looking. Com-posing dispenses a destiny,[2] as does every mode of the self-disclosure [of Being]. Bringing-forth, *poiesis*, is also destined in the sense just delineated" (FT, 25/24–25). This simply means that *Being* dispenses to us our destiny. Heidegger says, "Com-posing dispenses a destiny," but we know that "com-posing" is Heidegger's name for Being in its current mode of self-disclosure. Com-posing, like every mode of the self-disclosure of Being, dispenses to us a certain manner of disclosive looking. That is precisely what Heidegger means by destiny. Modern technology is one such way of looking, and *poiesis*, i.e., ancient technology, is another. In each case, what is destined is our theoretical outlook, our ontology, which is to say: our technology.

We can then begin to see what concern Dasein has in the essence of technology; it is the concern anyone has in his or her destiny. For Heidegger, however, the concern is not simply the natural interest people have in their factual destiny. On the contrary, the concern is over destiny as such; the concern is over the sense in which Dasein is at all destined— i.e., determined—rather than free. The genuine concern is freedom. What is at stake in the essence of technology is not the factual destiny of Dasein, or the possible threat to human existence posed by high-tech things, but the essential dignity of Dasein as a free agent, as a determiner of destiny rather than a slave entirely under the control of destiny. Heidegger's essay asks for the essence of technology so as to raise the question concerning the freedom of Dasein. That is what the question genuinely concerns.

For Heidegger, Being never *imposes* itself, and the partnership between Being and Dasein is always a genuine partnership in which both parties make an active—i.e., free—contribution to the disclosure of the meaning of Being. Being leads, but a leader requires a follower. For Heidegger, the dignity of Dasein lies in its role as the *indispensable* follower of Being. That is to say, the dignity of Dasein is precisely to be the place *required* by Being for its own self-disclosure. For Heidegger, however, what is indispensable is not merely the disclosive powers of Dasein, its consciousness or intelligence, but, on the contrary, its *freedom*. The dignity of Dasein does not reside simply in its unique disclosive powers but in its free exercise of those powers.

Heidegger's essay now proceeds to these issues, i.e., to questions concerning human freedom. The first paragraph of the discussion of freedom is a typically rich and demanding one:

> The unconcealedness of beings always proceeds by way of a disclosive looking [on the part of man]. The destiny to look disclosively in a certain way—that always holds sway over man.[3] But this destiny is never a compulsory fate. For man is free precisely in the way that he belongs indispensably [*gehört*] to the working of destiny, namely by giving a hearing [*ein Hörender wird*] to destiny instead of merely being a slave [*Höriger*] to it. (FT, 25–26/25)

Let us read this passage with due care. The first sentence is a summary expression of the indispensability of humans for the self-disclosure of Being. The sentence asserts that the unconcealedness of beings necessarily occurs through the participation of Dasein. Being may offer itself as wholeheartedly as possible, yet no disclosedness will arise without a place prepared to receive that offering. There is no giving without an accepting, no leading without a following, no disclosedness without a disclosive looking.

Heidegger next proceeds to identify—or, rather, reidentify—what is destined in humans, namely, their disclosive looking, their understanding of the meaning of Being in general. Heidegger then says that this destiny holds sway over man. What is the sense of the holding sway here? It must be understood as a sending in a certain *direction*. The general direction of humanity's disclosive looking is determined by the events of history, by the initiatives of Being. Humans are *led* by Being onto the path of a certain general outlook with respect to beings. Being is in the lead, and destiny holds sway over humans in the precise sense in which Being leads. But Being does not lead by forcing itself on us, which is to say that Being is *primarily*—yet not entirely—determinative of human disclosive looking. Humans are followers but still retain the freedom specific to followers. To lead is not to compel, and that is why Heidegger immediately remarks that destiny is not a compulsory fate. Destiny is not imposed by way of coercion; nor is it merely offered in a neutral sense, as one among many alternatives. Being offers itself with a strong motive force. Yet to motivate is never to compel, and destiny, while indeed primarily out of human hands, is not completely so. Humans retain a certain restricted freedom in the face of destiny, a certain freedom within a given general directedness, a certain freedom over their own destiny. To twist Hamlet's words, we could say that, for Heidegger, there is a divinity that rough-hews our ends, but their final shape is a matter of our freedom.

In the last sentence of the passage under consideration, Heidegger characterizes that freedom in terms of hearing. His point is that humans do not hear destiny in the manner of a slave hearing a command. What a slave hears is indeed a command; i.e., the slave is precisely the one who has no choice but to listen to the master and obey. For Heidegger, humans do *not* hear destiny in this way. Being does not hold sway over humans so thoroughly as to issue commands and thereby inflict itself. According to Heidegger's precise formulation, humans do not purely and simply *hear* destiny but instead "give a hearing" to it. Humans "entertain" destiny, grant it an audience, give it a "fair hearing." A slave does not *grant an audience* to the master; a slave is forced to listen. A slave hears in an entirely passive, receptive way. But that is not how humans hear Being. For humans to hear Being, humans must actively open themselves to Being. Humans must go out and meet Being partway, must make an effort to listen to Being, must engage themselves with all their disclosive powers in the search for the meaning of Being. That is to say, Being does not *inflict* itself upon humans but only elicits their free assent. Being, unlike the master of a slave, does request a hearing and does not force humans to listen. In terms we employed earlier, Being is a nurturing cause, an eliciting cause, and not an efficient, impositional cause. Consequently, if Being is heard at all, it will be, in part, on account of mankind's freely granting it an audience. For Heidegger, Being cannot disclose itself unless humans *assent* to look disclosively; Being cannot lead unless humans *agree* to be followers. This required assent is, for Heidegger, the *original domain of human freedom*; all other free choices depend on this original one, since they depend on an understanding of what it means to be in general—i.e., we cannot choose in favor of something unless we have some sense of its existence and, prior to that, some sense of existence in general. The crucial point is that a sense of existence cannot be forced upon humans and will arise only if it is freely accepted. That acceptance is the original exercise of freedom.

Dasein is thus indeed required for the self-disclosure of Being, but "required" must be taken here in a specific way. What is required is a place of disclosedness that freely assents to be the place, that freely takes on its role as place. What is indispensable to the working of destiny is not merely humans, or the human disclosive faculties, but human freedom. The required participation in the disclosedness of Being would raise humans above all other beings and would be a source of human dignity. Yet, for Heidegger, it is not simply that humans are required, that some hearer be on hand to receive the address of Being. A slave is required by a master, but there is little or no dignity in being a slave. For Heidegger, humans are not the slave of Being. Mankind has a higher dignity, which resides in the fact that humans are *free* partners of Being, genuine contributors to the self-disclosure of Being, and not mere passive receivers, simply there to be imposed on by Being. What is required for Being to lead is indeed that humans be followers, but to be a follower of Being means to be an authentic follower, an active receiver, one that freely assents to the request for a hearing on the part of Being. In Heidegger's eyes, it is the notion of free assent or authentic following that expresses the dignity and high vocation of humans.

In what, then, does human freedom consist? As I understand Heidegger, the most basic exercise of freedom is nothing other than the acceptance of the self-offering of Being. That would be the meaning of Heidegger's claim that "man is free precisely in the way he belongs indispensably to the working of destiny." The first of all freedoms is the decision to look disclosively upon beings, for that begins the work of destiny. The first and most basic choice is to open one's eyes and ears to beings, to enter into partnership with Being, to become a place where an understanding of Being arises. The first of all freedoms is the choice to "be there" for Being, which is not simply to occupy a certain place in space but to deliberately make one's disclosive powers available for the self-offering of what it means to be. In terms Heidegger uses elsewhere, the first free choice is the choice to be a being-in-the-world.

The most significant part of this last expression is the little word "in." That word must be taken not in the physical sense, such as a chip is in a computer, but in an intentional sense, i.e., in the sense of "into," such as a person might be into sports or into photography or into Shakespeare. To be a being-in-the-world means to be *into* the world, engaged in it, interested in it, enthused about it; it means to pursue the world with all—or at least some—of one's might.

The essential point is that one can only *freely* exercise one's might. Enthusiasm or interest cannot be compelled. Being, or the world, may entice us, may elicit our interest, but that simply amounts to an appeal upon our freedom. To be "into" the world, to pursue any being, is a matter of free choice.

Yet what sort of choice is this, the choice to be "into" the world? It is certainly not what we usually mean by free choice. It is not a deliberate choice, explicitly made after weighing alternatives and deliberating over consequences. It is not a willful choice in the usual sense. That is why Heidegger now says: "The essence of freedom does not originally pertain to the will and certainly does not pertain merely to the causality of human willing" (FT, 26/25).

The free choice at issue, the one that assents to receive the self-disclosure of Being, the choice to grant Being a hearing, is the choice a human being makes to become Dasein—or not to become Dasein.[4] The choice is not an exercise of the will in the ordinary sense of a deliberate taking up of a position. It is an implicit choice, made at the level of feeling rather than will. It is made first in childhood and then implicitly reaffirmed (or, possibly, revoked) each day. Most basically, it is the choice to be involved in the world of beings at all, *rather than* encapsulate oneself in one's own ego. Not all human beings make this choice, not all humans are Dasein, not all are beings-into-the-world, not all go out of themselves and open themselves to Being. It is a matter of free choice. There are those humans who withdraw from the world into their own shell or who never display the least interest in the world from birth. We call them mad, but madness, as a peculiarly *human* possibility, shows that there are all degrees of human engagement in the disclosure of Being—from the extreme of the madman (the null point) to the other extreme of the philosopher (who makes the meaning of Being her explicit concern). In between are the everyday modes of understanding what it means to be. These are all normal, ordinary, average; they are content with an everyday, implicit grasp of Being.

For Heidegger, the terms "human being" and "Dasein" are not equivalent. It is true that only humans can be Dasein. Indeed, Heidegger stresses that in each case Dasein is some human being's own, Dasein is in each case owned by some human being. That is Heidegger's concept of "ownness" (*Jemeinigkeit*). But Heidegger never says that every human being is Dasein, that a human being is in each case Dasein. The concepts are not convertible, and Dasein is the more restricted term, for it is restricted to those humans who freely choose to be Dasein. Indeed, these are almost all people, almost all people have some understanding of what it means to be, but there remains the possibility of extreme forms of human existence, such as severe madness, that are lived in total oblivion of the world of beings. I take such madness to be partially a freely chosen mode of existence, and the opposite choice, the decision to be a being-into-the-world, is also a free choice. And thus it is along those lines that I would understand Heidegger's claim that freedom is an ontological affair: "It is to the occurrence of disclosedness, i.e., to the occurrence of truth, that freedom stands in the closest and most intimate kinship" (FT, 26/25).

What Heidegger is saying here is that freedom is required for the occurrence of truth, i.e., for the self-disclosure of Being. Freedom has to do primarily with ontology; there would be no destiny, no ontology, no disclosive looking upon beings, no technology, without the exercise of human freedom. Since disclosive looking makes Dasein be Dasein, we can say that there would be no Dasein unless that mode of existence were freely chosen. The primordial free choice is to look disclosively, to open oneself to Being, to show an interest in beings, to get "into" the world, to be Dasein—or not. Here, in the essay on technology, Heidegger speaks of this free choice in terms of a disclosive looking within an open space. The primordial exercise of freedom is to step into a clearing, a lighted glade, and look disclosively upon what is lit up there:

> Freedom is carried out in an open space, understood as a lighted glade, i.e., in disclosedness. . . . All disclosing overcomes a closing and a concealing. Yet that which opens the open space—the mystery—is concealed and is always concealing itself. All disclosive looking comes out of an open space, goes into an open space, and brings us into an open space. The freedom to enter the open space neither consists in the unbounded arbitrariness of free will nor is it simply bound to occur by law. The openness of the open space conceals while lighting up; i.e., in the lighted glade there flutters the veil that hides the essence of all truth, and yet in the glade the veil itself appears as so hiding. The openness of the open space is the domain of destiny, and destiny in each case brings a disclosive looking on a particular way. (FT, 26/25)

A favorite image of Heidegger's later thought is that of a clearing (*Lichtung*), a glade open to the sunlight in an otherwise dense forest. The idea is that we humans can look disclosively only upon that which stands in light. A thing has to stand in a cleared, lighted space in order to be available to us. For Heidegger, that which provides the light, the open area, is Being. The self-offering of Being is the glade within which we can see beings, or, to put it less metaphorically, the understanding of what it means to be is the general notion in terms of which we can grasp any particular being. Any particular being can be grasped only if Being in general is already disclosed to us. This disclosure of the meaning of Being in general is the clearing. For Heidegger, Being may well offer itself, may form a cleared, open space for beings to be visible, may shed light on beings, and yet no disclosedness will arise unless humans make the effort to step into the glade, open their eyes to the light, pay heed to what stands in the light. To step into the glade, to accept the self-offering of Being, is, for Heidegger, the primordial exercise of human freedom. This exercise of freedom makes a human a disclosive being, i.e., it makes a human Dasein. That is how freedom stands in the most intimate kinship with the occurrence of disclosedness.

Armed with this basic meaning of the passage just quoted, we can, with some difficulty, make sense of it all. Otherwise, the entire paragraph becomes the densest of fogs. In particular, a very close reading is required to recognize that Heidegger here uses the word *Freiheit* ("freedom") in two senses. On the one hand, it refers to human freedom. On the other hand, Heidegger characterizes the lighted glade as *das Freie*, the "open space," and he then speaks of *die Freiheit des Freien*. That means "the openness of the open space" and refers not to human freedom but to the self-offering of Being. Of course, the two senses of *Freiheit* are related; indeed for Heidegger human freedom stands in the "closest and most intimate kinship" with the disclosedness of Being. Yet the two senses must also be kept distinct, or else the passage will be hopelessly confused.

Heidegger says here that "that which opens the open space—the mystery—is concealed and is always concealing itself." For Heidegger, Being is that which opens the open space or lights up the lighted glade. And Being is *the* mystery. What is most mysterious about it is precisely that it opens and conceals at the same time. Just as light is that by which we see, but which almost always recedes in favor of the things seen in the light, so Being offers itself only to withdraw in favor of that which it makes graspable, namely, beings. Being is closest to us, but its manner of self-offering motivates us to bypass it in favor of what is next closest, beings. For the most part we overlook Being, overlook the open space, in favor of the beings which stand in that space. The understanding of the meaning of Being in general must come first—it is the condition of the possibility of grasping any being—but we ordinarily leave the meaning of Being implicit and attend instead to what comes second, namely, individual beings. That is how Being conceals while lighting. It opens up an open space, and it does so by disclosing itself. At the same time, Being mostly veils itself in favor of that which it lights up and thereby allows us to grasp, namely, beings.

Heidegger's reference to the veil, in the passage under consideration, is now intelligible. Heidegger says that in the lighted glade there flutters a veil. The words "flutter" and "veil" are well chosen; they both imply a play of concealing and revealing. In the glade, "the essence of all truth" is veiled over. The essence of truth is the self-unconcealment of Being, and that is veiled over in the sense that Being does not ever present itself fully and openly. Being steps behind a veil, or recedes, in favor of beings. Being offers itself in a way that motivates us to overlook Being itself. On the other hand, in the glade "the veil itself appears" as hiding Being. In other words, Being veils itself in such a manner that we see the veil for what it is, *viz.*, precisely as fluttering over Being. To see a veil as fluttering over something is to get a glimpse of that which it covers. A veil—as in a veil-dance—is a means of flirtation; a veil is meant to conceal, yet in such a way as to reveal that something is indeed there to be concealed. What Heidegger is saying is that it is in this flirtatious, revealing/concealing way that Being offers itself to us. Being does show itself, we are afforded some understanding of it, but it presents itself only through a veil, i.e., in an enticing glimpse.

According to Heidegger, our free choice is precisely enticed. We are enticed to step into the open space and look disclosively. We are invited by Being to enter into a disclosive partnership with it. Our choice to do so is free, but this choice is not a matter of the "unbounded arbitrariness of free will." Nor, on the other hand, is it "bound to occur by law." It is neither entirely free nor entirely compelled. That is to say, it is enticed or motivated. The original exercise of our freedom is a response to an invitation; it is an acceptance (or refusal) of the self-offering of Being. We are motivated to be disclosive beings, we are enticed into the domain of destiny, into the domain of disclosedness. Still, to motivate is not to compel. Destiny, in Heidegger's words, is not a compulsory fate. This indeed means that our destiny does not rule us in the manner of a strict determinism. On a more fundamental level, however, it means that we are not even compelled to have a destiny; destiny itself is not compulsory. To have a destiny, to possess an understanding of the meaning of Being, to step into an open glade, to be Dasein—these are all synonyms, and they occur, if and when they do occur, by our free choice, by our free assent to the self-offering of Being.

Heidegger concludes the passage under consideration by joining its beginning and end; i.e., he joins together human freedom, the openness of the open space, destiny, and disclosedness. The passage began by asserting that human freedom is carried out in an open space, and at the end Heidegger says that the openness of the open space is "the domain of destiny, and destiny in each case brings a disclosive looking on a particular way."

What Heidegger is expressing here should now be apparent in its simplicity. Human freedom is carried out, or exercised primordially, in the choice to step into the open space, the one lit up by the self-disclosure of Being. The primordial free choice is the assent to be a disclosive partner of Being, to look disclosively at that which is lit up in the open space. This open space is the domain of destiny, since our destiny amounts fundamentally to our understanding of what it means to be in general. To step into the open space is to accept a certain destiny, a certain self-disclosure of Being. In other words, destiny, *in each case* (in each case that it does occur, in each case that it is freely chosen, in each case that a human being steps into the open space), puts the destined one on the path of certain disclosive looking upon things. That is how, for Heidegger, freedom, the open space, destiny, and disclosedness belong together. The self-offering of Being is the opening of the open space; the primordial free choice is to accept (or decline) the invitation to step into the open space and look disclosively; and to accept the invitation is to become Dasein, to become a being-into-the-world, to become a place where the meaning of Being in general is understood, or, in short, it is to assume a destiny.

Hastening

Thus we return to the concept of destiny and to Heidegger's view that humans, although destined, are not thereby deprived of freedom. Quite to the contrary, destiny even *requires* human freedom. Destiny, as an ontological affair, as a matter of the understanding of the meaning of Being, requires a free exercise of disclosive looking on the part of humans. That is the first, and more original, sense of Heidegger's statement that destiny is not a compulsory fate. It means that humans are not compelled to have a destiny; in other words, humans are not compelled to be Dasein, to step into the open glade, to look disclosively, to see things, to be "into" the world. Destiny, the complicity of mankind in the self-disclosure of Being, must be freely chosen.

For Heidegger, of course, human freedom does not exhaust itself in the choice to accept the self-offering of Being. That is the first of all freedoms, but it is *only* the first. By freely choosing to enter into a disclosive partnership with Being, we assume a destiny, we become destined. But destiny is not a compulsory fate, now understood in a second sense. Destiny brings us on the path of a certain general understanding of the essence of things; i.e., destiny holds sway in general. In our current age, com-posing holds sway, such that we are strongly enticed to look upon things as disposables. The self-disclosure of Being is primarily responsible for the current look of things, and we could not, on our own, radically alter that look. Our freedom is limited, since Being plays the leading role in the partnership that constitutes disclosedness. For Heidegger, however, this is a genuine partnership, and we are not compelled to follow passively. We are free partners, and we do have an influence over the way things in general show themselves. For Heidegger, we cannot wrest a new mode of disclosedness out of Being, but we can exercise a more subtle influence. We cannot impose but we can nurture. For Heidegger, to express it in a preliminary way, what we are free to do is to *hasten*—i.e., to hasten (or impede) the advent of a new epoch in Being's own self-disclosedness.

Doom

The remainder of Heidegger's essay on technology is devoted to working out this second sense in which destiny is not a compulsory fate, i.e., the sense in which we are free in relation to modern technology once we have freely stepped within the lighted glade and accepted the self-revelation of Being as com-posing. To consent to follow Being, to assume a destiny, is not to surrender oneself to a henceforth inevitable course. We retain a certain freedom—Heidegger wishes to have that established at the start. Thus he now repeats his view that it is our destiny to pursue modern technology, i.e., to look disclosively upon things in a certain way, but he stresses that destiny is not doom: "The essence of modern technology rests on com-posing. Com-posing pertains to the destiny to look disclosively in a certain way. These sentences express something different from the frequently blared prattle that technology is the doom of our age, where 'doom' implies the inevitableness of an unalterable course" (FT, 26/25).

Or again, Heidegger distinguishes destiny from "constraint." Our destiny is to look disclosively in a certain way, the way of modern technology, but this destiny "by no means constrains us, in the manner of a debilitating compulsion, to pursue technology headlong or, what comes down to the same, to rebel impotently against it and curse it as the work of the devil" (FT, 26/25–26).

Thus, for Heidegger, we are not compelled to surrender outright to modern technology. Yet neither is confrontational opposition to it the proper exercise of human freedom. Indeed, to be totally against technology "comes down to the same" as totally capitulating to it. How so? Perhaps we could say that to rebel against technology is in fact a kind of capitulation to it, a way of surrendering one's freedom to it, since to rebel is still to be entirely dominated by that which one is rebelling against. Heidegger says elsewhere that "Everything 'anti' thinks in the spirit of that against which it is 'anti'" (P, 77/52–53). To be "anti" technology is not to take up a freely chosen position toward it; it is to let technology itself dictate the terms of engagement. It is still to be ruled by technology, still to think in the spirit of technology, still to look upon things as disposables, except now the disposables are given a negative value. Capitulation and rebellion are the positive and negative sides of the same coin, of the same basic outlook on things. The one turns toward disposables and the other turns away, but they both need to look upon things as disposables in order to get their bearings. Thus both capitulation and rebellion are headlong (*blindlings* = blind to everything else), impulsive, unreflective: the one unreflectively obeys, the other impulsively resists. For Heidegger, both of these are slavish attitudes; they are heteronomous, they take their law from outside. The genuinely free relation to modern technology must be more authentic; i.e., it must involve an autonomous, self-chosen attitude toward it.

What then is the properly free relation to technology? Presumably, it will lie somewhere between capitulation and rebellion. In order to understand what it might be *in concreto*, we first need to see how modern technology poses a threat to our freedom.

The danger

Heidegger now launches an extended discussion of the danger inherent in modern technology. It needs to be underlined that for Heidegger the threat is not simply to human existence. The prime danger is not that high-tech devices might get out of hand and wreck havoc on their creators by way of a radioactive spill or an all-encompassing nuclear holocaust. The danger is not that by disposing of so many disposables we will defile the planet and make it uninhabitable. For Heidegger the danger—the prime danger—does not lie in technological things but in the essence of technology. Technological things are indeed dangerous; the rampant exploitation of natural resources is deplorable; the contamination of the environment is tragic. We need to conserve and to keep high-tech things from disposing of *us*. Yet, for Heidegger, conservation, by itself, is not the answer. Conservation alone is not radical enough. Conservation is aimed at things, technological things and natural things, but it does not touch the outlook or basic attitude that is the essence of modern technology, and it is there that the danger lies. It may well be that conservation will succeed and that technology will solve its own problems by producing things that are safe and nonpolluting; nevertheless, the prime danger, which lies deeper down, will remain. For the danger is not primarily to the existence of humans but to their essence: "The threat to man does not come in the first instance from the potentially lethal effects of the machines and devices of technology. The genuine threat has already affected humans—in their essence" (FT, 29/28).

In a sense, the threat inherent in modern technology has *already* been made good. Though we have thus far averted a nuclear disaster, that does not mean the genuine threat has been obviated. Humans still exist; they are not yet on the endangered species list. It would of course be tragic if humans made that list. Yet, for Heidegger, there could be something more tragic, namely for humans to go on living but to lose their human dignity, which stems from their essence. Here lies the prime danger, the one posed not by technological things but by the disclosive looking that constitutes the essence of modern technology. The prime danger is that humans could become (and in fact are already becoming) *enslaved* to this way of disclosive looking. Thus what is primarily in danger is human freedom; if humans went on living but allowed themselves to be turned into slaves—that would be the genuine tragedy.

The danger in modern technology is that humans may fail to see themselves as free followers, fail to see the challenges directed at their freedom by the current guise of Being, and fail to see the genuine possibilities open to them to work out their destiny. Then, not seeing their freedom, humans will not protect it. They will let it slip away and will become *mere* followers, passively imposed on by modern technology, i.e., slaves to it, mere cogs in the machine.

For Heidegger, there is an essential connection between seeing and freedom. The way out of slavery begins with seeing, insight. But it is the right thing that must be seen, namely, one's own condition. The danger is that humans may perfect their powers of scientific seeing and yet be blind to that wherein their dignity and freedom lie, namely the entire domain of disclosedness and their role in it. Humans would then pose as "masters of the earth," and yet their self-blindness would make them slaves.

The highest danger

Let the foregoing serve us as a guideline in working through Heidegger's account of the danger. In general, the danger has to do with disclosedness and disclosive looking. What is threatened is the proper disclosive looking on the part of humans, the proper human response to the self-offering of Being. There is always the danger that humans may inauthentically play their role as partners of Being. That is to say, human disclosive looking as such is threatened—in each and every epoch of the history of Being: "The destiny to look disclosively is as such, in every one of its modes, and therefore necessarily, *danger*. In whatever mode the destiny to look disclosively may hold sway, the respective disclosedness in which beings show themselves harbors the danger that humans may misconstrue what is disclosed and misinterpret it" (FT, 27/26).

Even in the first epoch of history, when Being presented itself more wholeheartedly to the Greeks, there was danger, for there was still required a free human response to the self-disclosure of Being. The Greeks could have misconstrued (*ver-gesehen*, "mis-seen") what was offered to them. The Greeks were not compelled to look disclosively in the appropriate way. They were not compelled to be authentic followers, to receive the self-offering of Being with the proper exercise of their disclosive powers. For Heidegger, humans are always free in their role as partners of Being, free to recognize and accept their subsidiary role, as did the Greeks, and also free to harden their hearts and pose as masters, the way humans do today. There is always danger, always an appeal to human freedom, even though it was doubtless easier for the ancients to respond appropriately, on account of the more wholehearted self-offering of Being to them. When Being is reticent, the danger is heightened, and thus the passage just quoted continues: "Yet when destiny holds sway in the mode of com-posing, it is the highest danger"(FT, 27/26).

According to Heidegger, the current, heightened danger attests to itself in two respects. The first concerns the relation of humans to things and to themselves:

> [1.] As soon as man has to do with unconcealed beings no longer as self-standing objects, but exclusively as disposables, and man in the midst of objectlessness is nothing but the imposer on disposables, then he comes to the extreme verge of the precipice; that is, he comes to the point where he will take himself merely as one of the disposables. Meanwhile, man, precisely as the one so threatened, struts about, posing as master of the earth. In this way the illusion spreads that everything man encounters exists only insofar as it is his construct. This illusion gives birth to one final delusion: it seems as though man everywhere and always encounters only himself. Heisenberg has with complete correctness pointed out that reality must present itself to contemporary man this way. *In truth, however, precisely nowhere does man today any longer encounter himself, i.e., his essence.* Man stands so decisively in attendance on the challenging of com-posing that he does not perceive com-posing as a claim, fails to see himself as the one claimed therein, and hence also fails in every way to understand the extent to which he ek-sists, by his very essence, in the realm of a claim addressed toward him, so that he *can never* encounter only himself. (FT, 27–28/26–27)

I will take up this passage by proceeding back from the end. Why, according to Heidegger, can humans never encounter only themselves? Furthermore, how could such a delusion arise at all—that humans everywhere and always encounter only themselves? Why is it even a forceful one today, such that Heisenberg could keep insisting on it in his lecture not as a delusion but as the truth? For Heidegger, it is a delusion, but one that possesses a certain necessity: it will arise in the present epoch as long as humans do not genuinely encounter themselves. That is to say, if, in our technological era, humans are heedless of their essence, they will misconstrue themselves as the authors of the disposables round about them. Technology itself will be taken in an anthropological sense, as a human product, and technological things will appear to be entirely of human doing, entirely a human construct. Even natural things will seem to be human constructs, since, according to Heisenberg's principle of indeterminacy, we have no access to a supposedly independent nature. Nature is now abstract, reduced to scientific formulas of our own devising. What, if anything, the formulas apply to is unknown. Thus all things, the so-called natural ones and the man-made ones, are our own handiwork; they are mirrors in which we see ourselves, see our own creative activity. That is how we would necessarily encounter only ourselves, wherever we look. If we take ourselves to be the masters of all things, then no matter what we encounter, we will find no autonomous things, no self-standing objects, but only ourselves, only our own creations, only the results of our own mastery. All things will become ob-jects, and in them we will find only our own posing activity.

For Heidegger, of course, we are not the masters, and so things are not our constructs. Indeed, he differs from Heisenberg *toto caelo*: even high-tech, disposable things, let alone the things of nature, are not our constructs. High-tech things are not our creations, not mirrors in which we behold ourselves. In these things we never encounter only ourselves. Since Being is the master, com-posing is the genuine author of the disposables. In encountering them we should encounter Being, not ourselves. We *should* do so, except for the fact that we are oblivious to the realm of disclosedness and to our subservient role therein.

According to Heidegger, the human imposition upon things is a response—a response to a more encompassing imposition that stems from beyond mankind. Humans, in their impositional activity, are claimed by Being in its current guise. That means humans, in looking upon things as disposables—and subsequently turning them into actual disposables—are only following the lead of the self-disclosure of Being. In Heidegger's words just quoted, man "ek-sists, by his very essence, in the realm of a claim addressed toward him." The essence of humans consists in their standing out from themselves (*ex-stare*) by standing in relation to something that comes toward them, i.e., something that originates beyond them. The essence of humans is to be on the receiving end of a claim or address. The essence of humans is to be followers of the lead of Being. Insofar as humans are blind to this essence, they will see themselves as the leaders, the claimants, the masters, and then they will seem to encounter only themselves. But that will be a delusion.

victim of delusion

Thus the first danger is that humans will fall (or have already fallen) victim to this delusion, namely that of being the master of all things. In other words, humans are here victimized by the delusory experience of absolute freedom, complete mastery, the ability to impose their will everywhere. For Heidegger, this attitude is a delusion, because, in attempting to be master, humans are actually altogether "in attendance on the challenging of com-posing." That is, to impose on things is really to comply passively with the demands placed on humans by Being in its current guise. To impose on disposables, to pursue technology headlong, is actually to surrender one's freedom to the all-encompassing imposition. It is to be a slave to the all-encompassing imposition.

This first delusion, that of mastery over things, also poses a danger for the relation of humans to themselves. As Heidegger says at the beginning of the passage presently under consideration, in our impositional attitude things are no longer self-standing objects. They become posed ob-jects. As posed, ob-jects have no autonomy; they are entirely determined from the outside, by the one who poses them. Now, if humans view all things as determined, then humans stand on the brink of an understanding of themselves in the same terms. Humans will be tempted to apply their science to themselves and thereby reduce themselves to the formulas they apply to things. Like determined things, humans will become the outcome of exterior forces. Then, e.g., humans will understand themselves as computers, complex ones, perhaps, but with their output still entirely determined by their input. This input will take the form of various outside forces, such as social, biological, and psychological ones. Humans will become the ob-jects of their own sciences of sociology, biology, and psychology. Humans will see themselves as included among other disposables, as posed by exterior forces over which they have absolutely no control. Consequently, humans will view themselves not as masters but as slaves, not free but determined, mere cogs in the great machine of forces around them.

This latter view, too, is a delusion. It is no less delusory to think of oneself as entirely lacking in freedom than it is to consider oneself absolutely free. For Heidegger, these two delusions, the one concerning the human relation to things (humans as the masters of all things) and the one concerning the relationship of humans to themselves (humans as disposable things), are founded on a misunderstanding of, or obliviousness to, a more basic relation, namely the relation of humans to Being. What is most concealed in the age of modern technology is the relation between the self-disclosure of Being and human disclosive looking. That concealment is the second respect in which the danger of our current destiny is attested:

concealment of relation b/w self-disclosure of Being & human looking

[2.] But com-posing does not simply endanger man in his relationship to things and to himself. As a destiny, it relegates man to the kind of disclosive looking which is an imposition, and where that holds sway, it dispossesses every other possibility of disclosive looking. Above all, com-posing conceals that disclosive looking which, in the sense of *poiesis*, *lets* things come forth into visibility. Compared to that, the imposition which challenges thrusts man into a rigidly oppositional relation to things. When com-posing holds sway, the controlling and dominating of disposables thoroughly imbue all disclosive looking and do not even let that which they characterize appear, namely, this disclosive looking as a disclosive looking.

Thus the challenging com-posing not only conceals a former way of disclosive looking (bringing-forth) but also conceals disclosive looking itself and, as going along with it, That whereby disclosedness, i.e., truth, occurs. (FT, 28/27)

The "That" whereby disclosedness occurs is Being; i.e., truth or disclosedness occurs primarily on account of the self-offering of Being. And disclosive looking is the human response to the self-disclosure of Being. Thus Heidegger is saying here that modern technology conceals the way these two—human disclosive looking and the disclosedness of Being—go along together. In other words, what is concealed today is the partnership between Being and humans with regard to the understanding of what it means to be in general. The outlook characteristic of modern technology obscures the disclosive partnership between humans and Being; most importantly, it is mistaken about the roles of leader and follower in that partnership. For Heidegger, the disclosive partnership is the domain of the essence of humans, and the human role in disclosedness is the locus of human dignity and freedom. Therein lies the danger, for if humans do not see their essence, if they are mistaken about their freedom, then neither will they see how to fulfill their essence and how to exercise their freedom. Humans will not even see how modern technology threatens their freedom. Their oblivion will place humans in danger of relinquishing their freedom and becoming blind slaves.

These are the issues at the heart of Heidegger's concept of danger. In order to work through them, let us first ask *how* the essence of modern technology conceals human disclosive looking and conceals the relation between that looking and the self-disclosedness of Being. Heidegger says that the impositional outlook "dispossesses" all other possible ways of disclosive looking. In particular, imposition dispossesses *poiesis*, or, as Heidegger will also say, it deposes (*verstellt*) *poiesis*. The essential idea here—upon which will hinge Heidegger's forthcoming redetermination of the very sense of essence—is that the two kinds of disclosive looking do not exist concurrently, with one merely enjoying an ascendancy over the other. Imposition dispossesses or deposes *poiesis* not only by dethroning it but by going further and exiling it. That is to say, when imposition holds sway, *poiesis* no longer even presents itself as a possibility. Imposition commandeers the entire field of disclosive looking and runs *poiesis* off that field. Thus imposition dispossesses *poiesis* in the literal sense of leaving it with no possessions, no rights. For instance, today final causes have been dispossessed in this sense, and so has the notion that matter might be pregnant with a form.

The general difference between the two ways of disclosive looking is, of course, that imposition sees things as there to be dominated, whereas *poiesis* sees things themselves as dominant, i.e., as demanding to be respected and abetted. The poietic way of technology is pious; it is midwifery, actively *letting* things come forth. The impositional way is the imperious one of control and dominance.

For Heidegger, the controlling and dominating attitude of modern technology dispossesses *poiesis* and *thereby* dispossesses the entire notion of a disclosive partnership between Being and humans. Imposition so thoroughly commandeers the field of disclosive looking that the phenomenon of disclosive looking is itself covered over: "When com-posing holds sway, the controlling and dominating of disposables thoroughly imbue all disclosive looking and do not even let that which they characterize appear, namely, this disclosive looking as a disclosive looking." That is to say, modern technology is so intent on controlling and dominating things that it sees only how to make and manipulate disposables but does not see *itself*—from an outside, more encompassing perspective.

Modern technology is understood today as a practical matter and as a purely human accomplishment. It is a way of doing or making things, and it is entirely of human creation. That is the instrumental and anthropological view of technology Heidegger spoke of at the beginning of the essay. This view is anthropological—or, better, anthropocentric—in the sense that it looks upon technology entirely from the human perspective, and, indeed, for Heidegger, today all other perspectives are dispossessed. The anthropological or humanistic view considers humans the authors of technology, the subjects of technology (in the sense of the ones solely responsible for technology). That is to say, on this view humans are autonomous, the ones in control, the dominators, the posers, and things are entirely passive, merely there to be imposed on.

For Heidegger, this dominating, impositional attitude does not allow itself to be seen "as a disclosive looking." Modern technology may very well appear in its impositional character but does not show itself as a disclosive looking. What does that mean? Or again, what does Heidegger mean when he says that the essence of modern technology conceals "disclosive looking itself," i.e., disclosive looking as such, the entire phenomenon of disclosive looking? What is disclosive looking? And what is the significance of the concealment of disclosive looking in our technological age?

Heidegger introduced the concept of disclosive looking in his discussion of ancient technology; it is the correlate of *aletheia*.[5] This latter names the self-disclosure of Being, the self-offering of Being, and disclosive looking is the human appropriation of that offer. For Heidegger, technology is this disclosive looking and is thus primarily theoretical, a matter of seeing or understanding, and is only secondarily practical. Nevertheless, the concealment of the basically theoretical character of modern technology would, by itself, be of little significance. The significance derives from the way in which, for Heidegger, the theory or onlooking is carried out, namely, as an active receptivity. Disclosive looking is an active exercise of disclosive powers, and yet it remains a response, a receiving. What is disclosed in the disclosive looking, *viz.*, the meaning of Being, is determined primarily not by our disclosive powers but by the self-offering of the gods, of Being itself. Disclosive looking is an acceptance of the overture stemming from Being, a consent to the offer of a disclosive partnership originating from Being. It is a way of looking back at Being, once Being has first looked at us.

The crucial point in the present context is that humans, in looking disclosively, are *not* autonomous. Disclosive looking is a following, not a leading. Disclosive looking is an *active* receptivity and is indeed active and creative. But it is not dominating or in control; it is primarily receptive, primarily under the control of Being. Now, what the impositional attitude conceals is precisely the receptivity, the following, on the part of humans and the activity or initiative on the part of Being. That concealment *is* significant. This, then, is what Heidegger means by the concealment of disclosive looking in the age of modern technology: the concealment is a failure to see humans as the followers and Being as the leader. It is a failure to see the superficiality of the anthropocentric view. It is, most fundamentally, an obliviousness to Being, a blindness to the peculiar way in which Being is in the lead, namely by leading and yet also leaving free.

The concealment of Being, the absconding of the gods, is, for Heidegger, equivalent to a concealment of truth. That accounts for the many instances in which Heidegger identifies the danger of modern technology with its covering over of the truth. For example: "Com-posing deposes the shining-forth and holding sway of truth. The destiny that sends into imposition is consequently the extreme danger" (FT, 29/28).

This says that the essence of modern technology does not allow the truth to manifest itself. And that means it does not allow the disclosive partnership to show itself. It does not allow Being to show itself as the leader, and it conceals the proper human role of (free) following. Or again, Heidegger says: "Com-posing challenges us into the frenzy of imposition, which deposes every view into the event of disclosedness and so endangers the very foundation of our relation to the essence of truth" (FT, 34/33).

This passage and the previous one express essentially the same idea: the impositional attitude does not allow us to see disclosedness—i.e., the self-disclosedness of Being. It does not allow us to see Being as ascendant. Thereby our human role, our proper way of responding to this offer of a disclosive partnership, our proper way of relating to the truth, is endangered.

To consider a third passage on the same theme, Heidegger says: "The holding sway of com-posing threatens man with the possibility that it could be denied him to participate in a more original disclosedness, which means to experience himself as addressed—by truth in the primal sense" (FT, 29/28).

The truth, for Heidegger, is the self-disclosedness of Being. If the truth is concealed, then humans will not experience themselves as addressed, as claimed by Being. Instead, humans will consider themselves the claimants, the posers. And that is precisely what makes the concealment of disclosive looking, the covering over of truth, the concealment of Being in its leading role, dangerous. Let us attempt to see exactly how this is so.

If we are unaware that Being is in the lead, if we consider ourselves the claimants, then we will mistake our human freedom. That mistake is what is dangerous. For the most part, our impositional attitude will motivate us to exaggerate our freedom. If all things are at our disposal, if they are entirely posed by us, then we will see ourselves as completely in control. This hubristic view, as we have already indicated, is threatened by a nemesis. If all things become disposables, we will stand on the verge of a precipice: we will be tempted (and have perhaps already yielded to the temptation) to take *ourselves* as disposables, entirely posed by forces *out* of our control. Thus if we do not see the disclosive partnership between Being and humans, if we do not see Being as in the lead and the peculiar way Being is in the lead, we will mistake human freedom either by excess or defect. The positive exaggeration of human freedom is oblivious to Being, blind to Being in its role as leader. The deterministic view, on the other hand, does recognize humans as followers of a sort but is oblivious to the freedom proper to a follower. The one view is blind to disclosedness (the self-offering of Being) and so is blind to the limits of human freedom. The other is blind to disclosive looking (the free, human response) and so is blind to the very possibility of human freedom. In either case, these views are blind to the relation between disclosedness and disclosive looking, blind to the disclosive partnership between Being and humans. Consequently, they are blind to the peculiarly limited human freedom.

The two views under consideration are exaggerations, opposite exaggerations. Yet they are merely complementary expressions of the same basic outlook, namely, a rigid, all-or-nothing attitude. They both, in their own way, exemplify the oppositional, confrontational attitude of modern technology. They are both blind to *poiesis*, unaware of a genuine alternative to impositional causality. If we are dispossessed of *poiesis*, then we will see only two alternatives as regards human freedom: all or nothing. Then we will understand mankind as dominating or dominated, imposing on things or imposed on by things, the master or the mastered—with no middle course.

This uncompromising attitude, which is motivated by the impositional outlook of modern technology, will, for Heidegger, recoil back on technology. That is to say, the impositional outlook will be applied to the very impositional outlook of modern technology. In other words, when imposition holds sway, humans will take up a rigidly antithetical relation to modern technology itself. At first, the impositional character of modern technology will appear to serve our domination of things; accordingly, technology will be appraised as wholly good and will be pursued headlong. Eventually, we are likely to see ourselves as one of the things dominated by modern technology. In that case, modern technology will be understood as entirely negative and will be opposed headlong. For Heidegger, neither of these attitudes of total pursuit or total opposition is a properly free one; both are slavish: "We ever remain slavishly chained to technology, whether we passionately affirm or deny it" (FT, 7/4).

The key word here is "passionately." For Heidegger, passion is intrinsic to our current attitude toward technology; we cannot avoid being passionate about it. To be passionate means to be headlong, blind to compromise or alternatives. According to Heidegger, the holding sway of imposition dispossesses the alternative to an all-or-nothing attitude, namely, *poiesis*. Consequently, our attitude toward modern technology, as long as imposition holds sway, as long as we are in the age of modern technology, is bound to be passionate. Both of the currently possible attitudes—affirmation and denial—will be uncompromising. Both will be passionate, and that will also make them slavish.

If we are passionate about technology, then technology itself will dictate the terms of our engagement with it—hence the enslavement. Whether we are passionately pro- or passionately anti-technology, we will be too tightly bound to it to take up an autonomous, freely chosen stance. We will constantly take direction from technology; which is to say that technology will constantly dictate to us or impose on us, whether we pur-

sue it or oppose it. Freedom, for Heidegger, will involve distancing ourselves from technology, detaching ourselves from it, not by opposing it
(which is not a detachment) but precisely by extricating ourselves from a
passionate, uncompromising, antithetical attitude toward it. That is to say,
if we are to be free, we will need to find (or, rather, we will need to be
given or be shown the way to) a nontechnological or nonimpositional attitude toward the very attitude of imposition. We will need to take up a
poietic stance toward modern technology, which means that we will need
to be undispossessed of *poiesis*.

In Heidegger's eyes, the alternative to passionate affirmation and
denial does most explicitly not consist in viewing technology as neutral.
That too is a slavish, indeed most slavish, attitude: "We are delivered
over to technology in an even worse way when we consider it something
neutral" (FT, 7/4).

To consider technology neutral is to view it as neither good nor bad
in itself; what is good or bad is the use we make of it. As neutral, technology is a mere means to our good or bad (or perhaps neutral) ends. In
any case, to see technology as neutral is to take it as a means, an instrument, lying there for us to wield; it is something open to our domination.
Accordingly, the view of technology as neutral is not the genuine alternative to the impositional attitude; to consider it neutral is still to think in
terms of mastery: "Everything will depend on our wielding technology, as
a means, in the appropriate way. We will, as we say, acquire rational control over technology. We will master it" (FT, 8/5). "As long as we represent technology as an instrument, we remain caught up in the will to
master it" (FT, 33/32).

Thus, for Heidegger, whether we think of modern technology as
good, bad, or neutral, we remain within the technological outlook of imposition. We still think of exercising our freedom through mastery and
domination. Consequently, the view of technology as neutral is not dis-
passionate. It is still passionate; it is blind to any other than the impositional attitude; it is not *poiesis*. There is here an *apparent* distance from
technology, an apparent freedom in relation to technology—namely, the
freedom to overpower it—but there remains the same underlying view
that imposition/domination/overpowering is the only way to accomplish
something, the only way to be free. And it is this underlying view that
Heidegger finds enslaving. The idea of technology as neutral does not distance itself from that impositional outlook; it is still entirely caught up in
it. In other words, to conceive of technology as neutral is just another enslavement to the technological outlook. It is an enslavement precisely to
that (*viz.*, technology) which it purports to be free to overpower. By
equating freedom with the capacity to overpower, this view is ipso facto
enslaved to the technological attitude, which is precisely the attitude of

mastery and overpowering. Consequently, the view of technology as neutral does not free us from technology but, on the contrary, delivers us up to it and even does so "in the worst way." It is more enslaving than the view of technology as wholly good or bad, because "this conception of technology as neutral, to which we especially like to pay homage today, constitutes utter blindness to the essence of technology" (FT, 7/4).

I suggest that we like to pay homage to this conception exactly on account of its apparent freedom from passion. Only fanatics go to the extremes of considering technology a panacea or a curse. To avoid these extremes and take a position directly in the center seems rational and open-minded. For Heidegger, however, that view is not open but, on the contrary, essentially closed. It closes off or conceals, more thoroughly than ever, the essence of technology. That is to say, it hides from us the phenomenon of disclosive looking, which means that it hides Being in its ascendancy over us. As perfectly neutral, modern technology has no power of its own; it does not lead, it does not even tend in any particular direction. It is a sheer instrument, an inert tool, something to be ordered about, a slave. To consider technology neutral is to think emphatically in terms of a master-slave dichotomy; technology is our slave.

This view of technology as neutral is thus the most hubristic. It makes us not only the leaders but the masters. It is most mistaken about the roles of leader and follower. Accordingly, it is, for Heidegger, "utterly blind" to the essence of technology, i.e., blind to our subsidiary role in carrying out technology. As blind, however, this conception also delivers us up to technology "in the worst way," since the technological attitude is precisely the hubristic one of imposition and mastery. The view of technology as neutral, as something to be ordered about, is the furthest removed from the attitude of *poiesis*; that is why it is the worst. It utterly fails to see where our genuine freedom lies: namely, not in opposition but in authentic following, exercising an influence within a general stance of obedience.

The occultation of poiesis

For Heidegger, modern technology *as such* conceals *poiesis*. Or, to express it more properly, modern technology could arise only in an age which has been dispossessed of *poiesis*, an age in which *poiesis* has been withheld. That is to say, modern technology is a *response* to the self-concealment of *poiesis*. If *poiesis* is *thoroughly* concealed, then that response will take the form of the completely opposite attitude: imposition. The essence of modern technology is the outlook that sees imposition as the only relation between beings. The only way to be free is to confront, dominate, master, and the only way to be subservient is to *be* dominated and mastered. When com-posing holds sway, it commandeers the entire field of vision, and no alternative is visible. Here, for Heidegger, is the danger. What is endangered is human freedom, since the impositional attitude exaggerates that freedom either by excess or defect; it makes freedom all or nothing. And both these views of human freedom—as absolute or as nil—are bound to bring disillusionment. They do not express the properly human way of being in the world, and it is ultimately unsatisfying to try to live according to an ideal of perfect freedom (or perfect slavery). The antidote, for Heidegger, the way to true human fulfillment and maturity, is to see a genuine alternative to imposition. We need to see authentic freedom as a matter *neither* of domination *nor* of being dominated. We need to see our genuine freedom as *poiesis*, as free and yet subservient, as in service to something greater and yet not under domination. Our ideal needs to be *poiesis*. But how, in the age of modern technology, when imposition holds sway exclusively, can we see *poiesis* at all? How can we see Being as in the lead, how can we see the phenomenon of disclosive looking? How can we see the properly human attitude of authentic following? What might save us from imposition? These are the questions Heidegger is about to broach in asking about "that which might save."

Let us first conclude our discussion of the danger as such by repeating, as Heidegger does, that it is not technological things that are dangerous (and so the danger is not to our mere existence), but, on the contrary, what is dangerous is the essence of technology, the exclusively impositional way of disclosive looking: "What is dangerous is not technology. Technology is not demonic; but its essence is indeed occult. The essence of technology, as a destiny to disclosive looking, is *the* danger. . . . Thus where com-posing reigns, there is danger in the highest sense" (FT, 29/28).

The essence is occult in the sense that is has been hidden, eclipsed from our view. To speak in astronomical terms, as Heidegger is about to do, there has been an occultation of the essence of technology, an occultation of Being in its way of leading, an occultation of *poiesis*, and that is what is dangerous. In a certain sense, the antidote Heidegger will suggest is to wait, *actively* wait, for the occultation to pass. Active waiting is *poiesis*; that might save us.

That which might save

Immediately upon concluding his discussion of the danger—by asserting that where com-posing holds sway, there is danger in the highest sense—Heidegger invokes a pair of lines from a work of poetry:

"But where danger is, there also grows
That which might save." (FT, 29/28)

Heidegger appeals to this poetry only for the sake of a clue. If the poem is true, which remains to be seen, then com-posing itself would harbor, perhaps deeply hidden, the means for us to be saved from composing. Com-posing itself would allow us to glimpse the genuine alternative to imposition, namely, *poiesis*. If the poem is true, then modern technology could reveal to us the essence of technology as such, namely a disclosive looking in response to the self-disclosure of the meaning of Being in general. Modern technology could show us the disclosive partnership between Being and humans not as a matter of imposition but as an instance of *poiesis*, where Being is in the lead and we humans play the indispensable role of free, authentic followers of that lead. Furthermore, if we could see in this role our genuine freedom (and not exaggerate human freedom either by excess or defect), it would then be possible for us to live in accord with our essence, in accord with our genuine human dignity. All this is what the poem suggests; it is but a clue that Heidegger will follow up.

He begins by asking what the poem means by "saving":

> Let us reflect carefully on these lines from Hölderlin. What does it mean to "save"? Usually we think that it merely means to seize hold of something threatened by ruin in order to preserve it— in the continuation of its former state. But "to save" says more. "To save" something is to bring it home, i.e., home into *its* essence, and to do so by bringing that essence for the first time into its proper appearance. (FT, 29/28)

This means, as applied to us humans, that to be saved is not equivalent to being preserved in our former state, preserved in our ongoing existence. We are not saved if we merely avoid nuclear accidents and continue living. On the contrary, to be saved is to be brought into our genuine state, into our home, into our essence. We will be saved when we can live in accordance with our essence, in accordance with our human dignity. But for that to happen we would need to see our essence; the essence would have to be brought to a proper appearance. For Heidegger, of course, our essence resides in the role we play in the disclosure of the meaning of Being; our essence is to be the place where Being discloses itself. Thus, we could be saved only through an illumination of disclosedness, through an appearance of the disclosive partnership between Being and humans, or, in short, through a shining forth of truth: "If the essence of technology, com-posing, is the extreme danger, and if, at the same time, Hölderlin is here uttering something true, then the holding sway of com-posing cannot exhaust itself solely in deposing every illumination of disclosedness, every shining forth of truth" (FT, 29/28).

On the contrary, com-posing must also, in some way, illuminate disclosedness, illuminate the disclosive partnership between Being and humans and the respective roles of humans and Being in that partnership. In other words, com-posing must in some way show itself adequately, for what it is, *viz.*, an eliciting of a certain disclosive looking: "Precisely the essence of technology must harbor in itself the growth of that which might save. But in that case, would not an adequate look into what com-posing is, namely, a destiny to disclosive looking, make appear that which might save in the place where it comes into view?" (FT, 29/28).

That which might save comes into view exactly in the disclosure of the essence of technology as a disclosive looking, as an active receptivity of the self-offering of Being. If com-posing can illuminate disclosive looking, then modern technology would not simply and solely depose the truth, depose *poiesis*. The essence of modern technology would also be a place where, as the poem says, there grows that which might save.

Having determined the sense of "saving," Heidegger now asks what the poem means by "growing": "In what way does there also grow, precisely where the danger is, that which might save? Where something grows, there it takes root, and thence it develops. Both of these happen in concealment, silently, and in their own time. The words of the poet do not mean that where the danger is we can expect to grasp immediately, and without preparation, that which might save" (FT, 30/28–29).

Heidegger is here issuing a warning against taking "growth" in a facile sense—i.e., in a sense that would make it facile for us to grasp that which might save. To grow does not here mean to bloom, to burst forth in the open. Heidegger is not referring to the growth that is visible above the ground at all; he means the taking root that occurs deep down. In other words, that which might save is still growing under the surface; its growth is its rooting of itself. It is developing but has not yet sprung up all the way to the surface. Consequently, we shall have to look deep to find that which might save. We shall have to look all the way down to that which is most hidden, most below the surface, namely the essence. Indeed, we shall even have to look at what is deepest within the essence, the essence of the essence. In other words, for Heidegger, we will discover in the essence of modern technology that which might save, but only if we strike all the way down to the essence of that essence, i.e., only if we root out the sense in which the essence of technology is an essence at all:

> We must now first consider in what way that which might save does
> even most deeply take root and start to develop where the extreme

danger lies—in the holding sway of com-posing. In order to consider this it is necessary, as a last step upon our way, to look with still clearer eyes into the danger. Accordingly, we must once more ask technology to show itself. For, according to what has been said, it is in the *essence* of technology that that which might save takes root and develops.

But how shall we behold, in the essence of technology, that which might save, as long as we do not consider in what sense of "essence" com-posing properly is the essence of technology? (FT, 30/29)

Heidegger's strategy will now be to argue that the essence of technology is not an essence in the usual sense. Thinking about technology thus requires us to redetermine the sense of essence. Accordingly, where the danger is, there does grow that which might save, for this redetermined sense of essence is one that illuminates the truth. That is to say, this new sense of essence reveals disclosedness, the disclosive partnership between Being and humans, and allows us to understand the role proper to each of the partners. Thereby, we may behold genuine human freedom and not exaggerate it either by excess or defect. With our sights properly fixed, we may possibly "sojourn in the highest dignity of our essence," as Heidegger will claim. The new sense of essence thus leads to a genuine alternative to the impositional attitude; it does so by reacquainting us with *poiesis*. That is how com-posing, the essence of modern technology, may, if thought through deeply enough, save us from com-posing.

The sense of essence

Its essence is that which makes something be whatever it is. Ordinarily, we think of the essence as a *one* which many things have in common; the many human beings have the one essence, "humanity," in common, and the many trees have the one essence, "treeness," in common. The essence of a tree is what makes anything be a tree, that which anything must have if it is to be a tree, that which is imparted to all trees in common. The essence of a tree is then the universal concept or the genus, and the many particulars are the various species (e.g., sequoias) or single cases (e.g., the General Sherman). These particulars are said to "fall under" the genus:

> Thus far we have understood "essence" in its ordinary meaning. In the language of academic philosophy, "essence" means *what* something is; in Latin, *quid*. *Quidditas*, whatness, provides the answer when we ask for the essence. To take an example, what is

imparted to all species of trees—oaks, beeches, birches, firs—is the same treeness. Under this common genus—the "universal"—fall all actual and possible trees. (FT, 30/29)

Such an essence, as a genus common to many, is called, in scholarly parlance, "discursive." We ourselves fashion this essence by "running around" (= *dis-cursively*). That is to say, in order to grasp what many things have in common, we must first go about and see the individual things. We must gather experience of them, and then we can abstract out from the individuals that respect in which they are alike. With a discursive essence (essence in the ordinary sense, genus), the many individuals come first; we must be acquainted with the individuals first, for it is *from* them that we abstract out their commonality, their essence.

Furthermore, the individuals that fall under a common genus are all related in the same way to the essence; they are all precisely *instances* of the essence. The fat and the skinny are different types of humans, and Socrates and Plato are different individual cases of humanity, but all of these are human in the exact same way, precisely in the sense of being particular instances of the essence.

With regard to the usual sense of essence, then, two conditions hold: the individuals precede the essence in our experience, and the individuals are instances of the essence. Is com-posing an essence in this ordinary sense? Is com-posing related to technological things as a common genus? Do we "run around" looking at technological things in order to conceive their essence by abstraction? Obviously not. Neither of the usual conditions holds. For Heidegger, the essence of technology, as a disclosive looking, *precedes* technological things. We do not run around looking at technological things in order to conceive the essence of technology. On the contrary, the essence of technology is the outlook that *subsequently* sends us running about making composites and disposable things. By the same token, technological things are not instances of the essence, they are not individual com-posings, individual ways of disclosive looking. The things of technology are related to the essence of technology in various ways and none of these ways is that of instantiation:

> Is then the essence of [modern] technology, com-posing, the common genus for all [modern] technological things? If this were so, then, e.g., the steam turbine, the radio transmitter, and the cyclotron would each be a com-posing. But the word "com-posing" does not here mean a "composite," i.e., a gadget or contrivance. Still less does it mean the general concept of such disposables. The machines and contrivances are not species or instances of com-posing, any more than are the man at the switchboard and the engineer in the drafting

room. All of these, in their own respective way, are indeed caught up
in com-posing—as something imposed on, as the resultant disposable, or as what does the imposing. But com-posing is never the
essence of technology in the sense of a genus. Com-posing is a way of
disclosive looking. . . . (FT, 30/29)

Rather than "fall under" com-posing, technological things are
"caught up in" composing, i.e., engulfed by it, commandeered by it,
pressed into its service in various capacities. Thus the individual beings do
not fall under the essence of technology as instances, nor are they all related to the essence in the same way. The individual beings that are
"caught up" in technology (and, for Heidegger, these are all beings extant
today) are related to it in sundry ways: the human engineer is the one
who carries out imposition, the natural raw material is what is imposed
on, and composite plexiglass is the end-product of the imposition, the resultant disposable. Humans, nature, and high-tech things are all technological beings, all encompassed by the all-encompassing imposition. But
these beings are related to com-posing in different capacities, and com-
posing is not their genus. Accordingly, com-posing is not a discursive
essence, not a common genus, not an essence in the usual sense.

Since com-posing is that to which all technological beings are related,
in various ways, is com-posing then an essence in the sense of a πρὸς ἕν
(*pros hen*) equivocal? For Aristotle, Being is not a genus but is instead related
to individual beings in a *pros hen* way. The essence of beings is Being, in the
specific sense that what makes a being a being is its relation "to one," to
Being, to the highest instance of being, to what most properly is. Likewise,
all healthy things are what they are, precisely as healthy, on account of their
relation, different in each case, to the one most proper instance of health,
namely the health of the organism. For Heidegger, com-posing is indeed that
to which all technological beings are related, but com-posing is not the highest instance of a technological thing. Com-posing is not a technological thing
at all, com-posing is nothing technological. Therefore com-posing is not the
essence of technological beings in the sense of a *pros hen* essence.

For Heidegger, com-posing is a disclosive looking, an impositional
one. Com-posing is the looking upon things as potentially disposable, a
looking that motivates the subsequent actual imposition upon things and
the turning of them into actual disposables. Com-posing is related to
technological beings in a motivational—or, rather, a *strongly* motivational, commandeering—way. All beings are "caught up" in com-posing,
engulfed by it. As a first formulation, we could say that com-posing is an
essence in a novel, commandeering sense.

Yet we recall that *poiesis*, the essence of ancient technology, is also
a way of disclosive looking. We are acquainted with two kinds of disclosive looking, two general outlooks on things, two kinds of technologies.

If we then consider technology as such, abstracting from both its modern and ancient species, can we not understand disclosive looking itself as the essence of technology, the common genus of both ancient and modern technologies? In other words, does not the concept of disclosive looking show itself as the essence of all technology, the essence of technology as such? Moreover, it would be an essence precisely in the usual sense of a discursive concept, a universal, a common genus. *Poiesis* and com-posing would fall under it as its instances.

For Heidegger, it is true that disclosive looking is the essence of technology in general, while *poiesis* and com-posing, bringing-forth and challenging, are its kinds. But Heidegger's contention—one that is absolutely crucial to understand if we are to grasp at all his redetermination of the sense of essence—is that disclosive looking is not a discursive concept; the two kinds do not fall under it: "Com-posing is a way of disclosive looking that is destined; it is, specifically, the way of disclosing looking that challenges. The disclosive looking that brings forth (*poiesis*) is another destined way of disclosive looking. But these ways are not kinds that fall under a concept of disclosive looking—i.e., fall under it side by side, concurrently" (FT, 30–31/29).

All Heidegger is saying here is that disclosive looking is not a concept the two ways would "fall under." Com-posing and *poiesis* are not *instances* of disclosive looking. Disclosive looking is not their essence in the usual sense of a common genus, a universal, a discursive concept. *Why* do the modern com-posing and the ancient *poiesis* not fall under a concept of disclosive looking? According to Heidegger:

> On the contrary, the disclosedness [of Being] is that destiny which, abruptly, and inexplicably to all thinking, dispenses itself now in the disclosive looking that brings forth and now in the disclosive looking that challenges. It is in these respective ways that disclosedness allots itself to man. The disclosive looking that challenges has its destined [i.e., historical] origin in the bringing-forth type of disclosive looking. But, at the same time, com-posing is destined to depose *poiesis*. (FT, 31/29–30)

This says that the two ways of disclosive looking, the two ways of technology, are not concurrent; on the contrary, the one is subsequent to the other. Being reveals itself now in one guise and now in another, motivating two different ways of disclosive looking and two different technologies. The original way was the bringing-forth type of looking; that way is the origin of the challenging, impositional type. But the challenging type then deposes the earlier one, dispossesses it; i.e., it not only dethrones the earlier type but also exiles it, sends it into seclusion. That is how the two types do not exist concurrently, arrayed side by side. And that is also why, for Heidegger, disclosive looking is not an essence in the sense of a common genus. The instances of a genus do not exclude one another. Oaks and birches may exist side by side. But com-posing and *poiesis* do not exist simultaneously. They are mutually exclusive, for Being does not show itself to mankind in two different manners, whole-heartedly and reticently, at the same time.

Then in what sense of essence is com-posing the essence of modern technology? It is not an essence in the usual sense of a common genus, nor is it an essence as a *pros hen* equivocal. Nor is disclosive looking it-self, of which com-posing is one of the types, an essence in any usual sense. And that is precisely because com-posing is not a type or species in the usual sense. The species of a genus do not exclude or dispossess the other species, but com-posing does depose *poiesis*. Com-posing is thus an anomaly in the realm of essences. It does not fit into our usual thinking about essences. And so com-posing calls on us to rethink the meaning of essence: "Thus com-posing, as a destiny to a disclosive looking, is indeed currently the essence of technology, but it is definitely not an essence in the sense of genus, *essentia*. If we pay heed to this, something wondrous strikes us: it is [modern] technology that calls on us to think in another sense what is usually understood by 'essence' [*Wesen*]. But in what sense?" (FT, 31/30).

We see here how Hölderlin's words are coming true. Modern tech-nology is the extreme danger, but in it there also grows that which might save, provided "to grow" means to be rooted deep within. If we peer deeply enough into the essence of modern technology, into com-posing, we become motivated to rethink the notion of essence. We will, presum-ably, then come to a more genuine understanding of the essence and of the relation between the essence of technology and technological beings, ourselves included. We may then see how technology makes demands on us but also requires our free complicity; and so we may understand our-selves as followers but not slaves. And that would amount to grasping (with the possibility of safeguarding) our genuine human dignity, which is exactly what we are in danger of losing. In other words, by redeter-mining the sense of essence we may find holding sway a different relation between things, not one of imposition but of *poiesis*. And so, in the midst of the danger, within com-posing, within the impositional outlook, *poiesis* might also grow.

Enduring

Heidegger begins his redetermination of the sense of essence the way he customarily begins an inquiry, namely by letting language lead the way. He appeals to two words in which the term for "essence" (*das Wesen*) occurs, although the words do not mean essence in any straight-forward sense. The words are *das Hauswesen* and *das Staatswesen*. Literally, the words say "house-essence" and "state-essence." But *das Hauswesen* does not mean the "essence of a house"; it means "domestic affairs" or "household management." Likewise, *das Staatswesen* does not mean the general essence of a state but, instead, "public affairs," "administration of a state," "political system." Thus, according to Heidegger, already in these words, although we use the term for "essence," *Wesen*, "we are not referring to a universal or genus; instead, we mean the ways in which a household or a state holds sway, how they are run, how they unfold, how they run their course to the end. In short, we mean the ways in which they abide [*wie sie wesen*]" (FT, 31/30).

Thus Heidegger is appealing to the verb *wesen* to clarify the noun *das Wesen*. And to understand the verb, which I have just translated, by way of anticipation, as "abide," Heidegger invokes, as is even more customary with him, poetry. He appeals to the early nineteenth century German poet, J. P. Hebel, who uses the "old word," *die Weserei*, to name the town hall.

Die Weserei is a most obscure word; presumably, we are to understand it in analogy with other German terms ending in *-erei*. That suffix signifies the constant carrying on of some activity (*die Schreiberei*, endless paperwork; *die Schwarzseherei*, pessimism, always looking on the dark side), or it may refer to the place especially devoted to carrying on some activity. *Die Druckerei* is a print shop, a place where printing (*drucken*) is carried on. By analogy, then, *die Weserei* is the place where *wesen* goes on. But, if so, why should *die Weserei* be the name of the town hall? According to Heidegger: "*Die Weserei* signifies the town hall inasmuch as there the life of the community is concentrated and village existence is constantly in play, i.e., abides [*west*]" (FT, 31/30).

What is most important for Heidegger here is the idea of constancy. Compared to any other place, the town hall is the one where the life of the village is most continually carried on. Town life is there most ongoing, most nearly always in play. The town hall is the place where the town most abides as a living town, as an establishment for communal life. What goes on at the town hall is an abiding of the town. *Die Weserei* then means "the *abiding* place," the place for the activity of abiding, *wesen*.

According to Heidegger, this verb, *wesen*, is the source of the noun, *Wesen*, and the verb, he now says explicitly, is equivalent to another, common word that means "to endure": "It is from the verb *wesen* that the noun [*das Wesen* = essence] is derived. In its verbal sense, *wesen* is equivalent to *währen* [to endure, perdure, persist], not only in terms of meaning, but also in terms of the phonetic structure of the word" (FT, 31/30).

Therefore the noun means that which does the abiding, that which endures. And so, by taking a clue from language, we find that the essence is "the enduring." Heidegger now seeks to confirm this clue, and he has no difficulty finding confirmation in the history of philosophy:

> Socrates and Plato already think of the essence of something as the abiding, in the sense of the enduring. Indeed, they think of what endures as what endures perpetually (ἀεὶ ὄν) [aei on, "eternal being"]. And they find what endures perpetually in what persists, what perseveres throughout all that may happen to a thing. That which persists they then discern in the outward look (εἶδος, ἰδέα) [eidos, idea]: for example, in the Idea "house."
>
> The Idea "house" exhibits what everything of that type is. In contrast, particular houses, actual or possible ones, are merely various changing and transitory instantiations of the "Idea" and thus belong to the non-enduring. (FT, 31–32/30)

For Plato, what is common to all things of a certain type is their physiognomy or basic look, which in Greek is termed *eidos* or *idea*. These words are derived from the verb "to see." The Idea is what is most properly seen, most properly visible. Which is not to say that the Idea is visible in the ordinary sense, visible to the physical eyes. On the contrary, the Idea is like the light that allows us to use our eyes. The Idea gives visibility to the particular things which exemplify that Idea. We grasp individual things in light of the Idea. The Ideas must be seen first; that is how they are "most properly" visible. Accordingly, the Ideas are not discursive concepts; for Plato, we do not run around looking at individual houses and then abstract out the essence "house." We need to have an Idea of what a house looks like first; it is a condition of our running round and recognizing particular things as houses. If we were not guided by an Idea, our running around would be aimless. In other words, we cannot gather together or make a collection of individual houses and *then* determine what they have in common. Unless we already knew what they had in common, unless we already knew their basic look, how could we collect them?

If they are not discursive concepts, then in what sense are the Ideas essences? To grasp that, we need a deeper understanding of the difference between Ideas and individual things. We need to understand the basis of the difference. For Plato, the fundamental difference is that the Ideas are changeless, whereas things change. The Ideas ever remain the same; they are radically self-same. Individual houses are changing and transitory; but the Idea "house" ever remains the same with itself. Even if all extant houses should perish, even if there never was a single house, the Idea "house" would remain what it is. As Heidegger puts it, "the Idea perseveres throughout all that might happen to a thing." The changes occurring in the things have no effect on the Ideas.

Thus Ideas and things exist in radically different domains, the domain of nonchange and the one of change. Consequently, Ideas and things stand in radically different relations to time. Changing things are in time; unchanging Ideas are outside of time. Everything in the domain of change—i.e., everything subject to change, whether actually changing or momentarily at rest—is temporal. Change (or rest) takes up a certain amount of time. But time does not pass in the domain of the Ideas, since they are radically self-same, changeless in principle. The Ideas are timeless, untouched by time, which we express by calling them immortal or eternal. In other words, they endure perpetually.

Heidegger does agree that it is distinctive of an essence to endure or abide, in a way that is not permitted to individual things. Yet he questions whether the Platonic Idea captures the genuine sense of enduring and the genuine sense of essence: "Every essence is something enduring. But is enduring only perpetual enduring? Does the essence of technology endure in the sense of the perpetual enduring of an Idea, one that would float above all technological things, thus making it seem that 'technology' is the name of a mythic abstractum?" (FT, 32/30–31).

The Heideggerian answer to these obviously rhetorical questions is "No." The essence of technology is not an essence in the sense of an Idea. Heidegger does not expressly formulate a critique of the Ideas, and, in fact, he himself will soon invoke the Platonic Idea of beauty. Here, however, he speaks in pejorative terms of the Idea as "floating above" things and as a "mythic abstractum." Presumably, Heidegger is referring to the usual understanding of an Idea as a reified universal, i.e., as an abstract concept, an "airy nothing," given a "local habitation and a name." In other words, the Idea would be *a* being, existing in some vague way and in some vague place, haunting things like a specter. For Heidegger, the essence of technology is not a being and does not float above technological beings in some vague way. The essence of technology relates to technological things in a very definite way, and that way is nothing like the relation of a specter to haunted things. Therefore the essence of technology is not a Platonic Idea as commonly understood.

For the moment, Heidegger retains from Plato the notion of the essence as something especially enduring, but he himself will determine the sense of the enduring—by considering the way the essence of technology actually does hold sway over technological things: "The way in which technology abides can be gathered only from that perduring by which com-posing actually holds sway as a destined way of disclosive looking" (FT, 32/31).

Bestowal

In order to determine the manner in which the essence of technology endures, or, more generally, the sense in which any essence is something enduring, Heidegger again appeals to a poet for a clue: "Goethe in one place . . . uses the mysterious word *fortgewähren* [to bestow perpetually] in place of *fortwähren* [to endure perpetually]. He hears *währen* [to endure] and *gewähren* [to bestow] here in one unarticulated accord" (FT, 32/31).

That is the clue, a possible affiliation between enduring and bestowal. The confirmation of the clue derives from reflection on the matters at issue themselves: "And if we now ponder, more thoughtfully than we did before, what it is that properly endures, and perhaps alone endures, we may venture to say: *only what is bestowed endures, and what endures primally, from the earliest, is that which does the bestowing*" (FT, 32/31).

Here we have Heidegger's redetermination of the sense of essence. The essence is to be understood in terms of the phenomenon of bestowal, i.e., in terms of the interplay between bestowing and bestowed. Moreover, for Heidegger, an appreciation of the phenomenon of bestowal is precisely what might save. The phenomenon of bestowal is what has been withheld from us for so long. It is the genuine alternative to imposition; it is a poietic phenomenon. If we recall that we have been led to the notion of bestowal by reflecting on the essence of modern technology, then we can see how the extreme danger harbors, deep within, that which might save. Hölderlin's verse will thereby prove true: that which might save, bestowal, does grow where the danger, imposition, is. All this, of course, needs clarification, and to that end let us begin with the beginning, with the very notion of bestowal and its place within technology.

The German word is *Gewähren*. It means a kind of giving, in the sense of allowing, affording, indulging; it is a kind of letting, letting someone have something desirable. A translation that very nearly captures the nuance Heidegger intends would be "vouchsafe." To vouchsafe is to grant something to someone as a favor, to give by way of grace, to give graciously. The crucial nuance is that of leniency or gentleness. Heidegger is referring to a kind of gentle giving, a furnishing of something already desired, and not a forcing upon. Another possible translation would be "tender," in the sense of proffering, i.e., presenting or holding out something for someone's acceptance. *Gewähren* is the opposite of imposition. That is why Heidegger says, "Challenging is anything but a *Gewähren*." To challenge is to force upon, to place a demand upon; that is anything but a gentle proffering. Heidegger has in mind here a giving of something that comes to the receiver as a boon, which, moreover, the receiver remains free to accept or reject. To give as a boon is to bestow or endow. The words "endure" and "endow" correspond very closely to the German pair *währen* and *gewähren*. The term "bestow" is not related phonetically to "endure"; nevertheless, I find "bestow" slightly superior to "endow" in expressing the crucial nuance of lenient giving, and so I propose it as the translation of *gewähren*.

Now, what does bestowing have to do with modern technology? At first sight, nothing: "As the essence of technology, com-posing is something that endures. Does com-posing hold sway at all in the sense of something that bestows? The very question seems blatantly mistaken. For according to everything we have said, com-posing is a destiny that encompasses us into the disclosive looking which challenges. Challenging is anything but a bestowing" (FT, 32/31).

Encompassing, too, is anything but a bestowing. Com-posing, the all-encompassing imposition, imposes on us an impositional outlook upon things in general. The essence of technology seems to be pervaded by imposition, the opposite of bestowal. Yet if we recall that technology comes to us as a destiny, which is something sent, then even if we are sent into an impositional attitude, the sending itself remains a bestowing, an offering of a certain self-disclosure of Being. This offering comes to us with strong motivational force but still requires our ratification. Therefore it is only at first glance that the essence of modern technology seems not to be a bestowing:

> So it does seem, as long as we do not attend to the fact that even the challenging into an imposition upon beings as disposables always remains a sending and, accordingly, leads man upon a path of disclosive looking. As this destiny, the essence of technology lets man into Something which, on his own, man can neither invent nor in any way make. For there is no such thing as a man who would be a man if left on his own. (FT, 32–33/31)

"Man" is to be understood here in the sense of Dasein. No human could, on his or her own, become Dasein, for Dasein is the place of ontological knowledge, the place of a disclosure of the meaning of Being. Therefore Dasein requires Being; no human being would be Dasein if left alone, if not addressed by Being. As Heidegger now puts it, in order to be Dasein a human must be "let into Something," i.e., given access to Being.

What role does technology play in the making of Dasein? Technology is precisely that which does the letting, the letting into the "Something," Being. Technology, as a general understanding of things and their possibilities, is the access to Being, the access a human needs to be Dasein. There would be no Dasein without technology. There is no such thing as a nontechnological Dasein. Hence it could be said that technology makes a human being Dasein. That is the boon technology confers. Technology endows upon humans that which they could never, on their own, "invent or in any way make," namely, the meaning of Being. That is precisely what a human needs to be properly human, in the sense of Dasein.

Technology is an intermediary between Being and humans. Technology possesses, as it were, two faces, one directed toward Being and one toward humanity. In relation to Being, technology is something bestowed; in relation to humans, something that bestows. Technology is a bestowed bestowing. Thus technology is pervaded by bestowal: "Every destiny to a disclosive looking occurs out of a bestowing and as a bestowing" (FT, 33/32).

Technology is the destiny to disclosive looking. Technology occurs "out of a bestowing," in the sense that it is a gift from Being, bestowed by Being. Being is what primarily bestows; i.e., Being is what bestows "from the earliest" and so is "what endures primally." Technology occurs "as a bestowing," in the sense that it in turn endows us with a certain general outlook on things, and this outlook is a genuine endowment, a genuine boon. It is the favor that makes a human being Dasein. Technology is sent and, in turn, sends. It is a sent sending or a bestowed bestowing. Technology, even modern technology, exists in the interplay between bestowing and bestowed; technology exists in the element of bestowal. Technology endures within bestowal; even modern technology is permeated by bestowal.

Thus a reflection on technology, and precisely on impositional technology, has brought us to the notion of bestowal. We now need to return to Heidegger's claim that an essence is to be understood in terms of bestowal, and then we need to see how the notion of bestowal might save us from the danger.

The essence as something bestowed

Immediately after drawing a clue from Goethe, Heidegger claimed, quite peremptorily, that "only what is bestowed endures." Furthermore, that which is earlier than the bestowed, namely, that which does the bestowing, Being, endures in an even more primal sense. Accordingly, what endures is Being as well as that which is bestowed by Being. Heidegger does not elaborate, he offers no evidence, and he certainly provides no proof. He merely presents his claim as the result of "pondering more thoughtfully than before that which properly endures," namely, an essence. He then leaves it to us to ponder along with him.

Does it make philosophical sense to say that only what is bestowed endures and that Being, the bestower, endures even more primordially? What makes an essence more enduring than an individual thing? What does the enduring of an essence have to do with bestowal? Just what is bestowed on an essence that is not bestowed on an individual being?

Heidegger leaves the answers to these questions implicit, but if we think through the issues, we might be able to make sense of his position. Let us begin with the essence of technology. The essence of technology is disclosive looking; by essence, technology is theory, the most general understanding of what it means for something to be. In other words, then, the essence of technology is the place of the *self-bestowal* of Being on us. In grasping an essence, we grasp what it means to be, either very generally (in the essence of technology) or with regard to some particular domain, such as houses (in the essence of a house, we grasp what it means *to be* a house) or beauties (in the essence of beauty, we grasp what it means *to be* beautiful), etc. An essence is a theory, a way of looking upon or grasping not individual beings but what it means to be an individual being as such or as some particular kind. The point is that Being holds sway in an essence. Being, so to speak, places itself in an essence, inhabits an essence, be-stows itself in an essence. That is why nothing can change an essence, except Being. An essence is not subject to the changes affecting individuals, since an essence is, as it were, on the side of Being; an essence partakes of the most proper enduring of Being. An essence is more enduring than an individual thing because Being bestows *itself* in an essence.

On the other hand, precisely since the essence is the place of a bestowal, it is not an Idea. An essence may change, if Being bestows itself differently, if Being has a history.

An Idea endures perpetually; it is always self-same. For Heidegger, an essence may change. As an example, the essence of technology has changed over time. Nature used to offer itself as something to be respected and now appears as something to be imposed on. For Heidegger, we humans could never, on our own, intentionally or through lassitude, bring about such a change. We are not primarily responsible for this change in the general appearance of things. On the contrary, what has changed is the self-bestowal on the part of Being. The essence endures because it is something bestowed, but it also changes for the very same reason, i.e., because it is something bestowed and, as such, dependent on the bestower. (The bestower has more autonomy, and that is why Being endures most properly.) If the bestower withdraws its countenance, if it bestows itself reticently, if it does not wholeheartedly give of itself, then our understanding of what it means to be will change. We may even fail to see Being as bestowing itself on us and may think of ourselves as wresting out from things their meaning. We will then be motivated to see ourselves as ascendant over Being, over things in general. Consequently, we will take up an impositional attitude toward things, which is to say that the ancient outlook will change to the modern one.

Thus, the essence of technology, our understanding of things in general, both endures and changes on account of the history of Being. The notion of bestowal not only accounts for the enduring of the essence but also for its peculiar sort of nonperpetual enduring.

Accordingly, it does make sense to say that only what is bestowed endures, provided the notion of a history of Being makes sense. That is admittedly a large proviso, and its questionableness shall have to remain in force here to the end. According to Heidegger, it is not an exceptionally profound notion; on the contrary, it is a simple one that seems obscure because we are overly sophisticated and have lost our ears for what is simple. I suggest we should be unwilling to despair of ever grasping it more adequately and be unwilling to declare that it is inherently obscure, until we are certain we do possess the eyes and ears that would enable us to fathom the dicta of the other great thinkers in whose tradition Heidegger stands, the pre-Socratics.

Bestowal as what might save

I now turn to the second question I raised in regard to Heidegger's notion of bestowing: exactly how is the phenomenon of bestowal that which might save? Heidegger reasons as follows: if we recognize the phenomenon of bestowal, i.e., if we understand that technology comes to us as something bestowed (rather than being either imposed on us or imposed by us), then we can see and therefore possibly safeguard our proper human freedom and dignity. Bestowal can show us our genuine freedom and save us from an exaggerated view of it as either all or nothing. In the phenomenon of bestowal we can see that Being has an ascendancy over us, that we are not the leaders. But we also see that this ascendancy is not domination. It is solicitation, proffering, tendering. Technology is given to us in the manner of *poiesis*, not by way of imposition. Therefore, deep within modern technology there is rooted the genuine alternative to imposition, *poiesis*. The self-offering of Being requires our free response, and so we are free—indeed not free to dominate but free to play the necessary role of abetter. As poietic, bestowal teaches us our role, which is that of abetting, and shows us the dignity of our role, which dignity consists in a certain ascendancy we enjoy over Being, precisely insofar as Being *requires* us and so is, to that extent, dependent on us. Thus bestowal teaches us that we are secondary partners—but, nevertheless, genuine, free partners—of Being in the event of disclosedness. In other terms, bestowal acquaints us with disclosive looking as such, i.e., as an active receptivity of the initiative on the part of Being. Thereby we can see what disclosive looking should be, namely a *most* active receptivity, a receptivity exercised with all our diligence. Thus bestowal shows us that our essence, freedom, and dignity lie in authentic following or abetting. For Heidegger, only if we "behold" our essence will we be able to see how it is endangered and then be able to protect it and "sojourn" in it. That is how the phenomenon of bestowal, which we have been led to by thinking through the all-encompassing imposition, might save us from being overwhelmed by the impositional attitude.

It takes Heidegger two dense pages to express how the phenomenon of bestowal might save us, but the primary statement is the following paragraph, which I will present as a whole before taking it up in detail:

> But if this destiny, com-posing, is the extreme danger, not only for man's essence, but for all disclosive looking as such, should this sending still be called a bestowing? By all means, and especially if in this destiny that which saves is supposed to grow. Every destiny to a disclosive looking occurs out of a bestowing and as a bestowing. Bestowal first acquaints man with his participation in disclosedness, a participation required for the very event of disclosedness. As so required, man belongs indispensably to the event of truth. Bestowal, the sending into one or another kind of disclosive looking, is in itself that which might save. For this [the phenomenon of bestowal] lets man behold and sojourn in the highest dignity of his essence. This dignity lies in tending to the unconcealment—and, along with that, to the prior concealment—of all essence on this earth. It is precisely com-posing, which threatens to inundate man in imposition as the ostensibly sole way of disclosive looking, and so thrusts man into the danger of the surrender of his free essence, it is precisely this extreme danger that may make us aware of our innermost, indispensable belonging to that which bestows, provided we, for our part, learn to see the essence of technology. (FT, 33/31–32)

In the first sentence, Heidegger joins together the essence of humanity (as Dasein) and disclosive looking as such. Both are endangered by the all-encompassing imposition. In fact, there is only one threat here, for disclosive looking does precisely constitute the essence of humanity as Dasein. The danger to disclosive looking *is* the danger to that essence. What exactly is the danger to disclosive looking? Heidegger expresses it as follows: "The essence of [modern] technology threatens disclosive looking, threatens it with the possibility that all disclosive looking will collapse into imposition and that all things will present themselves in only one mode of unconcealment, i.e., solely as disposables" (FT, 34/33).

Thus the danger is that all disclosive looking will be impositional and all things will be disclosed as there to be imposed on. Disclosedness and disclosive looking will collapse into (Heidegger's term literally means "to go up in," the way something may go up in smoke) imposition.

How is this collapse a danger to humanity's essence? According to Heidegger, as just quoted, if humans are inundated by imposition as the sole way of disclosive looking, then they will be thrust "into the danger of the surrender of their free essence."

To speak of a human being's "free essence" is pleonastic. Freedom is essential to humans; to lose one's freedom is to lose one's essence. How is a threat to disclosive looking a danger to freedom? For Heidegger, freedom directly depends on disclosive looking. Unless we *see* where our freedom lies, unless we grasp the possibility of a genuinely free exercise of our powers, we will not be able to act freely. If all things are disposables and all disclosive looking is impositional, then we will see ourselves in terms of imposition: as the imposers or the imposed upon, as entirely determined or totally free. Both of these views are illusory and ultimately lead to disillusionment. To attempt to live in accord with these views of freedom is to surrender the possibility of genuine human maturity. The antidote is a more adequate understanding of our freedom; that is what the phenomenon of bestowal may afford us.

For Heidegger, *all* disclosive looking occurs "out of a bestowing and as a bestowing." The problem, the danger, is that this fact has been hidden by the all-encompassing impositional attitude. What might save us is that which might unconceal bestowal and bring it home to us: "Bestowal, the sending into one or another kind of disclosive looking, is in itself that which might save." Ironically, it is precisely com-posing, the essence of modern technology, that motivates us to rethink the meaning of essence and thereby acquaints us with the phenomenon of bestowal. It is modern technology that allows us to see all technology, all disclosive looking, as a poietic phenomenon, as soliciting and requiring our acceptance of the self-proffering of Being. The all-encompassing imposition discloses the fact that imposition itself is not imposed on us. On the contrary, by thinking deeply enough about the essence of modern technology, we come to realize that technology is pervaded by bestowal.

How does the phenomenon of bestowal show us our genuine freedom? "Bestowal first acquaints man with his participation in disclosedness, a participation required for the very event of disclosedness," i.e., required for the event of truth. What is our participation in disclosedness, taking the latter as a process of bestowal? What role do we play as the ones bestowed upon? Since bestowal is a gentle giving, there is no bestowal without an acceptance on the part of the one to whom the bestowal is made. In other words, our participation is *required*. It is required but not compelled. Bestowal leaves us free to accept the bestowal, free to receive what is proffered. What bestowal requires of us is authentic following, active receptivity. We are free to follow the lead of Being with all—or with less than all—our might. In other words, our freedom in disclosedness is the freedom of the follower.

Now, this, for Heidegger, is our genuine freedom. As followers, our role is secondary; it is basically a receptivity. As free followers, our receptivity is active, creative, and we make a genuine contribution to the event of truth. Authentic human freedom then consists in the most active exercise of our receptive powers. In this resides "the highest dignity of our essence." Bestowal is what might save, because it lets us "behold and sojourn in" this dignity of our essence. To behold our essence is to see where our genuine freedom lies, *viz.*, in active receptivity. To sojourn in our essence is to carry out the active receptivity with all our might. That would be a genuinely mature human life. It would be a life without illusions.

In Heidegger's words, our dignity "lies in tending to the unconcealment—and, along with that, to the prior concealment—of all essence on this earth." To tend to the unconcealment of all essence means to be active recipients, to be abetters, to receive the self-offering of Being with all possible diligence. Our dignity lies in our role of *tending*, nurturing, actively letting the meaning of Being (= the unconcealment of all essence) come to its fullest possible self-revelation. This role is a dignified one, because it is required for disclosedness, because it is indispensable to the self-offering of Being. Truth, therefore, is beholden to us. Our tending to truth is required indispensably for the occurrence of truth, and this fact raises us above all other beings.

The preceding is relatively straightforward. Yet Heidegger also says that our dignity resides in tending to the concealment of all essence. That is much more problematic. Heidegger cannot mean that we are to tend to concealment in the same sense that we tend to unconcealment, namely by fostering it, helping it to increase, making it more widespread. On the contrary, we would tend to concealment merely by at-tending to it, respecting it, giving it its due. Even so, it is not clear how we can or why we should attend to concealment. Here, in the essay on technology, Heidegger does not say more about it. To understand what Heidegger means, we need to turn to his writings on Greek philosophy, since, for Heidegger, that is exactly what the pre-Socratics did attend to, concealment as prior to unconcealment.

Consider the original Greek understanding of truth. The Greek word for "truth," *aletheia*, is, according to Heidegger, a negative word, formed by an alpha privative and λήθη (*lethe*), from λανθάνω (*lanthano*), which does not mean "to forget," as it is usually thought of and translated, nor does it mean "to conceal," in the sense of the human activity of concealing something, but instead means precisely "to be concealed." For the Greeks, truth, *a-letheia*, then means "a-concealment" or "dis-concealment," in the specific sense of "being dis-concealed," "that which has been dis-concealed" (not "that which we dis-conceal"). Thus the Greeks express with a negative (and passive) term (*a-letheia*) what we express with a positive one ("truth"). Is this at most an interesting linguistic quirk?

> What we see here is more than just "interesting." It is decisive—namely, for an understanding of the primordial essence of truth, whose Greek name, *aletheia*, is derived from the word *lanthano* . . . For precisely the way *lanthano* is the ruling word tells us that what it names, "the concealed," has a priority in the experience of beings, and, indeed, as a character of beings themselves it is a possible "object" of experience. (*P*, 40–42/27)

This says that the concealment of things can be experienced, in some unusual way or other (whence the scare quotes around "object"), and even has a priority in experience. But how can that be? Something needs to be unconcealed in order for us to experience it. For Heidegger, to experience the concealment of beings means indeed to experience their unconcealment, but it means to experience that unconcealment in a special sense, namely, as primarily not of our own doing. We attend to the concealment of things when we recognize their unconcealment as primarily the work of Being. We experience the veiledness of Being when we recognize the veils as in the hands of Being itself. That is precisely what the pre-Socratic Greeks did recognize. They were aware of a concealing and an unconcealing over which they had no control and which, instead, had a priority over their own human efforts at uncovering and grasping things. They saw Being as in the lead with regard to the disclosure of beings, whereas we moderns recognize nothing as ascendant over our own subjective powers of observation and research.

One way Heidegger illustrates the distinction between the ancient and modern attitudes is the following. In the *Odyssey*, Homer says that, at a certain banquet, Odysseus was weeping *elanthane*. We usually say that his weeping was "unnoticed" by those round about him. But in the genuine Greek sense, according to Heidegger, it means that his weeping was wrapped in concealment:

> In the case of the weeping Odysseus, the Greeks do not consider that the others present, as human "subjects" in their subjective comportment, fail to *notice* the crying of Odysseus, but the Greeks do think that round about this man, in his current state, there was hung a con-

cealment, bringing it about that the others present were, so to speak,
cut off from him. What is essential is not the apprehension on the
part of the others but that there exists a concealment of Odysseus,
now keeping the ones who are present far from him. That a being, in
this case the weeping Odysseus, can be experienced and grasped depends on whether concealment or unconcealment comes to pass in it.
(P, 41/27–28)

The crucial point is that our experiencing a thing does not depend,
or at least does not primarily depend, on whether or not we are observant. It does not depend on our powers, our subjective comportment; it
depends on whether there hangs over the thing a veil or whether the veil
is lifted. The Greeks were aware of this veil; i.e., they recognized something ascendant over their own powers of observation. They recognized
Being, or the gods, as in the lead. To tend to the prior *concealment* of all
essence is therefore not to help spread ignorance but to recognize the visibility of things as a gift rather than our own accomplishment.

We can now understand Heidegger's assertion that human dignity
resides in a tending to both unconcealment and concealment. To tend to
unconcealment means to do all that is in our power to uncover truth. It
means to be active, authentic, observant. To tend, or attend, to concealment means to remember that we are followers in the event of disclosedness, that we are receivers of a gift of the self-disclosedness of Being, and
that we are to act appropriately. Thus, for Heidegger, human dignity lies
precisely in the role of authentic following, active receptivity, disclosive
looking as a response to the self-offering of Being. Both characteristics of
this role, the activity and the passivity, the authenticity and the following,
the looking and the being looked at, are essential and must not, either in
theory or in practice, be denied.

Heidegger concludes the paragraph under consideration from the
essay on technology by underlining the importance of our grasping
the essence of technology (as distinguished from technological things).
The essence of technology is disclosive looking, which is the correlate
of the self-offering of Being. Disclosive looking is the human response
to the lead of Being. Accordingly, disclosive looking is an active receptivity. If we begin to see technology in this light, then we become aware
that Being is a bestower, not an imposer, and it is brought home to
us that we are bestowed on, not imposed on. We begin to see ourselves,
then, as indispensable partners in a bestowal. As such partners, ours is
the freedom of the follower. Our freedom is not all or nothing; on the
contrary, our freedom is a poietic one. We are free to play a poietic role
within bestowal: to tend to bestowal, foster it, let it flourish. This is our
"intrinsic, indispensable belonging to that which bestows": we are by

essence midwives to the self-revelation of Being. The phenomenon of bestowal thus brings home to us a genuine, poietic alternative to imposition. Since the danger is precisely that we may be engulfed by imposition, this genuine alternative is what might save us. Surprisingly, then, in modern technology, in the all-embracing imposition, there also grows that which might save, and Hölderlin's words prove true: "Thus the essence of technology harbors in itself what we would least suspect, the possible emergence of that which might save" (FT, 33/32).

What about our poietic role of tending or fostering? In the first place, it presupposes a certain seeing. Before we can *do* anything to fulfill our role of midwife, we must *see* our role. We must first see technology as a phenomenon of bestowal, which is to say, once again, that we must see the essence of technology as distinguished from technological things: "Everything, then, depends upon this: that we reflect on its emergence [i.e., on the emergence of that which might save] and, in recollection, tend it. [Original version of the lecture: Everything depends on this, that we let grow that which might save.] How does that happen? Before anything else, by our seeing the essence of technology instead of merely gaping at technological things" (FT, 33/32).

We will postpone until the end a discussion of how we may, *in concreto*, carry out this poietic activity of "tending" and "letting grow" or, as Heidegger will also call it, "looking after" and "fostering." Indeed, in the essay we are considering Heidegger offers no more than hints with regard to a genuinely poietic technology, i.e., an authentic reception of the self-offering of Being. But Heidegger does make it very clear that what comes "before anything else," i.e., before any poietic *activity*, is a *seeing* of *poiesis*, which amounts to a seeing of the essence of technology. To grasp this essence as a matter of bestowal is to understand ourselves as free in relation to what is bestowed, i.e., free to receive it actively, free to follow it with all our might—or not. If we see the essence of technology and do not merely gape in thrall at technological things, then we find in modern technology a genuine alternative to the impositional outlook. That is how modern technology, the all-encompassing imposition, harbors what we would least expect, the growth of that which might save us from imposition.

The mystery

Heidegger proceeds to reflect on this peculiar circumstance that modern technology is by essence impositional and yet harbors deep within itself *poiesis*, the genuine alternative to imposition. The essence of modern technology is therefore, according to Heidegger, mysterious:

If, finally, we reflect that the unfolding of the essence occurs
in a bestowal and so requires man's participation by way of disclosive looking, then the following becomes clear:

The essence of [modern] technology is eminently ambiguous.
Such ambiguity indicates the presence of the mystery, the mystery of
all disclosedness, i.e., the mystery of truth.

On the one hand, com-posing challenges us into the frenzy of
imposition, which deposes every view of the event of disclosedness
and so endangers the very foundation of our relation to the essence
of truth.

On the other hand, com-posing occurs for its part in a bestowal that lets man endure therein precisely as one who is needed to
look after the essence of truth. (Although man does not yet experience himself as so needed, perhaps he may in the future.) In this way
appears the emergence of that which might save. (FT, 33–34/32–33)

I will comment on each of these four brief paragraphs, saving the
second one for last, since it is a statement of the conclusion.

The first paragraph speaks of the "unfolding of the essence." This
phrase refers to the self-imparting of Being, the self-revealing of the
essence of things in general. The unfolding of the essence occurs by way
of a bestowal, not by way of imposition. Accordingly, we humans are required, we must participate, we must respond by looking disclosively, if
the unfolding or self-revelation of the essence is ever to come to fruition.
An understanding of the essence of things cannot be imposed on us.

Thus com-posing, the essence of modern technology, shows itself
both as impositional and as just the opposite, namely, as a matter of bestowal. The third paragraph expresses the impositional character. Modern technology is by essence an all-encompassing imposition which
strongly motivates us to see beings exclusively as disposables, as there to
be imposed on. The impositional outlook deposes every view of the
"event of disclosedness." That is, if we see imposition everywhere, we
will be blind to the occurrence of disclosedness as a process of bestowal
and, consequently, blind to our poietic role in disclosedness. Modern
technology thereby endangers "our relation to the essence of truth," since
truth is disclosedness, understood as an accomplishment of, primarily,
Being itself. The truth is the relation between the initiative taken on the
part of Being to look at us and the free response on our part to look back.
The truth is that Being is in the lead and that we are free, poietic followers. "Our relation" to the essence of truth is our poietic service to the self-
revelation of Being. That service is what is endangered by modern
technology, since modern technology commandeers the entire field of disclosive looking, makes all disclosive looking impositional, and so blinds
us to the possibility of *poiesis*. If we see only imposition, we will do and

make things only impositionally. For Heidegger, unless we can envision *poiesis*, we cannot authentically fulfill our poietic role, wherein lies our essence, our freedom, and our dignity.

On the other hand, it is modern technology that has motivated us to rethink the meaning of essence and to recognize that an essence is something bestowed, not imposed. Thus in the midst of the danger there also grows that which might save us from the impositional outlook, namely a glimpse of our genuine relation to the essence of truth, our poietic relation to it. In the fourth paragraph, Heidegger calls this poietic service a "looking after" the essence of truth, which is another way of saying "abetting" or "nurturing," or "active letting." Heidegger also remarks that (on the whole) people today do not yet experience themselves as needed to look after truth, although perhaps they will in the future. That is to say, perhaps, if a third epoch in the history of Being dawns, if there comes to pass another beginning, if Being shows us its countenance once again, if the gods become again what they are supposed to be, namely, lookers, we will recognize our indispensable role, that of a free follower, and then be able to fulfill that role authentically, by summoning up all our powers. To the very restricted extent that modern technology does now show itself as a bestowal, we glimpse in it the "emergence of that which might save."

Thus modern technology both (emphatically) deposes *poiesis* and (deep within, reticently) manifests it. Heidegger concludes that the essence of technology is ambiguous and that "such ambiguity indicates the presence of the mystery, the mystery of all disclosedness, the mystery of truth." What is this mystery?

For Heidegger, Being is *the* mystery, and what is most mysterious about it is its ambiguous way of disclosing itself. It offers itself, but in its very offering of itself it holds itself back. In the very act of stepping forth, it recedes. Heidegger had already claimed, a few pages earlier, that "that which opens the open space—the mystery—is concealed and is always concealing itself." Being makes available an open space (an understanding of what it means to be), but just as the openness of the open space is most easily overlooked in favor of the things that stand in it, so Being withdraws in favor of beings. A knowledge of Being is first, closest to us, presupposed by all other knowledge. Yet Being offers itself in such a way as to recede in favor of what is next closest, beings. Being conspicuously sheds light on beings and very reticently sheds light on itself. What is mysterious about Being, about the self-disconcealment of Being, i.e., about truth, is this play of self-offering and self-receding. Being reticently shows itself and emphatically recedes. It is first to be experienced and last to be noticed, closest and furthest, most known and least known, most obvious and most overlooked. That is why Being is *the* mystery.

For Heidegger, modern technology manifests the same ambiguity, the same play of self-concealment and self-disconcealment. This, he says, indicates the presence of the mystery. It indicates that technology is a matter of the self-revelation of Being and is not merely some secondary, practical affair.

Modern technology is in truth a bestowal. Heidegger's point is not simply that modern technology shows itself, as a bestowal, imperfectly. There would be no mystery about that. Many things, indeed all things, show themselves imperfectly. What is mysterious, rather, is that modern technology makes something visible, just as Being makes beings visible; yet, in making something visible, modern technology makes itself invisible. Modern technology opens up the entire realm of disposables and, precisely in doing so, conceals itself. Just as beings overshadow Being (that which gives them visibility), so disposables overshadow the essence of modern technology (which is not one of the disposables but the bestowal of the entire realm of disposability). Modern technology motivates us to see *all* things as disposables; we will then apply to modern technology itself the outlook it has bestowed on us. In other words, our grasp of modern technology is the reason we do not grasp modern technology. That is the mystery. Our disclosive looking in the way motivated by the self-offering of Being is the reason we fail to look disclosively at disclosive looking, fail to see disclosive looking as such, as something poietic, as a free response to a bestowal. Instead, we understand it as something imposed. It is because we have responded appropriately to the way Being has bestowed itself on us, and thereby see all beings as disposables, that we cannot see either Being as bestowing itself or ourselves as having responded appropriately, poietically.

Modern technology insists on imposition. The impositional outlook is insistent, self-assertive, aggressive. Modern technology deposes *poiesis*. Yet it is the essence of modern technology that has motivated us to reflect more deeply on what it means to be an essence. Deep within, the essence of modern technology reveals its truth. What we had grasped implicitly— by responding appropriately to the way Being offers itself—can be made explicit. Our poietic response, our free following of the lead of Being, can be brought to light—precisely by reflecting on modern technology, by thinking about that which insists on the opposite attitude of imposition. That is the ambiguity, the mystery, the play of self-concealment and self-disconcealment in modern technology: in modern technology we find both imposition and its opposite, bestowal, *poiesis*. Modern technology harbors both. Where the danger is there also grows that which might save. Modern technology is therefore ambiguous, but the ambiguity is by no means a balanced one; it is heavily weighted on the side of the danger. Imposition is insistent; it thrusts itself forward. That which might save is reticent and well veiled. It takes the closest attention to find it; it requires attention to the *essence* of technology instead of enthrallment at the sight of technological things.

For Heidegger, this curious ambiguity clinging to modern technology indicates the presence of the self-disclosure of Being, the presence of the event of truth. It indicates that what is taking place in modern technology is not merely something *comparable* to the mystery of Being but *is* that mystery in its current guise. Modern technology is the current site of the mysterious interplay between beings and Being, between concealment and disconcealment. Today beings as such are nothing but technological beings, beings which present themselves as there to be imposed on. These are the things that Being currently makes visible. They are the things that are insistent, that blind us to all else, that overshadow the source of their own visibility. Being itself is that which withdraws in favor of these disposable beings. Yet Being does show itself, albeit reticently, and to grasp Being, over and against beings, is equivalent to grasping the essence of technology over and against disposables. The essence of technology is bestowal, and our role therein is the poietic one of active receptivity. For Heidegger, to understand technology as something bestowed, to understand ourselves as the recipients of a bestowal, is to glimpse that which does the bestowing, Being. It is in modern technology, as a phenomenon of bestowal, that Being discloses itself as the bestower, the leader with regard to our grasp of what it means to be. Therefore the interplay between imposition and bestowal is the ontological interplay, the interplay between beings and Being. Modern technology is the place of the ontological mystery, the place where Being offers itself in a strange interplay of self-revealing and self-concealing. That is again why, for Heidegger, technology is an ontological affair, a matter of truth, a matter of the self-disconcealment of Being, and the philosophy of technology is first philosophy.

The constellation

Heidegger proceeds to couch the ontological character of modern technology in an image drawn from astronomy or, rather, from stargazing:

> The insistence of imposition and the reticence of that which might save draw past each other like the paths of two stars in the course of the heavens. Yet their passing by is merely the other side of their nearness.
>
> In gazing at the ambiguous essence of technology, we behold the constellation, the stars in the mystery of their course.
>
> The question concerning technology is the question concerning the constellation in which concealment and unconcealment occur, in which the essence of truth comes to pass. (FT, 34/33)

How are we to understand this image of stars drawing past each other? Are not the stars fixed in their relation to one another? In fact, Heidegger's image makes sense, if taken in strict, astronomical terms. The majority of the stars we see do draw past each other; they are not single stars but binary ones, pairs of stars that are constantly revolving around each other and eclipsing one another. Yet this "drawing past each other" of the binary stars is exclusively a telescopic phenomenon. It is a discovery of scientific astronomy and is not available to ordinary stargazing. It is hardly likely that Heidegger would appeal to the stars as understood in science.

Heidegger must be referring to stars in a looser sense, whereby the term includes the planets and other heavenly bodies. He means "star" in the sense that we might call Venus the evening star. To the ancients, the planets were merely "wandering stars," πλάνητες ἀστέρες (*planetes asteres*), *stellae errantes*, a notion that survives in contemporary German, where a planet is a *Wandelstern*.

The planets do draw past each other. A conjunction of two bright planets is an impressive sight that requires no telescope. The approach, conjunction, and parting of two planets can be viewed in the course of three nights' stargazing. Presumably, this is the phenomenon to which Heidegger is referring.

Yet this way of understanding the image is beset by another difficulty. Heidegger calls the drawing past of the stars a "constellation" (*die Konstellation*); but only the fixed stars form constellations. There is no such thing as a constellation of planets; the constellations of the zodiac are precisely what the planets wander through.

We shall then have to take "constellation" in a slightly idiosyncratic sense, though, indeed, in the etymological sense. It would refer not to a fixed group of stars but to a "going together of the stars," again taking "star" to include the wandering stars. Then what Heidegger means by the term "constellation" is what in astronomy is called an "appulse," the "driving-toward" each other of two heavenly bodies.

The appulse of two planets is, of course, merely an apparent drawing near. They seem to approach one another only from our vantage point. Objectively, the distance between the planets may be increasing while they are lining up with the earth. Thus their coming together merely hides how far apart they are. Their coming into conjunction has a hidden, more genuine, side, the great distance separating them. Thus this sort of constellation is for astronomers one of merely apparent closeness and actual, though concealed, distance. For Heidegger, however, the phenomenon has the exact opposite significance.

He finds in the two stars that "their passing by is merely the other side of their nearness." That is to say, we see that the two heavenly bodies

do not collide, that they do not join together, that they pass each other by.
Their separation is apparent. But this does not mean they are actually
apart, isolated from each other. Their passing by hides the fact that they
belong together. For they could not pass each other by unless they were
near in their essence, i.e., unless they shared one and the same essential domain. Two unrelated things do not pass each other by. Ships may pass un-
seen to each other in the night, but they can do so only because they both
belong to the sea and so are connected to each other. For Heidegger, it is
only apparently that the stars are not near one another; if we consider
them more deeply, we realize they belong together by being assigned to the
same domain, and so they are close. Hence a "constellation" is for him a
phenomenon of apparent distance and deeper, more genuine, nearness.

Elsewhere, Heidegger even calls the night the "seamstress of the
stars." Objectively speaking, i.e., for the exact scientist, what might be
most impressive is the distance separating the stars. Yet "for the child in
man," for someone who bypasses scientific theory and goes straight to
the essence, the stars are close.

The reference to the night as seamstress occurs in a dialogue Heidegger composed. The line is spoken by the character in the dialogue
called the teacher. It is not said explicitly that Heidegger is this teacher,
but it becomes obvious that it could be no one else. The passage runs
as follows:

> Teacher: the night closes up the distances of the stars in the
>   heavens . . .
> Scientist: perhaps for the naive observer, although not for the
>   exact scientist.
> Teacher: For the child in man, the night remains the seamstress of
>   the stars.[6]
> Scholar: It joins together without stitch or weft or thread.
> Scientist: It is the seamstress because it only does close-work.
>   (G, 71/89–90)

Heidegger is here playing on the words *die Näherin* (seamstress), *die
Näharbeit* (sewing; literally, "close-work"), and *die Nähe* (closeness). The
seamstress is one who does close-work, not in the sense of meticulous work
that is held close to the eyes, but in the sense of work that closes up distances.
A constellation is then formed by two stars sewn together. The scientist
might deny that it happens; it is merely apparent. But for someone with
child-like eyes, eyes innocent of science, it is just the opposite. The distance
is mere appearance and the closeness, the belonging together, is genuine.

That is how the image of a constellation applies to modern technology. Modern technology is a constellation—in Heidegger's sense—of imposition and *poiesis*. These seem to pass each other by, to belong to

radically different worlds; the insistent impositional attitude seems to exile *poiesis*. But if we are permitted to look deeply enough into the essence of modern technology, deeply enough to see the ambiguity in that essence, we find imposition and *poiesis* near to one another. Just as the apparent passing by of the two stars has a hidden side, namely the truth of their belonging together, so the insistent outlook of imposition has another side, its true side, the fact that it is something bestowed. If the essence of modern technology discloses its depths, we will find the truth, the hidden bestowal. That is how the essence of modern technology presents itself as a constellation: its two stars, so to speak, apparently pass each other by, but in hiddenness they are sewn close together.

The nearness of imposition and bestowal is a mysterious one—in Heidegger's sense of mystery. In other words, their nearness has to do with Being, with the self-disconcealment of Being, with the coming to pass of the essence of truth. The constellation of modern technology is the ontological interplay between beings and Being, and that is why Heidegger says the question of technology is the question of the constellation "in which concealment and unconcealment occur." For Heidegger, concealment and unconcealment occur primordially in the interplay between insistent beings and reticent Being. And that is the interplay of modern technology. The insistence of the impositional attitude is the insistence of beings in their current guise as disposables. The reticence of modern technology to show itself in its essence as a bestowal is the reticence of Being to disclose itself as the bestower. The mystery, the ontological interplay, the coming to pass of truth, the process of the self-disconcealment of Being, the constellation, the ambiguity—these all name what is at issue in the question of technology, namely, theory, first philosophy.

Accordingly, imposition and bestowal are near in the same way that beings and Being are near to each other. Then they are not accidentally near, in the sense that imposition and bestowal, the danger and that which might save, just happen to be found together in one place, in modern technology. On the contrary, they are intrinsically near. There is no gazing at beings without an (at least implicit) understanding of Being. Likewise, there is no disclosive looking upon disposables without a latent grasp of bestowal as such, i.e., without noticing and responding appropriately to the look of Being. The more deeply we ponder over modern technology, the more do we make the phenomenon of bestowal explicit. The more clearly we see the ambiguity of modern technology, i.e., the more we gaze at the constellation, the constellation of the self-disclosure of Being, the constellation of truth, the more do we understand the impositional attitude as something bestowed. That understanding might save us, since it brings home to us our poietic role as free followers. That is the profit of being open to and gazing at the constellation: "What does it profit us to gaze at the constellation of truth? We look into the danger and glimpse the growth of that which might save" (FT, 34/33).

The profit is that we glimpse the phenomenon of bestowal, the alternative to the impositional attitude; we glimpse that which might save. Yet what sort of profit is that? That does not actually save us, does it? "In that way we are indeed not yet saved. But we are thereby summoned to hope in the growing light of that which might save. How can this growth happen? By our fostering it, by our fostering, here and now and in little things, the growth of that which might save. This includes holding always before our eyes the extreme danger" (FT, 34/33).

What are these little things? What, concretely, here and now, can we do to hasten the advent of that which might save? What is the proper human way to receive the self-bestowal of Being? We know that, for Heidegger, the genuinely free approach to things is *poiesis*, not imposition. And so he says that we are to "foster" the growth of that which might save. That is just another way of expressing what he had already proposed: we are to "look after," "tend," "let grow" that which might save. These terms all name the same poietic attitude; but what, specifically, does that attitude amount to? What actually should we do to foster the growth of that which might save?

Here, in the essay on technology, Heidegger does not say. The essay is open-ended. It invites us to take its lessons to heart and ponder how to put them into practice. That is, Heidegger leaves the practical application to us. He is much more concerned with theory, with that which precedes practice, namely the seeing of the realm of our genuine freedom. That realm is *poiesis*. Heidegger wants to open up that realm to our vision; he is concerned with what we "hold before our eyes." Presumably, if the realm of *poiesis* can be brought home to us with sufficient clarity, it will be a relatively easy matter to find our way in it in practice. Before we take up the issue of the appropriate practice, let us follow Heidegger to the end of his essay as he asks his final theoretical question: is there a privileged place where *poiesis* does show itself clearly, at least more clearly than it does in the essence of technology?

Transition to the question of art

In other words, is there a "more primordially bestowed disclosive looking," i.e., a disclosive looking, in the age of modern technology, that rivals the primordial disclosive looking, the one of the first epoch in the history of Being? Does the original disclosive looking survive somewhere? Indeed, for Heidegger, today all disclosive looking is impositional, and so, if this original outlook survives, it does so only in tatters. Can it perhaps be revived? Would it then allow us a clear view of *poiesis*, i.e., an understanding of Being as the bestower and of ourselves as active recipients of the bestowal?

What is endangered by modern technology is disclosive looking and disclosedness. The danger is that these will go up in imposition. For Heidegger, human activity by itself can never forestall this danger:

> Human accomplishments alone can never dispel [the danger]. But human reflection can ponder the fact that whatever might save must be of a higher essence than what is endangered, yet indeed of a kindred essence.
>
> Could there not perhaps be a more primordially bestowed disclosive looking, one able to bring that which might save into its first proper appearance in the midst of the danger (the danger which in the technological age is still more concealed than visible)? (FT, 35/33–34)

Heidegger is asking whether there is a disclosive looking that is of a higher essence than the impositional outlook, yet of a kindred essence. Heidegger will propose *art* as the higher disclosive looking. Indeed, in the modern age, the realm of art, too, is a disposable. It is there for what we can get out of it. We dispose of art for our cultural enrichment. Thus art has become incorporated into our impositional outlook. Yet, for Heidegger, art originally had a higher function, and a higher essence, and the question is whether, in the technological age, that function and essence might be bestowed again upon art. Will art allow us to glimpse the path leading toward that which may save us from the danger? Can art bring home to us that for the sake of which we are asking about technology, namely, our proper relation to things, our genuine freedom? Can art show us the phenomenon of bestowal and thereby prevent disclosive looking from going up in imposition?

Part IV

Art

Recall the setting for Heidegger's lecture on technology. The occasion was a colloquium devoted to the topic of "The arts in the technological age." The colloquium was sponsored by an institution dedicated to art, namely, the Bavarian Academy of Fine Arts, but it took place at a citadel of technology, a sort of German MIT, the Munich Institute of Technology. Thus, the colloquium literally brought art into the world of technology, and the seven invited speakers were to explore the proper role, if any, of art therein.

Heidegger finally takes up the designated topic of art in a passage that is less than two pages long, just prior to the conclusion of the speech. Coming so late, the passage on art is, understandably, cryptic. It runs as follows:

> There was a time when it was not technology alone that bore the name *techne*. Once that disclosive looking which brings truth forth into radiant appearance was also called *techne*.
>
> There was a time when the bringing forth of the true into the beautiful was called *techne*. That is, the *poiesis* of the fine arts was also called *techne*.
>
> At the outset of the destiny of the West, in Greece, the arts soared to the supreme height of the disclosedness bestowed on them. They brought the presence of the gods, and the dialogue of divine and human destinies, to radiance. And art was simply called *techne*. It was a single, manifold disclosive looking. It was pious, πρόμος [*promos*], i.e., submissive to the occurrence and holding sway of truth.
>
> The arts [*die Künste*] did not issue from artistry [*das Artistische*]. Artworks were not enjoyed aesthetically. Art was not one among other cultural creations.
>
> What was art—perhaps only for that brief but sublime age? Why did art bear the name *techne* pure and simple? Because it was a

disclosive looking that brought forth and, accordingly, belonged within
poiesis. Ultimately, what was awarded the name *poiesis* as a proper
name was poesy, i.e., poetry, that disclosive looking which holds sway
in all the fine arts, in all the arts that have to do with beauty.

The same poet from whom we heard the words,

> But where danger is, there also grows
> That which might save.

says to us:

> . . . poetically dwells man on this earth.

The poetical brings the true into the luster of what Plato in the
Phaedrus calls τό ἐκφανέστατον [*to ekphanestaton*], that which
shines forth most purely. The poetical holds sway in all art, in all disclosure of the essence through beauty.

Could it be that the fine arts are called to poetic disclosedness?
Could it be that such disclosedness lays claim to them most primally,
so that they in turn might expressly foster the growth of that which
saves, might awaken and found anew our vision of, and trust in, that
which bestows?

Whether this highest possibility of its essence may be bestowed
on art in the midst of the extreme danger, no one can tell. Yet we can
be in wonder. Before what? Before this other possibility, that the
frenzy of [modern] technology may entrench itself everywhere to
such an extent that the essence of [modern] technology, passing right
through all technological things, may someday hold sway over the
very event of truth.

Because the essence of technology is nothing technological, an
essential determination of technology and a decisive confrontation
with it must occur in a realm that, in relation to technology, is of a
kindred essence on the one hand, and yet, on the other hand, is of a
fundamentally different essence.

Such a realm is art—always provided that our approach to art
is not sealed off from the constellation of truth, concerning which we
are *questioning*. (FT, 35–36/34–35)

(Metaphysical) aesthetics versus (ontological) philosophy of art

The fundamental distinction at play in this passage on art is a typically
Heideggerian one. It is the distinction between a humanistic and an ontological view of art. The former makes humanity the measure of art: i.e., art
arises out of human creativity and exists to elevate human experience. Hu-

mans are thus the beginning and end of art. Versus this, the ontological view, to put it in a preliminary way, sees Being, the gods, at work in art.

The humanistic understanding of art goes by the name of "aesthetics." Today aesthetics is the predominant, not to say exclusive, philosophy of art. Everyone today thinks of art in aesthetic terms, which is to say in human terms, in terms of the effect of art on human sense-experience (*aisthesis*). We expose ourselves to art for the sake of a deepening of our experience. Art takes us out of our shallow, everyday world and expands the horizons of our experience, making us broader, deeper, more refined human beings.

This humanistic, aesthetic approach to art is nothing but the technological outlook: art is a disposable. We ourselves (or at least the artists among us) place artworks at our disposal, and we experience these creations precisely for what we can get out of them.

In Heidegger's view, however, aesthetics is not the only theory of art. It is merely the theory motivated by the second epoch in the history of Being: aesthetics arises when Being withdraws and is supplanted by human subjectivity. The original Greek attitude toward art was not a matter of aesthetics. The Greeks did not surround themselves with art for subjective reasons, i.e., for the sake of an elevation of their experience. The Greeks did not "appreciate" art, at least not in the etymological sense of valuing it for that which it brings "in return." Art was not something that brought returns; it had a higher provenance than human creativity and a higher function than refinement or culture. If art is there merely to be appreciated, then it has been debased, brought down to the human, subjective level. For Heidegger, in the first epoch of history humanity is not the measure of art; Being is. Art is under the sway of the self-disclosure of Being. Art in the first epoch is "pious," submissive to Being, not submissive to humans. That, in very broad strokes, characterizes the Greek approach to art as ontological rather than humanistic.

Heidegger expresses the difference between the ancient and the modern attitude toward art in three epigrammatic propositions, which we need to draw out. First of all: "The arts did not issue from artistry" (FT, 35/34). Heidegger employs here the ordinary German term for "arts," *die Künste*. What I have translated as "artistry" is an unrelated, nongenuine German word, *das Artistische*. That word is a borrowing from Latin, which is a strong clue that Heidegger means it in a pejorative sense. And the pejorative sense for him is the subjective sense. Thus the term refers to the artistic ability or creativity of the individual artist. *Das Artistische*, "artistry," should then be understood here in the sense of an artist's skill, dexterity, ingenuity, originality.[1] What the proposition expresses is that a human being, the subject, human genius, was *not* taken to be the source of art. Artworks were not viewed as human creations. As a result, art for the ancient Greeks was not a tribute to the creativity of the human artist. For the Greeks, humanity is not the beginning of art, and in viewing art we do not perceive evidence of human creative powers. Art, in the first epoch, is not meant to edify us by displaying the genius of our congeners, whose achievements we would all share vicariously. In the second, current, epoch, however, the humanistic view of art does most definitely include the sentiment that art is a paean to human genius.

The humanistic appreciation of art is an instance of the technological outlook, which is precisely the attitude of appreciating, i.e., looking upon things in terms of the returns they offer us humans. Artworks offer personal, not practical, returns. Yet, as Sartre writes, technological things, as well, can be taken personally:

> Humanism can refer to a theory which posits man as the end and as the supreme value. Humanism in this sense is visible in Cocteau's story, "Around the world in eighty hours." There a character, while flying over mountains in an airplane, declares, "Man is wonderful!" This means that I, who have not built airplanes, nevertheless receive personal returns from these particular inventions; i.e., I, inasmuch as I am a man, can consider myself personally responsible for, and honored by, the particular acts of some men. This presupposes that a value can be assigned to man on the basis of the highest acts of certain individuals. This sort of humanism is absurd, because only dogs or horses could make such a sweeping judgment about man and declare that man is wonderful, which they are careful not to do, at least not to my knowledge.[2]

Sartre is here expressing, and pillorying, an additional sense in which technological things are disposables. They not only benefit us in our practical tasks, such as our need to get over mountains as quickly as possible, but they also yield us *personal* returns. That is, technological things are at our disposal in the additional sense that they raise us in stature precisely as persons, as human beings. We can all take pride in technological achievements, since they show that humans are wonderful. We can all feel honored by the achievements of technological humanity, since we all share the same faculties that produced those achievements. Technology, like art, is a paean to humanity. That is to say, technological things, like artworks, are subject to humanistic appreciation. But if this humanism is absurd in the case of technology, it is no less so with regard to art. In other words, dogs and horses, as least to my knowledge, are careful not to declare that humans are wonderful—on the basis of either airplanes or masterpieces of art.

To return to Heidegger, what he means, most basically, by asserting that art did not issue from artistry is that the original Greeks did not relate art to the human subject. Heidegger says the same in the second of the three statements, this time with regard to the end of art instead of the beginning: "Artworks were not enjoyed aesthetically" (FT, 35/34). Elsewhere, Heidegger expresses this thought by claiming that the Greeks were fortunate in that they did not have lived experiences (N, 93/80). He does not mean that the Greeks were blasé or that they lacked deep feelings. Indeed, perhaps the Greeks' experiences were deeper and more lively than are ours today. What the Greeks did not do, however, is to search deliberately for experiences. The Greeks did not measure their lives according to the variety and intensity of their experiences. The very notion of subjective experience was foreign to the original Greeks. That is what Heidegger means by saying they did not have lived experiences: they did not understand their experience in terms of its effect on a subject, in terms of how a subject lives through the experience. The original Greeks did not think in terms of lived experience, and they were not trying to enrich their lives with experiences. That is why they were fortunate; something higher than the human subject revealed itself to them. The Greeks were occupied with something that transcended their experience. For Heidegger, it is precisely when this "something" withdraws that human subjectivity supplants it and humans become preoccupied with themselves, with their own experience.

Since the Greeks were not seeking enriching experiences, they did not relate art to themselves as subjects. The Greeks did not have art for the sake of more intense or broader experiences. These experiences of art are called aesthetic enjoyment, whether they are pleasurable or not. Thus when Heidegger says, "Artworks were not enjoyed aesthetically," he means that for the original Greeks the end of art was not its effect on the human subject, whether that effect be pleasure, pain, or any other lived experience. This again does not mean that the Greeks were blasé toward art or that art had a weak effect on their souls. On the contrary, precisely because they were not seeking to be affected, art may have aroused in the Greeks deeper feelings than the ones we today purposely seek out. What Heidegger does mean is that in the first epoch art had a higher function than the humanistic or aesthetic one of deepening the subject's experience. Art did not, as it were, point toward humans but away from them. The Greek attitude was not "Art for the sake of experience," or even "Art for the sake of art," but, rather, to put it in a still preliminary way, "Art for the sake of what it means to be." Being, not humanity, was the end of art, just as Being, not humanity, was its beginning. That is how, in a way we yet need to clarify, the Greek approach to art was a matter of ontology, not aesthetics.

[handwritten margin note: Greek ≠ aesthetic]

We come now to the third proposition in which Heidegger says explicitly what the Greek attitude toward art was not: "Art was not one among other cultural creations" (FT, 35/34). This does not mean that art was a *preeminent* cultural creation, rather than just one among others. It means that art was not considered in terms of culture at all. Art, for the Greeks. was not a cultural asset; art was not intended as an expression of culture, and its purpose was not to make people cultured—i.e., cultivated, refined, more humane. Today, however, art is indeed closely connected with culture. Arts programs are instituted in the schools for the sake of "cultural enrichment," art museums justify themselves as "bastions of culture," and life without art is disdained as brutality.

Thus Heidegger's three propositions all say the same: art in the first epoch was not understood in relation to the human subject. Art was not understood as stemming from the creativity of some subject, and its end was not to delight or shock or purge or acculturate human subjects. In other words, the original attitude toward art was not aesthetics. Aesthetics is the attitude that does relate art to humanity. It is our attitude today, the attitude motivated by the second epoch of history, the epoch in which humanity fills the vacuum left by the withdrawing of Being, in which humanism supplants ontology. Our epoch can also be called the age of metaphysics, i.e., the age that takes humanity as the subject of metaphysics, that makes the meaning of Being dependent on human subjective faculties rather than on Being's own self-disclosure. Accordingly, Heidegger elsewhere identifies aesthetics with metaphysical thinking:

> I am intending the *essence* of art here, and indeed not in general and vaguely, and to be sure not as an "expression" of culture or as "testimony" to the creative potential of man. My focus is how the work of art itself lets Being appear and brings Being into unconcealedness. This kind of questioning is far removed from metaphysical thinking about art, for the latter thinks "aesthetically." That means the work is considered with regard to its effect on man and on his lived experience. To the extent that the work itself comes to be considered, it is looked upon as the product of a creating, as a creation in which a "lived urge" comes to expression. Thus even if the work of art is considered for itself, it is taken as the "object" or "product" of a creative or imitative lived experience; that is to say, it is conceived entirely and constantly on the basis of human perception as a subjective act ($\alpha \ddot{\iota} \sigma \phi \eta \sigma \iota \varsigma$) [*aisthesis*]. The aesthetic consideration of art and of the work of art commences precisely (by essential necessity) with the inception of metaphysics. That means the aesthetic attitude toward art begins at the moment the essence of *aletheia* is transformed into $\dot{o}\mu o\dot{\iota}\omega\sigma\iota\varsigma$ [*homoiosis*, "assimilation"], into the conformity and correctness of perceiving, presenting, and representing. The transformation begins in Plato's metaphysics. (*P*, 170–71/115)

This passage repeats, in slightly amplified form, the claims of the three propositions from the essay on technology: art for the pre-Socratic

Greeks was not a matter of aesthetics. That is, art was not understood in relation to humans as subjects. Art did not arise from artistry (here called human "creative potential"), art was not pursued for its effect on human lived experience, and art was not an expression of culture. What then was art in the original epoch? The passage just quoted also repeats what has already been intimated: art "lets Being appear and brings Being into un-concealedness." At issue in art is therefore the meaning of Being; art is a matter of ontology, not of aesthetics. Art is related to Being, not to humanity. The question is: How so?

To prepare an answer, we need to explicate the second main idea expressed in the final pages of "Die Frage nach der Technik," namely, that poetry is—or at least was originally—the fundamental form of art. How and why was poetry fundamental, and what does that say about the Greek attitude toward art?

Art as most properly poetry

To show that poetry is the fundamental form of art, Heidegger presents, in the essay on technology, an extended argument that can be articulated into four steps:

1. Art is *techne*.
2. *Techne* is *poiesis*.
3. *Poiesis* is, most properly, poesy, i.e., poetry.
4. Therefore art is, most properly, poetry.

The first two steps are relatively straightforward. It is true on simple linguistic grounds that art is *techne*: the Greeks extended the term *techne* to art. *Techne* refers to knowledge, but not to knowledge for its own sake. It refers to knowledge insofar as it issues in practice, including both technology in the usual sense, the making of practical things, and art, the making of beautiful things. Indeed art, rather than technology, is more properly *techne*; art, as Heidegger says, is *techne* "pure and simple." The reason is that *techne*, for the Greeks, issues in *poiesis*, production, bringing forth. If we understand correctly the productions of art, we will see why art is *poiesis* or *techne* in a preeminent sense.

Then what about the products of the fine arts? What about beautiful things? What was beauty for the Greeks? Heidegger does not say explicitly, but he does provide a clue indicating where we should look. That clue is his reference to Plato's *Phaedrus* (Φαῖδρος), a dialogue whose theme is beauty, understood precisely as the *phaedron* (φαιδρόν), the lustrous, the gleaming, the radiant. Let us then briefly review the Platonic understanding of beauty in order to account for the privilege the Greeks accorded to art among the forms of *poiesis*.

We need to begin with Plato's theory of Ideas, which, at least as conventionally understood, posits two separate realms, an otherworld and this world, a world "there" and one "here," namely the invisible, changeless realm of the Ideas and the visible, changing realm of physical things. The Ideas, for Plato, exist in heaven, in the divine realm, and changing things belong to the world in which we humans live. The Ideas, grasped by the gods, are the eternal essences; changing things, which we see, are mere transient instantiations of the essence. Plato separates these two worlds, but that does not mean we humans are totally excluded from the divine realm. The things of our world all do manifest to some small degree the Ideas. For example, a triangle drawn on paper gives us some intimation of the Idea of a triangle; the same is true for human beings and the Idea of a human being, for just actions on earth and the Idea of justice, for two equal sticks and the Idea of equality, etc. All the things of our world reflect the Ideas to some extent. If they did not, if we were entirely closed off from essences, we could not recognize any human being as human, i.e., as an instance of the essence, humanity, or any just action as just, as a (shadowy) example of justice itself, etc. In general, therefore, all beings disclose, *pro tanto*, Being itself, or, Plato would say, all beings *remind* us of Being itself.

Nevertheless, for Plato, the Ideas do not shine very brightly in the things of our world. Most of the Ideas lack "luster." They do not gleam very well through their instantiations in our world. Therefore most things of our world allow us only a very inadequate grasp of the realm of the Ideas. There is, however, one Idea that does have special luster, that does shine more or less adequately in our visible world. This Idea is the one that is most manifest to sense; it is the *ekphanestaton*, that which is most lustrous, or, as Heidegger has just translated, "that which shines forth most purely." Through the visible instantiations of this Idea we can gain a relatively adequate insight into the Idea itself. We can see what an Idea is like by grasping these particular visible things. In other words, these beings can, in a privileged way, disclose or remind us of Being. For Plato, the special Idea is beauty. Beauty itself has such great luster that it shines through visible beautiful things strongly enough to allow us a grasp of the invisible divine realm. To put it another way, visible beauties are inhabited so intimately by the Idea of beauty that they partake of its radiance and reflect beauty itself to us. That is why art, in producing visible things of beauty, is the highest form of *poiesis*, or at least the highest instance of human *poiesis* (leaving open the possibility that nature may be *poiesis* in an even more proper sense). Art has a privilege—e.g., over practical technology—since art brings forth something human that is most intimately inhabited by the divine. Artistic productions are highest, because they are the earthly beings that transport us most nearly to heaven.

In sum, the Greek understanding of beauty is this: beautiful things, such as those produced by the fine arts, have a special luster or radiance. They are so shiny that they reflect to us, in a privileged way, the Idea, the essence, the truth, the divine realm, Being.

It is on this Platonic/Greek background that Heidegger, in the already cited last pages of the essay on technology, characterizes what is accomplished by art insofar as it brings forth something beautiful. We can now make perfect sense of all those apparently obscure declarations, which claim that art:

brings truth forth into radiant appearance.
brings forth the true into the beautiful.
brings the presence of the gods to radiance.
brings the dialogue of divine and human destinies to radiance.
is submissive to the occurrence of truth.
brings the true to the luster of what shines forth most purely.
discloses the essence through beauty.
fosters the growth of that which saves.
founds our vision of that which bestows.

These quotations all say one and the same thing: art discloses what it means to be. The truth, the gods, the essence, that which bestows— these are all synonyms for Being. What Heidegger is asserting is that in the work of art, as a thing of beauty, Being shows itself. The work of art is the place of a radiant appearance of Being; Being shines in the luster of the work of art.

Four of the statements above refer to truth. For Heidegger, truth is the self-disclosedness of Being. More specifically, truth is the relation (of ascendancy) between the self-disclosure of Being and our own disclosive looking. Truth is, so to speak, the dialogue between the self-disclosure of Being and our own disclosive looking. That is what Heidegger expresses in his apparently most enigmatic statement about art: art brings the dialogue of divine and human destinies to radiance. The divine destiny is the sending of Being, the self-disclosure of what it means to be. Human destiny is the disclosive looking that is thereby sent on its way. The dialogue between these destinies is the interplay of sending and sent, bestower and bestowed upon, leading and following, initiative and abetting, self-disclosure and disclosive looking. Art, for Heidegger, brings this interplay or constellation to radiance. Art allows us to see Being—precisely in its ascendancy over us; art is *submissive* to the occurrence of this ascendancy. Furthermore, since the ascendancy is not an overpowering but is instead a matter of *poiesis* itself, art thereby shows us *poiesis*. Art brings to appearance an alternative to imposition. That, by way of anticipation, is how art might save us or how art, in Heidegger's words, fosters the growth of that which saves.

Heidegger's declarations about art are *understandable* on the background of the theory of Ideas. Heidegger himself even invokes Plato in this context. Nevertheless, Plato's opinion on the privilege of the Idea of beauty is an insecure foundation on which to build. Heidegger does of course not take literally what Plato says concerning the luster of the Ideas. Beautiful things on earth and the Idea of beauty in heaven are not connected by way of sharing luster. Indeed, Heidegger would no doubt reject the entire conception of heaven and earth in the theory of Ideas. Therefore the privilege of art in the disclosure of Being cannot derive from the simple fact that artworks are beautiful. Beautiful things have no special disclosive power. For Heidegger, art is indeed privileged, but its eminence derives from something else that is fundamental to art—i.e., not from beauty as such. It derives from poetry. Poetry is the fundamental art and is fundamental to all art; it is by being poetical that art is art. The disclosive power of art stems from its poetical character. Art is a bringing forth (of truth, of the gods, etc.) in virtue of its being poetical. In other words, art is what it is, *viz.*, *poiesis*, because it is poetry. *Poiesis* is fundamentally poetry. Heidegger might speak of art in Platonic terms, in terms of gods and luster, but the ground justifying those terms is not Plato's theory of Ideas but Heidegger's own theory of poetry. It is in the latter theory that we might find "proof" of Heidegger's characterizations of art.

Heidegger asserts quite straightforwardly that *poiesis* (and thereby art as such) is, most properly, poetry: "Ultimately, what was awarded the name *poiesis* as a proper name was poesy, i.e., poetry, that disclosive looking which holds sway in all the fine arts" (FT, 35/34).[3]

The ordinary German word for poetry is *die Dichtung*. That word is unrelated to the Greek *poiesis*. But the relation between poetry and *poiesis* is precisely what Heidegger wishes to express. He is saying that *poiesis* is most properly poetry and that even in the Greek language the term *poiesis* was ultimately applied in the most proper sense to nothing but poetry. The Greeks recognized many forms of *poiesis*, but the word became not a common name for any sort of bringing forth but a proper name for one kind, poetry. *Poietes* (ποιητής) came to mean not just any producer but, most properly, the poet. The Greeks understood *the* producer to be the poet. Likewise, *poiema* (ποίημα), "something produced," meant specifically a poem.

Besides the ordinary word *Dichtung*, there is another word in German for poetry, namely, the literary term *die Poesie*. *Dichtung* and *Poesie* mean the same, namely, poetry, but, obviously, only the latter is a cognate of the Greek *poiesis*. Heidegger therefore introduces the term *Poesie* to link *poiesis* and *Dichtung*. Thus the order of the terms in Heidegger's text is the following: *poiesis, Poesie, Dichtung*. The order says that *poiesis* is *Poesie*, which is *Dichtung*; that is to say, *poiesis* is poesy, which is poetry.[4]

Heidegger is saying that poetry is the privileged form of art; poetry "holds sway" in all art. Art is *poiesis*, and its proper name is poetry. Poetry makes art art. Poetry is the fundamental art. All art is fundamentally poetry.

I thus arrive at the conclusion of the syllogism in which I formulated Heidegger's argument concerning the priority of poetry. Art is *techne*, *techne* is *poiesis*, *poiesis* is fundamentally poetry, and therefore art is fundamentally poetry. Heidegger's argument is clear; at least it is clear in its intention. And the argument is valid, in the sense that the conclusion follows from the premises. But what about those premises, especially the claim that *poiesis* is, most properly, poetry? Heidegger has done no more than *declare* it is so. The historical, linguistic connection between "poetry" and "*poiesis*" is surely no proof that art is fundamentally poetry. Heidegger's observations amount to no more than a *claim* that poetry is the fundamental art, the fundamental form of *techne* and of *poiesis*. Yet this claim is so outré that it is questionable in the highest degree. It surely needs to be supported by some proffered evidence, since all the apparent evidence speaks to the contrary.

In the essay on technology, Heidegger does not provide the required evidence. He merely claims. He actually mentions poetry four more times in the essay. He cites a work of poetry to the effect that we dwell poetically on this earth, he asserts that poetry brings truth to the most lustrous shining, and he declares again explicitly that "the poetical holds sway in all art." Finally, Heidegger asks, rhetorically, whether the arts are called to poetic disclosedness, are even called "most primally" to such disclosedness. As rhetorical, these questions, along with all the other references to poetry, merely amount to claims that art is fundamentally poetry. In the essay on technology, Heidegger does no more than *assert* this claim.

There is another place, however, where Heidegger does attempt to demonstrate the holding sway of poetry in all the arts. Heidegger is there perhaps not as clear or explicit as we could wish, but it is a place to begin in trying to come to a decision for ourselves on the matter at issue.

I will turn therefore to a passage from a lecture course Heidegger presented exactly ten years prior to the essay on technology. It is a course on Greek philosophy, and Heidegger speaks there about art in relation to the ancients. What he says, however, insofar as it touches the essence, is applicable to all art. The passage (*P*, 171–173/116–117) in question begins with the apparent evidence that poetry holds *least* sway in art. Poetry is less immediate than architecture, painting, and sculpture; it is less impressive, more fleeting, and more ambiguous. That is so because the other arts have no need of poetry and its words:

> According to the usual opinion, there are different "classes" of art. Art itself is the forming and shaping and "creating" of a work out of some matter. Architecture, sculpture, and painting use stone, wood, steel, paint; music uses tones, poetry words. One might agree that for the Greeks the poetic presentation of the essence of the gods and of their dominion was certainly essential; yet no less essential and in fact more "impressive," because of its visibility, would be the presentation of the gods immediately in statues and immediately in temples. Architecture and sculpture use as their matter the relatively stable material of wood, stone, steel. They are independent of the fleeting breath of the quickly fading and, moreover, ambiguous word. Hence these classes of art—architecture, sculpture, and painting—set essential limits on poetry, on account of the fact they do not need the word, while poetry does.

Heidegger proceeds to call this view into question, and he implies that the other arts do need words: "Now, this view is quite erroneous. Indeed architecture and sculpture do not use the word as their matter. But how could there ever be temples or statues, existing for what they are, without the word?"

Heidegger says at first which words he does not mean: the other arts do not need what he calls "historiographical" words. That is, they do not need words *about* art. The Greeks did not need art critics or art interpreters or what we call art historians. In Heidegger's eyes, that is because the Greeks were not humanists. The Greeks were fortunate: human subjectivity did not yet supplant Being in their attention. The tasks of poetry, of philosophy, and of the other arts were "more than enough" for the Greeks. These tasks amount to the disclosure of the meaning of Being; accordingly, the Greeks were occupied with Being and not with the human mode of access to Being. The Greeks therefore did not need words telling them explicitly what their art was all about; the Greeks were already occupied with that which art is all about:

> Certainly these works have no need for the descriptions of the historiography of art. The Greeks were fortunate in not yet needing historiographers of art, or of literature, of music, or of philosophy, and their written history is essentially different from modern "historiography." The Greeks had more than enough to do just with the tasks given them by poetry, thinking, building, and sculpturing.

Heidegger next asserts explicitly that words are essential to the other arts, even if these arts do not work with words: (The scare quotes indicate that, for the Greeks, art was not a human work, not the product of human artistry.)

> But the circumstance that in a temple or in a statue of Apollo there are no words as material to be worked upon and "formed" by no means proves that these "works," in what they are and how they are, do not still need the word in an essential way.

Heidegger does not yet call the required word the word of poetry, but he does seem to exclude all other words: "The essence of the word does not at all consist in its vocal sound, nor in mere noise, nor in its service to idle chatter, and certainly not in its merely technical function in the communication of information."

Heidegger finally characterizes the word that is essential to art. He calls it the "silent word": "The statue and the temple stand in silent dialogue with man in the unconcealed. If there were not the *silent word*, then the looking god could never appear in the outward aspect and figure of the statue. And a temple could never, without standing in the disclosive domain of the word, present itself as the house of a god."

These lines are as daunting as any passage in Heidegger. One word that stands out is the term "looking," which I will employ as a key to the meaning. Heidegger refers to a looking god. We know that for him the looking of a god is not the god's gazing upon us but signifies, instead, the self-disclosure of the god. The look of a god is the look of Being, the self-disclosure of the meaning of Being. Therefore the dialogue mentioned here must be the interplay between the disclosedness of Being and the disclosive looking of man. It is the dialogue between divine and human destinies. What Heidegger now asserts about this dialogue is that it is a silent one; it transpires in the medium of the silent word. On account of the silent word, the statue is able to present to us the look of the god. That is to say, the silent word allows sculptures to disclose something about Being. Why? What is this silent word? How does it function?

Heidegger speaks here of the "disclosive domain of the word." He also says that the silent dialogue occurs "in the unconcealed." In the next lines he even refers to the "clarity of the word": "The fact that the Greeks did not describe and talk about their 'works of art' aesthetically bears witness to the fact that these works stood well secured in the clarity of the word, for without the word a column would not be a column, a tympanum a tympanum, a frieze a frieze." Clarity is, presumably, the height of disclosedness. In the next lines, Heidegger will again refer to the "disclosiveness" of the word. We can assume, therefore that the word is essentially connected to disclosure or unconcealment; the word establishes a domain of disclosedness. The word establishes a clearing, a lighted area, for the dialogue between human looking and the self-presentation of beings. We know that for Heidegger the clearing is constituted by the meaning of Being in general. That is the domain in which gods and humans can dialogue. The word is then that which conveys to us what it means to be in general. Which word is this? And why is it silent here?

The word must be the one spoken in poetry. For Heidegger, language has an ascendancy over our thinking, and the meaning of Being is primarily delineated in the words of our language. The history of Being, its approach and withdrawal, may occur primarily in the medium of language. There are words with special force as regards our understanding of what it means to be. These words are conveyed to us in poetry. The poets (and the thinkers) are entrusted with the task of presenting to us the best words, the words in all their force. The poets have a special relationship to the Muses; that means the poets are inspired to convey to us the self-disclosure of the divine, the meaning of Being in general, the essence of things as a whole. That would be how the word, the poetic word, establishes a disclosive domain.

Why then does Heidegger invoke a silent word? Recall the context, which is the realm of architecture and sculpture. For Heidegger, these are the arts that require the silent word. Presumably, the word is silent there because it has already been spoken. In order to convey anything to us, these arts rely on a word already given from elsewhere. These arts, to put it differently, are not the primary conveyers of the meaning of Being; they presuppose that we are already familiar with what it means to be in general. In short, these arts presuppose that we have already heard the word of poetry. That is how, as Heidegger says, these arts require the disclosive domain of the word and "need the word in an essential way."

Therefore, insofar as the other arts need an already spoken word, poetry has a priority over them. Insofar as art in general is meant to convey the meaning of Being, poetry is the privileged art. Yet it is certainly not the case that this privilege is an absolute one. That is to say, it is not the case that Being as such presents itself exclusively in poetry, while the other arts merely inform us about individual beings. In this sense, architecture, sculpture, and painting not only *need* the silent word but also, as it were, *speak* a silent word to us. That is, they partake of poetry, they convey to us the essence of things, they manifest the meaning of Being in general. The other arts, too, are the domain of the inspiring Muses. Painting and the other arts tell of the essence; they have a voice, an "essentially telling" voice. They are, however, in relation to poetry, silent voices; they are, as Merleau-Ponty calls them, "voices of silence."

The priority of poetry is therefore a highly nuanced one. It is not an aesthetic priority, as if poetry had a greater effect on our lived experience than do the other arts. It is an ontological priority. Yet it does not amount to an absolute priority *over* the other arts, as if the latter were excluded from poetic disclosedness. The priority is rather a holding sway of poetry *in* all the arts, a speaking therein—even if silently— of the poetic word, the word that tells the essence. Heidegger expresses this nuanced priority of poetry in the concluding part of the passage under consideration:

> In an essentially unique way, through their poetry and thinking, the Greeks experience Being in the disclosiveness of lore and word. And only therefore do their architecture, painting, and sculpture display nobility as something built and formed. These "works" *exist* only in the medium of the word, i.e., in the medium of the essentially telling word, in the realm of lore, in the realm of "myth."
>
> It is *therefore* that poetry and thinking have a priority. Yet we fail to grasp this priority if we represent it "aesthetically" as a priority of one class of art over others, for no art is the object of a "cultural" or lived drive; on the contrary, each and every art is the bringing into work of the unconcealedness of Being out of the holding sway of Being itself.

Surely Heidegger does not mean here that poetry is fundamental to the arts in the sense of providing them specific themes. Heidegger does not mean that sculpture needs poetry in the sense that we could not know to sculpt a statue of Apollo unless the poets spoke about that god, unless there were myths about him. On the contrary, the myths, the lore of a people, the words of the poet, are "essentially telling." They tell what is the essence of things as a whole. Through these words, Heidegger claims, people "experience Being," i.e., Being in general. It is only on the basis of this experience, or in the medium of these words, that architecture and sculpture, as Heidegger underlines, *exist*, i.e., occur at all. Without an understanding of Being as such, the architect or sculptor or painter could not form or produce any being whatever. Nor could a viewer who lacked this understanding take a statue as a statue or a frieze as a frieze, i.e., as a particular being. These other arts therefore arise within an already spoken word concerning what it means to be as such. That expresses again the priority of poetry. But what sort of existence is then enjoyed by the other arts? Heidegger characterizes it with this term: nobility.

To be noble is to be well derived, high born. As something "built and formed," i.e., built and formed *by humans*, paintings and sculpture are mere "works," merely objects wrought by humanity. Thus they are low born, mere human creations. They lack nobility. They do not derive from Being itself, they are not inspired, they do not disclose the essence of things. For Heidegger, however, to think in this way of the priority of poetry over the other arts is to fail to grasp it. Architecture, painting, and sculpture *are* noble. The last sentence of the lines just quoted is precisely an expression of that nobility: *each* of the arts is *not the product of human lived experience* but is the bringing into work of the unconcealedness of Being *out of the holding sway of Being itself*. Every art is the work of Being; every art is noble. At play in every art is a self-disclosure of what it means to be in general. Being speaks to us in all the arts. The priority of poetry is therefore not the priority of essences over facts. It is not that poetry is able to express the essence of things, while sculpture is limited to mere particularities, mere factually existing things. All the arts disclose something essential, something concerning what it means to be as such.

Then what remains of the priority of poetry? For Heidegger, poetry is still privileged—on account of the intimacy between language and Being, between words and the essences of things. For Heidegger, it is in words, not pictures, that Being *primarily* discloses itself. That is why painting, in its disclosedness, is fundamentally poetry, rather than poetry being fundamentally painting. It is why Heidegger speaks of the silent word in the other arts rather than an invisible picture in poetry.

What is the intimacy between language and Being? To take up that issue in any adequate way would draw us much too far afield. We can, however, indicate an obvious intimacy between words and essences: words are the habitat of essences, words are the expression of essences. Words are universals, they express concepts, meanings, Ideas; pictures, on the other hand, are always images of particular things. Words are abstractions; that is, they "draw out" the essence from the particular. There can be pictures of individual beings but, strictly speaking, no picture of what it means to be as such, since Being is not a particular being. Accordingly, it is poetry that sets essential limits on the other arts, not, as was apparently evident, vice versa. Their lack of the word makes *the other arts* ambiguous, restricts them to only the vaguest representation of what it means to be. Thus we could apply to all the nonlinguistic arts what Merleau-Ponty says about music: it is "too far on this side of what can be designated in speech to be able to represent anything but the vaguest outlines of Being."[5]

Painting and sculpture are too far on *this* side of what can be designated in speech; they do not reach the abstract level of words, they are too far on this side of universals, too immersed in the concrete world of particulars. It requires words in order to go beyond particulars to the essence. For Heidegger, that, at least in part, is why the other arts, insofar as they manifest Being in general, are emulations of poetry. In these arts, Being does speak—though improperly, in silent words. The priority of poetry derives from the intimacy existing between words as such and the essences of things. When allowed its full force by the poet, language is that in which Being most properly discloses itself.

Art and the history of Being

Let us return now to the essay on technology and to Heidegger's claim that poetry holds sway in all art. The claim is justifiable—provided it is made within the context of a theory of art that is no longer aesthetics. There is no aesthetic priority of poetry. Poetry does not affect us more intensely than do the other arts. Poetry is not superior in making us cultured. Poetry is not a more impressive instance of human creativity.

Thus the priority of poetry makes no sense from a humanistic standpoint, from a view of art as something wrought by humans. But it does make sense from a premetaphysical standpoint. On that view, artists are not so much creative ones as they are inspired ones. Inspiration is nothing but the self-disclosure of Being. Insofar as we all have some understanding of what it means to be, we are all, *pro tanto*, inspired. Artists are those who most diligently, most actively, and most "creatively" receive that inspiration. Artists are Dasein in a preeminent way and play a privileged role in the history of Being. That role is indeed to produce art, but "pro-duction" must be understood in the sense of *poiesis*. It does not mean to create art out of one's own ingenuity, nor, or course, does production mean to be the passive instrument of divine revelation. The artist's role is midwifery, active receptivity.

Artists must indeed develop and exert all their creative powers— just in order to be abetters, to nurture into fullness the self-disclosure of Being. Insofar as that self-disclosure takes place most properly in language, then the artist of language, the poet, plays the most privileged of all human roles in the history of Being. The poet is the one who most actively receives and most fully expresses the self-offering of Being to mankind.

In the end, Heidegger's claim regarding the priority of poetry is justified if there is sense in the notion that art issues primarily from "inspiration" (which is not passive reception of a revelation) rather than from human artistry. It is justified if art is the work of Being, if art is accomplished primarily by the self-disclosure of Being, by the self-disclosure, in words, of the essence of things. Briefly, it is justified if Heidegger's notion of the history of Being makes sense. And that remains an open question.

Art and technology

Recall, for the sake of summary and transition, that we have been searching for Heideggerian, rather than Platonic, grounds for the declarations Heidegger makes concerning art: namely, that it brings the presence of the gods to radiance, it is submissive to the occurrence of truth, it discloses the essence, it brings forth the true, etc. These declarations all signify, in more straightforward terms, that art reveals Being, what it means to be in general. If we were to base ourselves on the theory of Ideas, we could say that the products of art, beautiful things, partake intimately of the luster of the Idea of beauty. Art would on that account enjoy a special relation to the divine realm of essences, the realm of Being. It could then be said that art brings forth, in beauty, the presence of the gods, etc. Now Heidegger might indeed speak in Platonic terms, but his grounds are his own: it is because art is fundamentally poetry that it discloses Being.

Poetry is the most sensitive use of language, the most proper speaking of words. Formulated more in accord with the later Heidegger, the poet is the most active *listener* to words, the most authentic *receiver* of that which is expressed in language. What do words say? What speaks in them? Words express the essence of things. The meaning of Being is revealed most properly in language. Poetry, the art of language, therefore has a privilege in the disclosure of what it means to be. In poetry, the speaking of Being is allowed its richest expression. But insofar as all the arts are fundamentally poetry, insofar as they all partake of the art of poetry, they all express what it means to be. Being speaks in all the arts—properly in poetry and improperly in the others. All the arts reveal something about the meaning of Being in general; all art is a disclosive looking upon the essence of things. These are the Heideggerian grounds for saying that art produces the presence of the gods. Art, as poetical, produces what is highest. Therefore art is the epitome of *poiesis*; art is the highest form of production, the highest form of *techne*. Art, according to Heidegger, is *techne* pure and simple.

Thus the question arises: what about technology itself? Heidegger has maintained all along that technology is a disclosive looking upon the essence of things in general. Technology is the understanding of what it means to be. Technology is not a mere human or practical affair. Is technology, in Heidegger's sense, then the same as art? How is art related to technology?

In the two antepenultimate paragraphs of the essay on technology, Heidegger takes up the relation between art and technology:

> . . . an essential determination of technology and a decisive confrontation with it must occur in a realm that, in relation to technol-

anti-Plato

ogy, is of a kindred essence on the one hand, and yet, on the other
hand, is of a fundamentally different essence.
    Such a realm is art . . . (FT, 36/35)

Thus art and technology are akin in essence and yet are radically different
in essence. What is the kinship, and what is the fundamental difference?

Heidegger had already mentioned the essential kinship and difference when he spoke of the danger and of what might save us from the
danger. The danger resides in the essence of modern technology; modern
technology threatens to collapse all disclosive looking into imposition.
Heidegger asserted, characteristically, that humans on their own could
never dispel this danger. But, he went on, "human reflection can ponder
the fact that whatever might save must be of a higher essence than what
is endangered, yet indeed of a kindred essence" (FT, 35/33–34). If disclosive looking is endangered, i.e., if disclosive looking is in danger of col-
lapsing into the impositional type, the type of modern technology, then
what might save is a disclosive looking of a higher kind. Since this higher
kind cannot be a mere human accomplishment, it will have to be *bestowed* on humans. That is what Heidegger immediately proceeded to express, in the form of a question: "Could there not perhaps be a more
primordially bestowed disclosive looking, one able to bring that which
might save into its first proper appearance in the midst of the danger?"
(FT, 35/34). Heidegger then launched the discussion of art, and it became
clear that he is proposing *art* as this "more primordially bestowed disclosive looking." We could say then that, in general, modern technology represents the danger, and art that which might save. For Heidegger, there
must be a kinship of essence between the danger and what might save,
though the latter must be of a higher essence. Therefore the fundamental
difference between art and technology is a determinate one: art is of a
higher essence. Art and technology are akin in essence, yet the former is
higher in essence. What does all that mean?

Let us first ask what art and technology have essentially in common. For Heidegger, it is this: in essence, art and technology are theories, comprehensive theories, ways of looking disclosively upon beings as
a whole. Art and technology are in essence ontological; they are disclo-
sures of what it means to be. They disclose the essential possibilities of
beings in general. They each have practical implications, since we can
make of beings only what we can envision as essentially possible about
them. Fundamentally, however, art and technology are theoretical. They
are realms in which Being reveals itself to us. In other words, technology
brings to appearance the presence of the gods, just as do poems, lore,
paintings, and the rest of art. That is how art and technology are of a
kindred essence: art, as well as technology, is an outlook on what it
means to be as such.

How are they essentially distinct? Heidegger does say that art is of a higher essence and is the more primordially bestowed disclosive looking. But he does not say how that is to be understood. Perhaps we could find art to be of a higher essence in this sense: although art and technology are indeed each fundamentally theoretical, art tarries at the level of theory, whereas technology immediately descends to the practical. Art would be higher in the sense of being, so to speak, more purely theoretical. Art is *emphatically* theoretical: in art, the theoretical side of the disclosive looking is emphasized; in technology, the practical side. Art is a looking upon beings merely for the sake of seeing, for the sake of knowing, rather than for accomplishing practical tasks.

Accordingly, the difference is not a matter of *what* each theory sees, as if Being revealed itself one way to the artistic outlook and another way to the technological one. Art and technology see the same, they bring to appearance the same gods; neither is superior in its understanding of what it means to be. Art is not higher in terms of content. Its content is not more ample or more profound or more true. On the contrary, the difference is merely that art holds up that content for us to contemplate, whereas technology immediately turns that content into useful things.

To take an admittedly hackneyed example, let us consider trees. What does the technological outlook see in trees? It sees disposables: lumber, cellulose, marketable fruit, a tourist attraction, etc. Technology then sets out to turn the trees into actual disposables. What does the poet see in trees? The poet does not see anything beyond or different from lumber and the rest. What then distinguishes a poem from a logging prospectus is that the poem purposely disregards the lumber and informs us simply that only God can make a tree. What the poem holds up to our view is the tree—however understood—in the mystery of its emergence into existence.

What is the difference between a geological survey of the Mt. Sainte-Victoire and Cézanne's paintings of it? The artist does not deny that the mountain is a coal lode or an ore depository. Cézanne purposely studied the geological content of the landscapes he wanted to paint, believing that the geological "anatomy" should be represented in every stroke of his brush. Yet what he is trying to express is not this anatomy: "What I am trying to render you is more mysterious. It is entangled in the very roots of Being, in the impalpable source of sensations."[6] In Merleau-Ponty's terms, Cézanne is trying to render the mountain *naissant*, being born, emerging from its roots in Being.[7] What is mysterious is not especially the mountain as coal lode but the mountain—however understood—as having emerged into existence at all. What the painting renders us is the mountain in the mysteriousness of its existence as such; the painting expresses the mystery that we see anything at all, the mystery

that the visible has emerged from its invisible source, the mystery that
there are beings at all, that Being holds sway in them.

Thus art, in relation to technology, does not present things under an
alternative essence, if "alternative" means different but on the same level.
In our epoch, art does not *replace* the understanding of things as disposables with some other understanding. That is what Heidegger means by
saying that art and technology are kindred in essence. At one level they
remain the same: each is a disclosive looking upon disposables, upon beings as they currently disclose themselves. The difference is that art and
technology do not remain at that level but proceed from it—in opposite
directions. Art, as it were, proceeds up and technology down. That is why
art is of a higher essence. Art proceeds from the disposables one step
further up, one step closer to the origin, rather than descending down
from the origin to the practical. Art relates the disposables up to Being
rather than down to our human needs and desires. Art presents these disposables to our contemplation—i.e., art calls on us to attend to the mystery of their existence as such. In art, the disposables are indeed presented
as there at our disposal, but as *mysteriously* there. Art—all art—presents
to us the mystery of the there, the mystery that anything is there at all,
that beings are beings. Thus art is, in a sense, more ontological than technology, since it relates beings up to Being rather than down to humans.
Art presents beings simply *as* beings; i.e., it presents to our contemplation
beings in relation to their mysterious source, beings in relation to Being.

We can adopt—or, rather, adapt—here Kant's famous determination of beauty, which he applies to the beauty of the work of art, as a presentation of "purposiveness without a purpose."[8] In Heideggerian terms,
both art and technology look disclosively upon disposables; i.e., they
both present beings in their practicality or purposiveness. Yet, in contradistinction to art, technology has an ulterior motive, a purpose, a practical objective. Technology observes purposiveness while armed with a
purpose, the purpose of satisfying efficiently some human need or desire.
Art, however, is a disclosive looking upon purposiveness for the mere
sake of contemplation, with no ulterior purpose. In art we merely *observe*
the purposiveness. The beautiful work of art presents the purposiveness,
the disposables, as simply there, as having emerged we know not whence,
as uncannily there.

Thus it happens that art shows us something nondisposable about
the disposables. The very existence of the disposables is not at our disposal. Their emergence into being is mysterious, wonderful, impalpable,
beyond us. That there are disposables and disposable resources at all is
not our work but the work of Being. The existence of beings is a gift to
us. That is to say, art presents the disposables as bestowed upon us.
Technology turns the disposables into practical gizmos and gadgets; art

displays the disposables as indeed essentially disposables but as, so to speak, *more* essentially bestowals. In Heideggerian terms, it is *correct* to say that beings are today disposables, but it would be more *truthful* to say that they are bestowals. Art is higher than technology because art presents the higher truth of the disposables, namely, that in coming forth as disposables they are bestowals.

In offering us a sense of beings as bestowed, art brings us to look upon Being as the bestower. That is what Heidegger is referring to when he wonders whether the arts "might awaken and found anew our vision of, and trust in, that which bestows." Our vision of that which bestows is simply our grasp of truth, our understanding of the self-disclosure of Being as in the lead over our own efforts at disclosive looking. As the bestower, Being enjoys a certain ascendancy over us humans, the ones who receive the bestowal. Accordingly, art reawakens trust; if we understand Being as the bestower, then the experience of trust again makes sense. Trust is always a matter of reliance on something that is in some way ascendant. Trust makes no sense in a domain of total self-reliance. To trust in the bestower is to understand our subordinate role in the disclosure of what it means to be. Art therefore does not serve as a paean to humanity. It is exactly the opposite; art manifests the hubris inherent in humanism, the hubris of claiming that humans are ascendant over all things.

On the other hand, the ascendancy of Being over us is not a matter of domination or imposition. Our subordinate role is not without dignity. Being also relies upon us—to be authentic followers. To that extent, we in turn enjoy a certain ascendancy over Being. Accordingly, the lead or ascendancy of Being is a subtle and nuanced one. It is not unilateral or impositional but poietic. The truth of the dialogue of divine and human destinies is *poiesis*. In the last analysis, then, art might save us because art brings home to us *poiesis*, the genuine alternative to the impositional attitude, which is the danger.

At least, this presentation of beings as bestowed is, for Heidegger, the highest possibility of art. This is what art is called upon to accomplish. This is inspired art. But will art be inspired? Will art succeed in bringing home to us the mystery of the existence of things? Will art display beings as uncannily there? According to Heidegger: "Whether this highest possibility of its essence may be bestowed on art in the midst of the extreme danger, no one can tell" (FT, 36/35). Heidegger expresses himself very precisely here: it is a question of whether this possibility will be *bestowed* on art. In other words, it is primarily in the hands of Being, in the hands of the inspiring gods. That is why, ultimately only a god can save us. We humans shall have to wait. But we must wait in the manner appropriate to the receiving of a bestowal: we must wait with all our might. That means poets and other artists will never be inspired if they are passive; they must prepare themselves by working at their craft with all the skill and creativity they can muster. Indeed, we all have a role to play in preparing a place for the fullest possible self-disclosure of Being. All of us are at least called upon to be open to and respect what is revealed in art and poetry. We are all called upon to approach art in terms of truth, in terms of the relation between divine and human destinies, and not in terms of aesthetics. Art is that which might save, "always provided that our approach to art is not sealed off from the constellation of truth . . ." (FT, 36/35).

Questioning

The final two paragraphs of "Die Frage nach der Technik" form a kind of epilogue. In good rhetorical fashion, Heidegger ends his speech by returning to the beginning. He turns back to the topic of the first two sentences of the speech, namely, questioning. Indeed, this topic had already been announced prior to those opening sentences, in the very first word of the title.

The epilogue then deals with questioning and concludes with the declaration that "questioning is the piety of thought" (FT, 36/35). Heidegger had already indicated in what sense he takes piety; it means to be submissive, submissive to the occurrence of truth. But *all* thinking, or at least all serious thinking, needs to be submissive to the truth. All philosophical thinking must be submissive to truth. Otherwise, thinking is not in accord with its own essence. Submission to truth is what makes thought genuine thought. Thus Heidegger is saying that questioning is that by which thought is thought. Questioning is simply thought submitting itself to truth. But what is the truth? The truth is the ascendancy of the self-disclosure of Being over our disclosive looking. To be submissive to this ascendancy is to acknowledge one's proper role as authentic follower. That is what constitutes questioning for Heidegger. Questioning is submissive thinking rather than impositional or dictatorial thinking.

Questioning is therefore not simply a matter of posing questions, for questions can be captious, as are the questions the scientist poses to nature. Science is research, a posing of questions, but is very far from piety. Questioning, in Heidegger's sense, is docile thinking, or, to put it better, docile thinking is what Heidegger means by questioning. Docility, of course, is a nuanced concept and has to be understood in the sense that applies, for instance, to good students. A docile student is teachable, which indeed means able to be led. But it does not mean able to be led passively, willing to accept uncritically every word from the mouth of the teacher. An uncritical student is repugnant to a genuine teacher.

Docility, however, does entail openness to another's standpoint; it means not to be hardened, not to have a closed mind. If the uncritical student is a child, the hardened student is an adolescent. Docility, questioning in the most proper sense, is adult thinking, mature thinking. Questioning is equivalent to the most genuine thinking, which is philosophy. This thinking is not passive or effortless; indeed it asks the most penetrating questions. In that sense it is authentic. On the other hand, it is not hardened and restricted to the thinker's own standpoint; it is not immured within the human standpoint. In that sense, it is a following. To what, then, *in concreto*, is it attuned? To what is it open?

Presumably, an authentic questioning has taken place in the course of "Die Frage nach der Technik." Very few actual questions have been formulated, but, instead, what has occurred is a thinking about the essence of technology as distinct from technological things. Instead of being enthralled by technological things, Heidegger has inquired into the essence. Rather than looking at technology from the human standpoint, from the standpoint of how technology is related to human concerns, whether by solving them or exacerbating them, Heidegger has inquired from a viewpoint that transcends the human, from the viewpoint of the history of Being. Heidegger's questioning of technology amounts to a thinking about the truth of technology. Heidegger has attempted to be submissive to the occurrence of truth, submissive to the ascendancy of the self-disclosure of Being. Indeed, that is precisely what has been determined regarding the essence of technology: technology is essentially a disclosive looking upon beings as such, in *response* to the way Being addresses itself to humans.

The questioning of art in the essay on technology amounts equally to an inquiry into the essence. It is a thinking about the essence of art rather than a consideration of art from a human standpoint, from the standpoint of aesthetics. Heidegger has attempted to be submissive to the truth of art, i.e., to art not as a paean to humanity but as a mode of the self-disclosure of Being.

Therefore "Die Frage nach der Technik" is a questioning in the precise sense that it is a thinking which is attuned to the essence. Thinking about the essence *is* what Heidegger means by questioning. He is not referring to the posing of questions in the usual sense. Questioning is for him a thinking that springs from an attitude of piety, i.e., from submissiveness to something recognized as ascendant over the questioner. The only genuine question, the only question to which we do not already know the answer, is the one posed to something ascendant. That which is ascendant over humanity is Being, the truth, the essence. Accordingly, the epilogue begins with the connection between questioning and the essence: "Therefore it is in questioning that we bear witness to the predicament that in our sheer preoccupation with [the things of] technology we do not yet experience the essence of technology, that in our sheer aesthetic-mindedness we no longer heed the essence of art" (FT, 36/35).

It is in *questioning* that we distinguish the essence of technology from technological things, the essence of art from the human view of art. If we understand questioning as submissive thinking, thinking about the essence, then we can make sense of the rest of the epilogue. It continues:

> Yet the more we question and bring ourselves to think upon the essence of technology, the more the essence of art becomes full of mystery.
>
> The closer we draw to the danger, the more brightly do the ways into what might save begin to shine, and all the more questioning do we become. (FT, 36/35)

These two statements express the exact same idea. The first one says that the more we question, which means the more we think about the essence of technology, then the more we are able to see the mystery in the essence of art. The mystery of this essence is that art can disclose the mystery of things, their mysterious emergence into existence, their uncanny givenness, their being bestowed on us. Thus, questioning about the essence of technology, which is equivalent to thinking about the ascendancy of the self-disclosure of Being over our own efforts at disclosive looking, makes art more disclosive of the exact same mystery, the mystery of bestowal in which Being is the bestower, things are bestowals, and we ourselves are the bestowed upon. Questioning, or thinking, attunes us to art, and art, reciprocally, discloses just what we tried to think about.

The second sentence just quoted speaks of our drawing close to the danger. For Heidegger, the danger lies not in the hazards of technological things but in the essence of modern technology, in the impositional outlook. Our closer approach to the danger is not our more complete adoption of this outlook but our *recognition* of it as the essence of technology. Our drawing close to the danger is precisely our questioning or thinking about the danger, about the essence of technology. Therefore the second sentence says the same as the first. It says that the more we question technology, i.e., the more we think about its dangerous essence, the more we are able to come into that which might save. That which might save is art, so what Heidegger is asserting is that the more we question or think, the brighter does art shine. The closer we draw to imposition in thought, the more art can disclose what might save us from imposition, namely, the attitude of *poiesis*, the attitude that recognizes the ascendancy of Being over us and points the way to our proper role as authentic followers. Furthermore, Heidegger goes on to say, the more art brings *poiesis* home to us, the more questioning we become. This means that art reciprocates: as art becomes more disclosive, the clearer we are able to *think* about the essence, think about Being, think philosophically.

Therefore, Heidegger's conclusion is the intertwining of thinking and art, the intertwining of philosophy and poetry. They both disclose the same truth, the truth of Being as the bestower, and they derive from each other their disclosive power. What might save us from the danger of technology is then not simply art; it is art and philosophy intertwined. Neither is more original, neither is *the* more primordially bestowed disclosive looking; they are equiprimordial.

On the one hand, Heidegger has claimed that philosophy is a precondition for art to constitute a saving realm: "Such a realm is art—always provided that our approach to art is not sealed off from the constellation of truth, concerning which we are *questioning*" (FT, 36/35). *Provided* our approach to art is informed by our questioning, by our thinking, then art might serve to save us.

Thus it might seem that philosophy is foundational, but Heidegger also speaks of art as founding, for example when he calls upon art to "found anew our vision of, and trust in, that which bestows." Here art is the foundational disclosure; it founds our vision of Being as the bestower. Elsewhere, Heidegger even calls thinking or philosophy a scion of poetry, an offshoot of art.

Let us leave the last word on this issue, the relation between art and philosophy, to a poet, namely to Heidegger as a poet. Heidegger did publish a slim volume of his own poetry—in 1954, the year of publication of the essay on technology. He entitled the volume *Out of the Experience of Thinking*. The title refers to the book, the poems, as arising out of the experience of thinking. Thus the title indicates that poetry arises out of thinking, out of philosophy. Yet the poems themselves say that thinking arises out of poetry:

> Singing and thinking are neighboring stems, scions of poetry.
> They grow out of Being and stretch up into its truth.
> Their relation gives us pause and we think of what
> Hölderlin has sung of the trees of the forest:
> "And the neighboring trunks of the trees,
> All the while that they stand,
> Remain to each other unknown." (*AE*, 25/13)

Perhaps Heidegger then is ending "Die Frage nach der Technik" with a plea for a poetry and a philosophy that do not remain unknown to each other, with a plea for a synthetic unity of poetry and philosophy as mutually fulfilling, with a plea for what his poem calls "poetic thinking":

Veiled over still is the poetic nature of thinking.
Where it does appear, it is for a long time taken to be the
    Utopia of a half-poetic mind.
But in truth poetic thinking is not Utopia but topology, the
    topology of Being.
It discloses the place where Being has its essence. (*AE*, 23/12)

We are left to wonder what sort of practical effects, what sort of making and doing, what sort of technological things, would be set upon this topology—i.e., set on their way by a poetic thinking in which Being comes into its essence as the bestower.

Part V

Detachment

Let us now respectfully detach ourselves from "Die Frage nach der Technik." That is, let us attempt to move beyond the essay, specifically by way of a sympathetic response to it. The essay is open-ended; it issues in an invitation and needs to be carried on. What it leaves open, basically, is practice. The essay is theoretical, it provides a diagnosis, but it leaves open the practical therapy. If we accept Heidegger's diagnosis, namely, that the impositional attitude of modern technology is a threat—indeed today's greatest threat—to human freedom and dignity, then what practical steps can we take to ward off that threat?

Heidegger did offer a hopeful prognosis and did prescribe a remedy in very general terms: "We are summoned to hope in the growing light of that which might save. How can this growth happen? By our fostering it, by our fostering, here and now and in little things, the growth of that which might save" (FT, 34/33).

In general, the antidote to the impositional attitude is the one of fostering or abetting. But what exactly should we do if we wish to take up this attitude, and what should be the object of our fostering? What can we do "here and now"? What "little things" is Heidegger referring to? Are there any little things? All things today are disposables. What should we do with these things? What should be our attitude toward technological things? Most generally, how are we to live in the technological age and yet not fall victim to the technological outlook? How can we become free of imposition? Should we oppose technology, curse it, and attempt to smash it, in the manner of the Luddites? Should we perhaps offer passive resistance, benign neglect? Or, should we fully enter into the technological world and attempt to reform it from within?

213

Contemplation; Detachment (Gelassenheit)

Let us approach these questions by taking guidance from Heidegger himself. In another of his works on technology, Heidegger did propose a practical remedy to the danger. This work was a lecture delivered exactly two years after "Die Frage nach der Technik." The occasion was a public gathering to commemorate a musical artist from Heidegger's native district in Germany. Thus, in contrast to the setting of the earlier lecture, the audience was not composed of the most eminent philosophers and scientists of the day but instead consisted of average, everyday people, such as ourselves. Heidegger's speech on this occasion was appropriately simple and practical. It was a plea for all humans to do something here and now and in regard to little things or, as Heidegger reformulates it, "here and now and on the most inconspicuous occasions" (*G*, 21/53).

What Heidegger advocates that we do is think. That, most basically, is the antidote Heidegger proposes, and it is an antidote, he emphasizes, open to all human beings. Of course, Heidegger is not referring to just any sort of thinking. In the first place, he does not even mean thinking in the sense of a special mental activity. He is referring to an attitude toward things as a whole, a general way of being in the world. Heidegger names this therapeutic attitude "detachment," *die Gelassenheit*. That is Heidegger's prescription of the attitude toward modern technology that might serve to hasten the advent and foster the growth of that which might save.

His term *Gelassenheit* is borrowed from the German religious mysticism of an earlier age, where it meant to "let go" of the things of the world and cling to the things of God. Heidegger means it in a nonmystical and very nuanced sense. If still put in religious terms, detachment would mean to be *in* the (technological) world but not *of* that world, there in body but not in spirit, availing oneself of technological things but bestowing one's heart and soul elsewhere. Thus it involves being in the technological world and yet simultaneously withdrawing from it. Detachment (*Ge-lassen-heit*, from *lassen*, "to let") means letting things go, letting the things of technology go. But it is absolutely essential that this "letting go" be understood in a double sense: it means both to let go of technological things and also to let them go on. For Heidegger, detachment is an attitude that both says "no" to technology (lets go of it) and also says "yes" to it (lets technology go on).

Detachment might at first seem overly passive. It might not appear to be an attitude of active receptivity or nurturing. It might seem far removed from the attitude of abetting or midwifery. We therefore need to take a closer look at *Gelassenheit* and understand it as Heidegger presents it, namely, in terms of a distinction between two ways of thinking.

The commemorative speech in which Heidegger introduced the concept of detachment bore that name as its title; i.e., Heidegger entitled the speech *Gelassenheit*. It was published as the first part of a very small book that was itself entitled *Gelassenheit*. The other part is a dialogue[1] Heidegger composed and called "Discussion of *Gelassenheit*." Thus the book seems to be unitary and indeed single-minded: it is about nothing but detachment. Nevertheless, for the most part Heidegger is occupied here with a distinction between two ways of thinking. Detachment itself is surprisingly seldom mentioned. Presumably, that is why the title of the published English translation of the book is *Discourse on Thinking*. The translator gave the speech the name "Memorial Address," and the dialogue is called "Conversation on a Country Path about Thinking."[2] These English titles obviously call attention to the theme of thinking, but they misplace Heidegger's own focus on the attitude embodied in the thinking (embodied in one particular form of thinking), namely, the attitude of *Gelassenheit*, detachment from technological things.

In his speech on *Gelassenheit*, Heidegger distinguishes between calculative and contemplative thinking. Those are the two ways of thought. The former is in play whenever we "plan, research, organize, operate" (*G*, 12/46). This thinking is interested in results, and it views things as means to an end. Accordingly, what Heidegger calls calculative thinking is simply our everyday practical attitude toward things. Contemplative thinking, on the other hand, is detached from ordinary practical interests.

Calculative thinking, according to Heidegger, is not necessarily computational. It does not require calculators or computers. It is not necessarily scientific or sophisticated. It should then be understood precisely in the sense in which we call a person "calculating." We do not mean such a person is gifted in mathematics. We mean he is designing; he uses others—to further his own self-interest. A calculating person is not sincere. There is an ulterior motive, a selfish purpose, behind all his relations. He is engaged with others only for what he can get out of them. Heidegger's referral of this thinking to "operating" also allows us to call it operational thinking, in the sense in which we call a scheming person an operator.

Calculative thinking is therefore not so much a way of thinking, understood as reasoning or deliberating, but is rather a general outlook on things. It is the attitude that beings are there simply for what we can get out of them, that the world is there for us to exploit. In other words, what Heidegger here calls calculative thinking is precisely the attitude of modern technology, the impositional attitude. Calculative thinking amounts to an *attack* on things and sees in the world, as Heidegger now says, one gigantic filling station. It is our contemporary attitude, by which we approach the things of nature with our gas-guzzling self-interest and say,

"Fill 'er up." Calculative thinking is the way of disclosive looking Heidegger had earlier called challenging. It sees all things as there to be ravished and motivates their actual ravishment.

Today there is no dearth of thinking, in the sense of calculative thinking. Indeed there has never been so much thought, so much planning, research, problem-solving. People have never been so calculating. Yet, for Heidegger, ours is an age of thoughtlessness, if thinking is taken in the genuine and most proper sense, the sense in which it is what is most proper to humans. The most proper thinking is what Heidegger calls contemplation. For Heidegger, humans are by essence contemplative, and it is precisely that essence which is under threat in the age of technology.

For the most part, Heidegger characterizes contemplative thinking obliquely as an attending to what is closest. Heidegger also indicates that contemplation heeds the meaning of things, the essence of things. It does not have a practical interest, it does not view things as means to an end, but instead dwells on things for the sake of disclosing that which makes them be what they are. Contemplation is therefore not practical but theoretical.

What does contemplation attend to? That is to say, what is closest, closer to us than beings? For Heidegger, what is even closer, though ordinarily overlooked in favor of what is next closest, is Being. Being ordinarily withdraws in favor of beings. But Being must be closest, first known, because it is only in the light of Being, only in the clearing, only in terms of an understanding of what it means to be in general, that we can relate to beings as beings at all. Therefore what Heidegger calls contemplative thinking is an attending to Being. It is the most general theory, the disclosive looking upon what it means to be as such. It is thus paying heed, as Heidegger says, to the meaning of things, to the essence of beings precisely as beings, to that which makes them be beings at all.

The term "contemplation" captures Heidegger's intention especially well, since con-templation is what is carried out in a temple, namely a communing with the divine, a raising of the sight to the gods, a gazing into the realm of Being. In particular, the temple is a special place set aside to observe auguries. An augury is an omen, a being which bears a divine message, a being through which the gods speak to us, a being in which we can observe Being. Contemplation, as an observing of beings just insofar as they exist at all, is an attending to that which makes a being a being, the essence of beings as such, namely, Being. To contemplate is to take a being as an augury.

Heidegger emphasizes that contemplation does not require something extraordinary or "high above" on which to focus. It can occur on any inconspicuous occasion. It can take place with regard to the most unpretentious being. We can begin wherever we find ourselves, with what now appears closest, i.e., anywhere amid beings. What is essential to contemplation is the attempt to see what makes the being a being at all, the attempt to see its essence as a being, to see what it manifests about Being. What is essential to contemplation is the passage from the being to Being. We can focus on any given being; what counts is not the particular being but the way of focusing, namely the way that takes the being simply as such, simply insofar as it manifests what it means to be rather than insofar as it may serve our purposes.

Contemplation is therefore not reserved for specialists. Heidegger stresses that it is open, *pro tanto*, to all people. The reason would be that contemplation is simply a matter of making explicit that which is available to every Dasein. Contemplation is making explicit precisely that which makes Dasein Dasein in the first place, namely an understanding of what it means to be.

Contemplation is thus essential to humans. Humans, for Heidegger, are by essence thinking—i.e., contemplative—beings. To say that humans are contemplative is equivalent to saying that humans are instances of Dasein—beings to whom the meaning of Being is disclosed. The danger in the age of modern technology is precisely a threat to this essence of humans. The greatest danger, as Heidegger stresses again in his speech on *Gelassenheit*, is not that technological things, such as atom bombs, might get out of hand and destroy human life. Something more tragic is imminent, namely that calculative thinking, the impositional attitude, might depose contemplation. Calculation might commandeer the entire field of thinking, might be reputed the only valid mode of thinking. And then:

> What great danger would then be impending? Then the highest and most fertile acumen in calculative planning and invention might be accompanied by indifference toward contemplation, total thoughtlessness in the genuine sense. And then? Then man would have renounced and cast off what is most proper to him, namely that he is a contemplative being. Therefore what is at issue is the saving of the essence of man. That is why it matters to keep contemplation alive. (G, 25/56)

Contemplation is paying heed to Being; it is theory. It is not concerned with solving everyday practical problems by manipulating beings in ingenious ways. Contemplation is sincere; it does not look upon beings in terms of our own interests but instead seeks the meaning, the essence, of beings. But contemplation must then also be practical, since our understanding of Being, of the essential possibilities of beings, determines what we can make of beings and determines our role in the activity of making. Indeed, for Heidegger, contemplation is of the utmost practical use, since it may bring forth genuinely "lasting human works" (G, 26/57), in contrast to the disposables produced by calculative thinking.

Openness to the mystery, autochthony, lasting human works

Heidegger's speech on *Gelassenheit* shows—or at least suggests—
how contemplation might bear such fruit, and that is the real contribution of the speech to the practical problem of living genuinely human lives
in the technological age. The connection between contemplation and lasting human works is, of course, not an immediate one. Heidegger introduces a number of mediating terms. Contemplative thinking leads to the
attitude of detachment, and these two in turn produce what Heidegger
calls "openness to the mystery" and "autochthony." And lasting works
are autochthonous ones. So we now need to see how Heidegger knits all
these together. That is, in order to see how contemplation may lead to
lasting human works, we need to see how the following are unified:

> Contemplation
> Detachment
> Openness to the mystery
> Autochthony
> Lasting human works.

Most basically, all these phenomena are unified by reference to Being.
That is to say, they all arise from our paying heed to Being over and against
beings. It would be closer to the truth to say these are all *accomplished* by
Being, produced primarily by the self-disclosure of what it means to be.
They will come about if Being offers its true face to us and if we have prepared ourselves to be authentic receivers. They all derive from our consent
to be authentic followers, provided Being wholeheartedly leads.

Let us begin by asking how and in what sense contemplation de-
taches us from technological things. In general, for Heidegger, if we attend to Being, then technological beings will lose significance. They will
no longer seem absolute but, instead, relative and dependent. They will
thereby cease to enthrall us. That is Heidegger's general argument regarding *how* contemplation motivates the attitude of detachment, which
argument he couches here for the most part in terms of claims.

Technological things make a claim on us, an exclusive claim. Technological things do not present themselves in a reticent way or even in a
neutral way. They are insistent; they work upon us insidiously, and re-
lentlessly, until they make a claim that excludes all other claims. That is
to say, technology fascinates us and claims our undivided attention. In
other terms, calculation claims to be the only valid mode of thinking. It is
the *exclusive* claim that is dangerous, for it threatens us with bondage. To
ward off the danger, according to Heidegger, we must be attuned to
Being, to the meaning of technological things. Then we might see that

these things do not concern "what is most central and proper to us"; they are "nothing absolute" but depend on "something higher." We can then be free of technology—i.e., detached from bondage to it.

Admittedly, Heidegger is offering here little more than a suggestion as to how contemplation may allow us to see through the meretricious attraction of technological things. His point is that contemplation allows us to put technology into perspective, to relativize technological things, by opening up an even higher realm, the one of Being. What Heidegger is suggesting is that contemplation allows us to put technological things in their place, which amounts to detachment from them. Putting them in their place must indeed be understood in the sense of demoting them, dismissing them from the highest place. But it also means to put technological things in their proper place; i.e., it involves the recognition that they do have a legitimate place. Contemplation relativizes beings with respect to something "higher," Being, but does not render beings insignificant. While Heidegger is perhaps not as clear as we might wish concerning the motivating force of contemplation, the sense of the ensuing detachment is made very plain. In particular, Heidegger stresses that a detached attitude toward technological things is not rigid and extreme but is in fact nuanced and balanced. Heidegger is not opposed to technology as such; he is against bondage to technology:

> For all of us, for some to a greater and some to a lesser extent, the contrivances, apparatuses, and machines of the technological world are indispensable. It would be silly to rail blindly against technology. It would be shortsighted to condemn the technological world as the work of the devil. We depend on technological objects; they even challenge us to ever greater improvements. Nevertheless, we may unwittingly become so firmly shackled to technological objects that we end up their slaves. (G, 22/53–54)

If we recognize that technological things do not touch our essence, they can then be left to run their course on their own. Thus we may indeed use them without falling victim to them, and we may use them precisely as they were designed to be used. Heidegger is not opposed to the use of technological things, nor does he advocate that we should use them with reservations or in some idiosyncratic way. We can use technological gadgets unreluctantly and still be free of them. We will not fall into bondage to them as long as we deny them an exclusive claim:

> We can use technological objects, and even use them just as they were devised to be used, and yet we can thereby remain free of them, so that at the same time we let go of them. We can let the technological objects take their course as things that do not concern us in

what is most central and proper to us. We can say "yes" to the in-
eluctable use of technological objects and can at the same time say
"no" to them, insofar as we refuse to allow them to claim us exclusively and thereby warp, muddle, and, ultimately, lay waste our
essence. (G, 22–23/54)

Thus detachment is not a withdrawal from the technological world,
any more than detachment was for the mystics a flight or escape from the
world. Detachment is not the denial of the validity of the claim stemming
from worldly things; it is simply the denial of the exclusivity of that claim.
It is the recognition that there is a higher claim. Detachment for Heidegger amounts to leaving technological things outside the highest realm,
outside the realm of what gives meaning. Detachment is the recognition
that technology is not self-sufficient or exclusive but is dependent on
something else for its meaning:

> Yet if in this way we simultaneously say "yes" and "no" to
> technological objects, will not our relation to the technological world
> then become ambiguous and unsure? Quite to the contrary. Our re-
> lation to the technological world will become wonderfully simple
> and serene. We will let technological objects into our daily world and
> at the same time leave them outside; i.e., we will let them take their
> course as things that are nothing absolute but are instead always de-
> pendent on something higher. I would use an old term to name this
> attitude of a simultaneous "yes" and "no" to the technological
> world: *detachment in relation to things.* (G, 23/54)

What is the higher realm, the higher claim? That is, to what are we
*at*tached if we are *de*tached from technology? The mystics clung to God,
which is for Heidegger a closed possibility. Yet according to Heidegger
we do adhere to something mysterious in the attitude of contemplation or
detachment:

> In all technological processes there holds sway a meaning, one which
> claims human actions and omissions, a meaning man has not on his
> own invented or made. We do not know the actual meaning of the
> uncannily increasing dominance of atomic technology. *The meaning
> of the technological world conceals itself.* But if we now explicitly
> and constantly attend to the fact that a concealed meaning touches us
> everywhere in the technological world, then we are ipso facto stand-
> ing in the realm of that which conceals itself from us and indeed con-
> ceals itself precisely in approaching us. (G, 23–24/55)

It is a mystery how something may offer itself and withdraw while
doing so, be closest and furthest, most evident and most easily over-

looked, first known and only last known. Yet this is precisely how Being offers itself, and therefore *the* mystery is Being. Contemplation, paying heed to Being, thus amounts to an openness for the mystery. Accordingly, the passage just quoted continues: "To show itself in this way, while at the same time withdrawing, is the fundamental characteristic of what we call the mystery. I name that attitude in virtue of which we hold ourselves open to the concealed meaning in the technological world: openness to the mystery" (G, 24/55).

*D*etachment, as openness to the mystery, is *at*tachment to Being. Contemplation, detachment, and openness to the mystery are therefore one and the same. They all mean to attend to Being rather than be enthralled by technological things. They are names for the most basic human disclosive looking, the looking at what it means to be in general, which is a response to the way Being looks at us. As a response, contemplation is not primarily a human accomplishment; it does not occur by our unaided efforts at looking. Contemplation depends primarily on how wholeheartedly Being looks at us. On the other hand, of course, contemplation, detachment, and openness to the mystery do not occur without our extreme efforts: "Detachment in relation to things and openness to the mystery never ac-cede to us on their own. They are not ac-cidental. Both flourish only by means of unrelenting, courageous thinking" (G, 25/56).

Primarily, however, to attend upon Being requires that Being take the initiative and attend to us, disclose itself to us. Contemplation is primarily a matter of waiting, active waiting: "Contemplation must wait, as the farmer waits to see whether the seed will come up and ripen" (G, 13/47).

Contemplation, detachment, and openness to the mystery are accomplished primarily by Being. As human attitudes, they amount to an active *receiving* of the self-disclosure of what it means to be. They must await—i.e., actively prepare for—a wholehearted approach to mankind on the part of Being. If the self-disclosure of Being is ample enough, and if humans have prepared a place for this self-disclosure with sufficiently unrelenting courage, then the partnership between Being and mankind may yield the truth. That is to say, we might then understand the truth of Being, namely, that Being is the bestower and that we have a secondary, though dignified, role to play as the required receiver. Thereby we might become autochthonous and bear true fruit: "Detachment in relation to things and openness to the mystery give us the prospect of a new autochthony" (G, 24/55).

Autochthony is indigenousness; it means to be rooted in one's home ground. According to Heidegger, there is only one way for humans to be autochthonous, there is only one home ground for all

humans. That home ground is Being. To be autochthonous is to attend
to Being. Therefore autochthony is one with contemplation, detachment, and openness to the mystery. They all mean exactly the same
thing: to heed Being or, putting it more truthfully, to receive actively
the wholehearted self-disclosure of Being. Humans will not be autochthonous again until Being reapproaches them and they become authentic receivers. The *new* autochthony Heidegger speaks of is
therefore a return to the old epoch in the history of Being, an age in
which mankind was autochthonous.

Autochthony is equivalent to Heidegger's concept of dwelling in the
homeland (*die Heimat*). The authentic homeland for humans is not a certain country or other, not Germany, not Greece, but is instead a matter of
attending to Being.[3] Its main requirement is that Being disclose itself to
us. Today, in the second epoch of history, we are uprooted, our autochthony is threatened. This is not the case simply because so many people relocate from their native places to big cities. As Heidegger points out,
those who remain in their native places, in a physical sense, may be just
as uprooted, just as homeless, as those who have been transplanted
(*G*, 15/48). That is because to be close to home, to be on one's home
ground, to be autochthonous, is not a matter of physical location. It is a
matter of what we heed. What do we heed today? What is closest to us?
In Heidegger's words, what is closest now is: "all that with which modern technological instruments of communication hourly stimulate, assail,
and obsess man" (*G*, 15/48).

Closest to us now are beings, technological beings such as television
sets, the artificial worlds they present, and the disposables they advertise.
Technological things are not only closest; they are exclusively close. As
Heidegger says, they obsess (*umtreiben*) us. They besiege us from *all* sides
(*um-treiben*). They monopolize our attention. How can they do so? Why
can we not detach ourselves from them? Why are we unable to contemplate Being? Why is calculation threatening to commandeer the entire
field of thinking? For Heidegger, our lack of autochthony is not primarily our doing, or our omission, but is motivated by the current history of
Being: "The loss of autochthony is not simply caused by external circumstance and fortune, nor does it derive from negligence or from the superficiality of man's way of life. The loss of autochthony stems from the
spirit of the age" (*G*, 16/49).

The spirit of our age is fundamentally constituted by the reticent
self-showing of Being. It is on account of that reticence that we produce
disposables instead of lasting works. It is why we do not bear genuine,
mature fruit. Heidegger expresses this reason by quoting a poet: "We are
plants which must rise up from roots in the earth in order to bloom in the
ether and bear fruit" (*G*, 14/47).

According to Heidegger, "earth" here means "home soil." Thus the poet is saying that to bear fruit, to produce genuinely lasting works, to be mature human beings, we must not only be rooted but must be rooted in our native place, in our home ground. Home is our first dwelling place. Home is what was first close to us, first disclosed to us. That is Being. An understanding of what it means to be is still closest to us, though we usually overlook it and take it for granted in favor of our relations to what is next closest, namely, beings, disposables. To be rooted in our home soil, to dwell in our homeland, means to let beings go (in the double sense) and pay explicit heed to Being. This in turn requires that Being look at us intently, unveil its face to us. It requires that Being show itself in beings or, otherwise put, that beings become transparent and not, as they are for calculative thinking, opaque. For calculation, beings are the end-point; for contemplation, merely an augury. In contemplation, we see *through* beings, see Being through them. Indeed, for Heidegger, beings are the only path to Being. We mortals have no direct access to Being. But it is one thing to take beings as revealing Being and another thing to look upon beings as merely there to satisfy our self-interest. The first way is sincere, the other calculating. The sincere way is what Heidegger calls contemplation or detachment.

To be autochthonous is to be explicitly ontological. For Heidegger, if our ontology, our theory, is sound—i.e., if the truth is offered us, and if we have prepared ourselves to receive it—then a distinctive sort of practice will follow. Specifically, if we stand in the truth of Being our practice will then be genuine; i.e., we might bloom in the ether and bear fruit. How so?

First of all, what is it to pay heed to Being, to grasp the truth? Most basically, for Heidegger, it is to recognize Being as the leader and ourselves as followers. Disposables are produced by humans insofar as they take up the opposite attitude, i.e., insofar as they consider themselves lords of the earth. Human creativity, genius, produces disposables. In Heidegger's view, genuinely lasting works are those generated by Being: e.g., those nature would bring forth. Humans, of course, have a necessary role to play in this generation, and that role is an honorable one, but it is merely the role of the midwife. Human works are therefore autochthonous when they are precisely not autonomous. Human works become genuinely lasting fruits when they are rooted in home soil, in Being, and are thrust up by that soil. Human works are at their height when they are not so much works of humans, as they are works of Being. Humans are therefore at their height when they play the role of authentic followers, which amounts to abetting rather than imposing. That, at least implicitly, is how Heidegger concludes his speech on *Gelassenheit*: "If detachment in relation to things and openness to the mystery are roused up in us, then we will be brought on the way to a new ground and soil. If our producing strikes new roots in this soil, we might bring forth lasting works" (G, 26/56–57).

Contemplation, detachment, openness to the mystery, and autochthony must precisely be roused up if they are to occur at all. They cannot arise out of sheer willpower. They must be roused up by Being, by a new wholehearted self-disclosure of what it means to be. They must be bestowed by Being. Being is their genuine ground, though, of course, the bestowal also depends on our capacity to receive it. If contemplation is roused up by the self-offering of Being, then what is offered to our contemplation is precisely Being, the truth of Being; and this truth concerns the role of Being as that which does the rousing. In other words, contemplation, as a grasp of the truth, is the explicit understanding of Being as the ground of contemplation, as that which motivates the contemplation by means of its own self-disclosure. That is why Heidegger says that if contemplation and the rest are roused up, we will be led to a new ground. That new ground is actually the oldest ground, Being. To be led to this ground means to heed Being as the ultimate ground. It means, in general, to recognize Being as the bestower.

Heidegger then hopes our producing will strike roots in this ground. How is our productive activity to be rooted in Being rather than in ourselves, in our human creativity? Presumably, there is only one way: by our taking up the role of midwives or nurturers. If we pay heed to Being as the bestower, then we must necessarily recognize ourselves as the bestowed upon; and the proper role of the receiver of a bestowal is authentic following, active receptivity, abetting. For Heidegger, therefore, it is by accepting this authentically human role of nurturing that we might bring forth lasting works.

The connection we spoke of earlier in our discussion of Heidegger's speech on *Gelassenheit*, the connection between contemplative thinking and genuinely lasting human works, is thereby complete. Heidegger indeed presents it as a mediate connection. Contemplation leads to detachment from beings, which leads to attachment to the mystery, which in turn makes possible autochthony or rootedness in home soil. And autochthonous works, those we *nurture* into existence, are the genuinely lasting human works. Yet the mediating phenomena Heidegger introduces are in fact one with contemplative thinking. These attitudes do not "lead" to each other in the sense of something engendering something else. They are merely different implications of recognizing the one truth of Being, and that recognition by itself motivates a genuine human practice or at least shows us the secure path to such a practice.

In Heidegger's writings, the phrase "truth of Being" refers to the relationship between the self-disclosure of Being and the disclosive efforts of humans. The truth of Being is that the former has the lead over the latter. That is why Heidegger can designate the turn in his philosophy, the turn back from metaphysical to premetaphysical thinking, the turn from the ascendancy of humans over Being to the predominance of Being over humans, as a turn from Being to the truth of Being. That is to say, the turn in Heidegger's philosophy is one from Being as the object of an unveiling *accomplished by humans* to Being as the subject of the unveiling, as *self-unveiling*. For Heidegger, the truth of Being is that Being has a history, that Being unveils or hides *itself*, that Being is in the lead, that Being is the bestower.

Truth, for Heidegger, *is* the self-revelation of Being. This truth is the ground of all other possible truths, all those that have to with beings. Truth is the self-bestowal of the meaning of Being onto humans. In other words, reverting back to Parmenides, truth is a goddess, one that takes thinkers by the hand and *leads* them. The changes in this leading by the hand on the part of a goddess, i.e., the changes over time in the self-offering of Being, in the self-bestowal of truth, are *the* events of history, the genuinely autonomous events. That is a key to making sense of Heidegger's most famous writing on the event, his *Beiträge zur Philosophie (Vom Ereignis)* [*Contributions to Philosophy (On the Event)*]. For example, he there asks explicitly what the question of truth is "all about." He answers that it is not about a modification of the concept of truth or about a more original insight into the essence of truth. Instead, it is

> about the daring view that truth itself is autonomous [*die Wesung der Wahrheit*]. . . .
> And therefore it is in the first place about dignifying and empowering Being itself as the realm of *the* original event. (*BP*, 338/237)

Event for Heidegger means genuinely original event, that which motivates all "history" (= human chronicle) in the usual sense. *The* event is an occurrence in the history of Being. Heidegger is saying here that the question of the truth of Being is all about recognizing that Being has a history, that Being has the predominance. In other words, it is about recognizing that Being is empowered, that Being appropriates humans and not vice versa, which is precisely what Heidegger's turn is all about. Accordingly, the passage just quoted from *Contributions* concludes that the question of truth is also about the secondary—though essentially required—role of humans as Dasein, as the abetter of the self-offering of what it means to be. As required, humans are themselves a ground of disclosedness; as secondary, this ground is itself grounded in the *self*-disclosedness of Being. That, above all, is what the question of truth is about.

For Heidegger, contemplative thinking is precisely this attending to the truth, this recognizing of *the* event; or, expressed more truthfully, contemplation is the *receiving* of a self-disclosure of Being as ascendant over our disclosive powers. Contemplation then motivates a putting into perspective of our human role as secondary, as the role of abetter. To contemplate is to acknowledge the genuinely mature human role as one of authentic following. That role immediately demands on our part, to put it in familiar terms, *poiesis* rather than imposition. What Heidegger hopes, what he exhorts, is that humans take up that role with all their might. If they do, then, according to Heidegger, what might flourish is not only the works of humans but also the essence of humanity: "Is it not possible that a new ground and soil will be bestowed back on man, a ground and soil out of which the essence of man as well as all his work might flourish again, even in the atomic age?" (*G*, 21/53).

The new ground is precisely the understanding of Being as the ultimate ground, and of humans as the grounded ground, of what it means to be. If humans play their role of abetter with full diligence, then their works might be genuine. Abetting is *poiesis*. Thus, in the end, we could say that theory, contemplation of the truth of Being, motivates the practice of *poiesis*. Contemplation holds out to us the poietic attitude as the authentically human one. Contemplation shows us that lasting human works, versus disposables, are precisely ones produced poietically. Therefore contemplative thinking, as Heidegger indicated, is not out of touch but is of the highest practical utility. It motivates the attitude of abetting, and that attitude might bring forth genuine fruit: namely the saving of the essence of humanity. That itself would be the most genuinely lasting human work.

Conclusion: *phenomenology, improvisation on the piety in art*

In the final analysis, then, what exactly is Heidegger recommending to ward off the danger? Indeed, he is recommending contemplation and detachment. Yet in a certain sense these presuppose each other and form an apparently closed circle. Detachment from technological things can be seen as a precondition for contemplation; i.e., we cannot contemplate Being if we remain under the thrall of technological beings. On the other hand, it is precisely the contemplation of Being that allows us to relativize technological beings and escape from their thrall. Thus detachment requires contemplation, and contemplation detachment. They form a sort of hermeneutical circle, and the task is to find a way to break into it.

For Heidegger, it is not possible to enter this circle by means of human powers alone. Neither intelligence nor will can accomplish contemplation and detachment. They have to be accomplished by Being, and so, primarily, we need to wait. That is what Heidegger means when he

says only a god can save us. Only a more wholehearted self-revelation of
Being, only a new, third epoch of history, can save us. Yet Heidegger is
not suggesting that we should be so meek and few in the pod as to wait
supinely. We must wait actively; our waiting must be our preparing ourselves with all our might, with unrelenting courage. How are we to carry
out this preparation? What is the appropriate waiting? Toward what is
the activity of active waiting to be directed? In Heidegger's words, the
preparation for contemplation and detachment amounts to a "strenuous
exertion" (*G*, 13/47). Toward what are we to exert ourselves?

Basically, for Heidegger, we are to prepare for contemplation and
detachment by a kind of apprenticeship, by practicing them, by exercising them (*G*, 13/47). In a sense, this, of course, only begs the question, since exercising them presupposes an already completed
apprenticeship, an already completed self-revelation of Being. Heidegger goes on to specify the basic attitude we need to practice as "sensitive care" (*feine Sorgfalt*) (*G*, 13/47). Sensitive care is *poiesis*, which is
the pious attitude at the heart of contemplation and detachment. In
other words, *poiesis* is precisely what we need to prepare for, and so
Heidegger is saying that we are to learn *poiesis* by practicing it, which
returns us to the earlier hermeneutical circle: how could we practice
poiesis unless we were already granted an unveiling of Being as the
bestower and of ourselves as receivers?

The dilemma, put differently, is that if we are to learn something by
doing it, then we need an example to imitate. And that is just the problem; there are no good examples of *poiesis* today. Imposition has deposed
poiesis. Or does art still offer us examples?

Recall that the occasion of Heidegger's speech on *Gelassenheit* was
a public celebration to commemorate a musical artist, a composer. The
speech stands out from a background of art, as did the earlier discourse
on "Die Frage nach der Technik." During his speech on *Gelassenheit*,
Heidegger mentions, with approval, that music will immediately follow.
In fact, Heidegger says that the true commemoration, the real accomplishment of the day, will be the music. His speech is, as it were, a mere
prelude to the music. For Heidegger, it is most appropriate that immediately following his speech, which consists in an urgent exhortation to
contemplative thinking, the audience will be exposed to art. Indeed, twice
during the speech Heidegger brings art to the foreground, precisely when
the issue is how we could begin contemplation. For instance: "What does
this celebration suggest, in case we are ready to contemplate? In that case
we may heed the fact that out of home soil a work of art has been
brought forth" (*G*, 14/47).

The first, most impressive, thing brought up by the soil of the homeland is art. Heidegger also refers to home soil as bringing forth "poets

and thinkers" (*G*, 14/47). Let us say that the order here is important and that the home soil, Being, calls forth the poets first and then the thinkers. In other words, the way to contemplation is paved by art. It is in art that we might find the examples to imitate, the examples of the *poiesis* we need to practice in our apprenticeship. The practice of contemplative thinking, which is our preparation for receiving poietically the self-disclosure of Being (should it be offered), will consist in our taking up and practicing the poietic attitude we find expressed in art.

What will we actually find in art, and how are we to apply this to our own being-in-the-world, our own attitude toward things? Heidegger leaves it up to us to seek personal answers to these questions. Presumably, what will be required of us in this search is the respect and sensitivity embodied in sensitive care and, along with that, a great deal of thinking, which in this case means strong imagination. We will need to be sensitive to what is revealed in art, and we will need to improvise creatively if we are to imitate art in our everyday dealings with things.

What will be required of us is therefore comparable to the practice of phenomenology. The founder of the movement called its method "free variation in imagination." For Husserl, phenomenology works with examples. These are then to be varied in imagination until something essential, i.e., invariable, is seen to remain. We need to have good examples, and we need to have fertile imaginations so as to improvise on those examples. Husserl knows that the examples we might gain from our own experience are limited. So are the offerings of history. And our imaginations are usually sluggish. Therefore phenomenology, which wants to return "to the things themselves," must have recourse to the great works of art and, for Husserl, especially poetry. And so he claims that *the fictitious* (*die Fiktion*) is, paradoxically, "the element in which phenomenology lives"; the purely fabricated is "the source out of which the knowledge of 'eternal truths' draws its nourishment." Yet art does not merely provide us with the examples we might never experience and could never imagine. In addition, for Husserl, acquaintance with the great works of art serves to make our own imaginations fertile. Art, in other words, both provides the best examples and empowers our free imaginative improvisation on those examples.[4]

We need examples, and we need to improvise. Heidegger does not go beyond suggesting where we should look (art) and what in general we should find and improvise on (*poiesis*). He then leaves it up to us to make our own way, to find our own way of bringing *poiesis* (and its underlying piety) into our lives. His philosophy of technology thus ends with an appeal for us to wait, actively wait, which we are to do precisely by exercising—by exercising respect, sensitivity, and imagination. For the rest, for

the concrete embodiment of these in the lives we have to live in the technological age, Heidegger leaves us to our freedom.

I will here also leave the reader to his or her freedom. That is to say,
I will not plead for any particular concrete way of being in the world.
But I will make more specific Heidegger's and Husserl's appeal to art as
that which might free the imagination and provide it with examples. I
submit the following, then, as three works of art especially appropriate to
the task of finding a way to live in the age of technology without falling
victim to the attitude of imposition.

I commend the reader, first of all, to *Modern Times*, the film by
Charlie Chaplin. The great existentialist, Sartre, was deeply enamored of
this film, so much so that he chose its French title (*Les temps modernes*)
for the name of the journal he founded to propagate existential thinking.
The story of the film is certainly an existential one. An unnamed man gets
caught up in the dehumanizing world of machines and then literally becomes a cog in a machine. It is, however, not his life that is endangered
but his human dignity and sanity. He goes mad, which is to say that he
loses touch with what it means to be. Eventually, after numerous absurd
and hilarious vicissitudes, he is rescued, apparently by a woman's love,
and his sanity, or some measure of it, is restored. In the famous final
scene, the protagonist waddles confidently off into the sunrise. Indeed he
has not actually been saved but, in true Heideggerian fashion, is at least
"summoned to hope in the growing light of that which might save."

So much for comedy. As to tragedy, I suggest Dostoevsky's *Notes
From Underground* or, to translate the Russian title (*Zapiski iz podpol'ya*)
more literally, *Jottings From Under the Floor*. The edifice under whose
floor the jottings originate is the one of science or technology, called here
the "crystal palace." Within the palace, everything is crystalline, i.e., rational, calculable, predictable. But under the floor—in everyday experience—things are dark, chaotic, haphazard, irrational. The writer of the
jottings upholds the rights of the irrational, its resistance against the attempt to take it up into perfect rationality. The nameless writer stands for
the rights of freedom in the face of a growing determinism, the rights of
the body in the face of reason, the rights of naive experience in the face
of the scientific explanation of that experience. In a certain sense, he
stands for the rights of contemplative over and against calculative thinking. Versus all other, direct, practical, calculating people, he is excessively,
acutely, conscious. He is, as he says, philosophical; he is theoretical—i.e.,
he is *aware* that science is turning people into objects, into mere effects of
causes. That is why he feels insulted and why his entire life becomes a way
of returning the insult. In science, people are piano keys or organ stops,
they are mere automatic reposes to stimuli, and their whole lives can be

calculated in advance. In the face of this growing objectification, the writer represents the *last* ("I will have no readers") attempt at preserving personality, freedom, human dignity. He sees his whole life's work to consist in proving that he is a man and precisely not a piano key, even if that requires him to do something perverse and irrational on purpose. He will do anything, even go mad, to prove that not every action can be calculated beforehand by natural science and mathematics.

Such proof may come at the cost of one's own skin. The tragedy of the book is that it is precisely this cost which is paid by the author of the jottings. For example, he is suffering from disease, and he knows that medical science can cure him, but he will not consult a doctor, and his reason is a spiteful one: he will not allow doctors the pleasure of objectifying him. He will not turn himself into an object of scientific observation, he will not, we could say, turn his human heart into a stethoscopic object, he will not participate in the objective world at all, he will not, in his own mixed metaphor, contribute one brick to the building of the crystal palace. In the age in which he lives, it having become futile to resist the rising tide of scientific objectification, he has recourse to irrationality—out of spite. He eventually becomes a follower of Dionysus simply to demonstrate that not everything can be made Apollonian, simply to spite those who say it can. The tragedy of the book consists in its portrayal of the consequences of the attempt to make everything rational and calculable, namely that the irrational and chaotic will assert itself—with a vengeance.

I offer next a parable, but it is a most un-Heideggerian one; it is the foil against which to set off the poetry I will invoke in conclusion. The parable is from the Taoist sage, Chuang-Tse, and tells of a certain Tzu-kung, who came across an old man working in a garden. The old man had dug ditches for irrigation and was pouring water into them from a jar he filled by hand, climbing laboriously in and out of a wellspring. The old man was exerting himself to the utmost and yet was not accomplishing very much. Tzu-kung told him of a device with which a hundred fields can be irrigated in one day. It takes little effort and accomplishes much. He told the old man to make a wooden arm, with the back end weighted and the front end light (a counter-balanced lever called a shadoof), and said that it is thereby possible to draw water so fast that it will seem to be gushing out. The wise old man replied with derision that he would be ashamed to use such a thing, for those who use machines do all their work in a machine-like way. Furthermore, those who do their work like machines become machine-hearted. Those who have a machine-heart in their breast lose their pure simplicity. Those without pure simplicity are unsure in the stirrings of their spirit. And uncertainty in the stirrings of spirit is incompatible with the great way of truth. (Chuang-Tse, Book III, 11)

It is un-Heideggerian to suppose that those who do their work by machines necessarily become machine-hearted (or that the mere avoidance of machines guarantees a true human heart). It is un-Heideggerian to suppose that thinkers and poets will lose their pure simplicity if they write with ball-points or word-processors (or that the use of goose quills will foster such simplicity). Therefore, versus this parable, I commend the reader to the extensive poetry of Dannie Abse, a contemporary yet detached physician who has, for example, rhapsodized over the stethoscope, a modern "machine" without which no doctor works today. In "The Stethoscope,"[5] Abse celebrates his own ears and finds praiseworthy what he hears in the auscultation of the heart. That is because he does not merely hear "lub-dub," the pumping of a machine-heart, but also, as he puts it, "the sound of creation." In Heideggerian terms, the poet is referring here to the mystery that the heart, which is no doubt a pump, has been created—or bestowed—at all. What the poet finds praiseworthy is not simply that hearts are pumps, but that they are bestowals.

Thus the stethoscope does not need to connect machine-hearts. What counts is not the stethoscope as a high-tech gadget but what it is we are able to hear with it, which in turn depends on what kind of ears we have. If a doctor merely hears a machine pumping, then he himself or she herself has become machine-hearted. But it need not be so. Everything depends on what sort of hearing we cultivate; or, more basically, it depends on what sort of ears we have (been given) to hear with.

Notes

Preface

1. In this study I deal exclusively with primary texts and do not relate my findings to what other commentators have said. To spell out these relations would perhaps be a worthwhile task, though certainly an extraneous one. In the bibliography at the end, I list some of the major secondary sources on Heidegger's philosophy of technology and indicate, very generally, how my work stands in relation to them.

Introduction

1. "E coelo devocavit et in urbibus collocavit." Cicero, *Tusculanae disputationes*, V, iv, 10.
2. Heidegger finds the original pious attitude in its purest state in Homer and in the pre-Socratic philosophers Anaximander, Heraclitus, and Parmenides. Socrates marks a definite break, although vestiges of the earlier attitude are still clearly visible in Plato and Aristotle. The falling away, while swift, was therefore a gradual one.
3. For Heidegger, the gods are, primarily, the looking ones; θεοί are θεάοντες (*theaontes*, "ones who look"). Looking means here self-disclosure, and so the gods are the δαίοντες (*daiontes*), the "shining" ones par excellence, whence they are also called the δαίμονες (*daimones*), the ones who are "uncanny" (demonic) in their shining. What is uncanny is their peculiar self-withholding in the very act of self-showing. Therefore, according to Heidegger, "The Greek gods are Being itself as looking into [shining through, yet while withdrawing in favor of] beings" (*P*, 164/111).
4. Of course, truth never *completely* discloses or withholds itself to humans. To be Dasein is always to have an imperfect understanding of what it means to be. The goddess truth always veils herself to some extent. But the veils may be more or less lifted; Heidegger is saying that it is primarily the goddess herself who lifts them.

5. For the publication history of the original and of the English translation, see the list of Heidegger's works cited, p. 237. I will make some reference to the published translation, by William Lovitt, since it is in its terms that Heidegger's philosophy of technology is mostly known and discussed in the English-speaking world. Yet I have strong reservations about the adequacy of that translation and will for the most part use it merely as a foil. In fairness to Lovitt, it must be mentioned that he himself recognizes the insufficiency of his translation for scholarly work: "It goes without saying that anyone who wishes to know Heidegger's work well must read and study the German text" (p. xxi of the translator's Introduction).

Part I. Ancient Technology

1. Sophocles makes this same connection between begetting and nurturing. Oedipus refers to his (supposed) father as the one "who nourished me and begot me" (*Oidipous Turannos*, in *Sophocles I* [Loeb Classical Library 20] [Cambridge: Harvard University Press, 1994], 827). The order is important; the nourishing is—at a superficial level, paradoxically—placed prior to the begetting, so that the implied sense is: "who nourished me and *thereby* begot me (fully)." That is to say, nurturing is a prior condition of the father's begetting. We could therefore with equal justification speak of the *almus pater* as of the *alma mater*.
2. As Heidegger himself articulates it, causing in this sense amounts to "facilitating, inciting, offering reassurance and support, arousing, encouraging, stimulating by way of liberation and provocation, nudging, upholding, heartening, enticing" (*PI*, 127/94).
3. Jean-Paul Sartre, *L'existentialisme est un humanisme* (Paris: Nagel, 1964), 16.
4. We will see that modern technology is violent in a very different sense; it does violence not just to the superficial appearance but to the essence, the Being of the being. Modern technology *imposes* an essence on the being.

Part II. Modern Technology

1. At least some of the products of ancient handcraft were of course designed for violent ends. The ancients indeed produced implements of war, as do we, but there is an essential difference between the attitude toward nature embodied in forging a sword and the one involved in making a smart bomb.
2. To relate to Being in a disclosive way is to enjoy a friendship with Being, which for Heidegger is the literal meaning of philo-sophy. Heidegger goes on to argue that if even at the purely human level friendship cannot be controlled or compelled, then, a fortiori, the friendship that constitutes philosophy must come as a gift from Being itself (*H*, 3).

3. A careful reader of the English translation might wonder about the significance attached here to the capital letter, since, on page 4, "That" is capitalized when it refers to nothing more than the essence of a tree. But that capital appears only in the translation, not in Heidegger's original German.

4. The published English translation of this crucial statement on the relation between science and technology is as follows: "The modern physical theory of nature prepares the way first not simply for technology but for the essence of modern technology" (p. 22). This surely gives the mistaken impression that science is prior to the essence of modern technology.

5. *Grundfragen der Philosophie.* All the following quotations are from §38.

6. Werner Heisenberg, "Das Naturbild der heutigen Physik," in *Die Künste im technischen Zeitalter* (Munich: Oldenbourg, 1954), 62–63.

7. Maurice Merleau-Ponty, *L'Oeil et l'Esprit* (Paris: Gallimard, 1964), 9–10.

8. Heidegger himself interprets Socrates' cave-allegory in a pre-Socratic sense. For Heidegger, what is at issue here is not learning as a human accomplishment, but the possibility of a human being coming forth as Dasein, as a place of the disclosure of Being. And that is not a matter of humans possessing learning, retaining things, but of humans being possessed by, retained by, Being itself. Thus Heidegger translates as follows: "Next, then, form an image of our human essence, and understand this our essence accordingly, namely with respect to the possibility of its coming forth, as well as not coming forth, as something retained" (*VW*, 114).

Part III. *The Danger in Modern Technology*

1. Straus refers to the sedimentation of general *psychological* experience. See "The Upright Posture," in Erwin Straus, *Phenomenological Psychology* (NY: Basic Books, 1970), 156, n.

2. Throughout these central pages of "Die Frage nach der Technik," the published translation turns Heidegger's admittedly difficult German into even more difficult English. For example, the very important phrase, "Com-posing dispenses a destiny," is rendered thus: "Enframing is an ordaining of destining."

3. Published translation of these two sentences: "Always the unconcealment of that which is goes upon a way of revealing. Always the destining of revealing holds complete sway over man." I sympathize with the difficult task the translator faced, but I cannot see that he has here expressed the proper sense or, indeed, any determinable sense.

4. For a full discussion of the notion of Dasein as a freely chosen mode of human existence, see Richard Rojcewicz and Brian Lutgens, "A genetic (psychological) phenomenology of perception," *Journal of Phenomenological Psychology*, 27, No. 2 (1996): 117–145.

5. See p. 55. See p. 55.

6. The published translation does not use the word "seamstress," and this crucial line is rendered inexplicably as follows: "Ever to the child in man, night neighbors the stars."

Part IV. Art

1. Actually, Heidegger's text does not contain the neuter nominative *das Artistische* but the dative *dem Artistischen*. Grammatically, this could also be the dative of the masculine *der Artistische*. In that case the term would mean not artistry in general but "the artistic person," and Heidegger would be saying even more strongly that the artist (with his or her artistry) is not the source of art.
2. *L'existentialisme est un humanisme*, 90–91.
3. Readers of the English translation of Heidegger's essay on technology might well wonder whether he does in fact accord a privilege to poetry, for this crucial statement on the issue is mistakenly rendered as follows: "It was finally that revealing which holds complete sway in all the fine arts, in poetry, and in everything poetical that obtained *poiesis* as its proper name." My reading of the passage is confirmed by Heidegger's nearly identical, though more forcefully expressed, discussion of this same matter elsewhere (*N*, 203/165).
4. In English, the intermediate term, "poesy," is, of course, superfluous, since "poetry" is already a cognate of the Greek *poiesis*.
5. *L'Oeil et l'Esprit*, 14.
6. Reported by Joachim Gasquet, cited by Merleau-Ponty, *L'Oeil et l'Esprit*, exergue.
7. Merleau-Ponty, "La doute de Cézanne," in *Sens et non-sens* (Paris: Nagel, 5th ed., 1966), 29.
8. Immanuel Kant, *Kritik der Urteilskraft*, ed. Gerhard Lehmann (Stuttgart: Reclam, 1963), §§10–17.

Part V. Detachment

1. It is in this dialogue that the teacher calls the night the seamstress of the stars. See p. 180.
2. The latter is actually Heidegger's subtitle for the dialogue.
3. The homeland is presumably the same as the fatherland, and Heidegger says explicitly (*HG*, 121) that the fatherland is Being itself.
4. Edmund Husserl, *Ideen I* (Den Haag: Nijhoff, 1976) (Husserliana III), §70, *ad finem*.
5. Dannie Abse, *White Coat, Purple Coat: Collected Poems, 1948–1988* (New York: Persea Books, 1991), 187.

Cited Works of Heidegger

The following list includes only those works of Heidegger cited in the present study. Comprehensive bibliographies of Heidegger's writings are readily available. Posted on the Web at http://www.umr8547.ens.fr/Documents/HeidBiblio.html is an admirably exhaustive chronological bibliography.

I cite Heidegger by the page number of the German text, according to the abbreviations given below, followed, after a slash, by the page number of the published English translation, if one exists. All translations in this book are my own; page numbers of the published translations are provided solely for the convenience of readers who may wish to compare the two versions.

AE   *Aus der Erfahrung des Denkens*. Pfullingen: Neske, 1954. Translated by Albert Hofstadter as "The Thinker as Poet," in Martin Heidegger, *Poetry, Language, Thought*. NY: Harper & Row, 1971.

BH   "Brief über den Humanismus." In Martin Heidegger, *Wegmarken*. Frankfurt: Klostermann, 2nd ed., 1996, Gesamtausgabe (GA) 9. Translated by Frank A. Capuzzi and J. Glenn Gray as "Letter on Humanism," in Martin Heidegger, *Basic Writings*. NY: Harper & Row, 1977.

BP   *Beiträge zur Philosophie (Vom Ereignis)*. Frankfurt: Klostermann, 2nd ed., 1994 (GA 65). Translated by Parvis Emad and Kenneth Maly as *Contributions to Philosophy (From Enowning)*. Bloomington: Indiana University Press, 1999.

EM   *Einführung in die Metaphysik*. Frankfurt: Klostermann, 1983 (GA 40). Translated (from the unrevised 1953 edition) by Ralph Manheim as *An Introduction to Metaphysics*. NY: Anchor Books, 1961.

FT   "Die Frage nach der Technik." Originally published in *Die Künste im technischen Zeitalter*. München: R. Oldenbourg, 1954. Republished, in slightly modified form, in Martin Heidegger, *Vorträge und Aufsätze*, Pfullingen: G. Neske, 1954, and in Martin Heidegger, *Die Technik und die Kehre*, Pfullingen: G. Neske, 1963. (In 1967 Neske also issued *Vorträge und Aufsätze* in three volumes. "Die Frage nach der Technik" is found in Volume I.) The definitive, improved text (which I will cite) includes Heidegger's marginalia from earlier editions and is published under the aegis of the

Gesamtausgabe in *Vorträge und Aufsätze*. Frankfurt: Klostermann, 2000 (GA 7). Translated (from the first *Vorträge und Aufsätze* edition) by William Lovitt as "The Question Concerning Technology," in Martin Heidegger, *The Question Concerning Technology and Other Essays*. NY: Harper and Row, 1977. Republished in modified form in Martin Heidegger, *Basic Writings*. NY: Harper & Row, 1977. (I will provide page numbers of the original edition of the translation.)

G   *Gelassenheit*. Pfullingen: Neske, 3rd ed., 1959. Translated by John M. Anderson and E. Hans Freund as *Discourse on Thinking*. NY: Harper & Row, 1966.

GP   *Grundfragen der Philosophie: Ausgewählte "Probleme" der "Logik."* Frankfurt: Klostermann, 1984 (GA 45). Translated by Richard Rojcewicz and André Schuwer as *Basic Questions of Philosophy: Selected "Problems" of "Logic."* Bloomington: Indiana University Press, 1994.

H   *Heraklit*. Frankfurt: Klostermann, 3rd ed., 1994 (GA 55).

HG   *Hölderlins Hymnen "Germanien" und "Der Rhein."* Frankfurt: Klostermann, 3rd ed., 1999 (GA 39).

HI   *Hölderlins Hymne "Der Ister."* Frankfurt: Klostermann, 1992 (GA 53). Translated by William McNeill and Julia Davis as *Hölderlin's Hymn "The Ister."* Bloomington: Indiana University Press, 1996.

N   *Nietzsche: Der Wille zur Macht als Kunst*. Frankfurt: Klostermann, 1985 (GA 43). Translated (from the 1961 edition) by David Farrell Krell as *Nietzsche: The Will to Power as Art*. San Francisco: Harper & Row, 1979.

P   *Parmenides*. Frankfurt: Klostermann, 1982 (GA 54). Translated by André Schuwer and Richard Rojcewicz as *Parmenides*. Bloomington: Indiana University Press, 1992.

PI   *Phänomenologische Interpretationen zu Aristoteles: Einführung in die phänomenologische Forschung*. Frankfurt: Klostermann, 2nd ed., 1994 (GA 61). Translated by Richard Rojcewicz as *Phenomenological Interpretations of Aristotle: Initiation into Phenomenological Research*. Bloomington: Indiana University Press, 2001.

PS   *Platon: Sophistes*. Frankfurt: Klostermann, 1992 (GA 19). Translated by Richard Rojcewicz and André Schuwer as *Plato's Sophist*. Bloomington: Indiana University Press, 1997.

PT   "Phänomenologie und Theologie." In Martin Heidegger, *Wegmarken*. Frankfurt: Klostermann, 2nd ed., 1996 (GA 9). Translated by James G. Hart and John C. Maraldo as "Phenomenology and Theology" in Martin Heidegger, *Pathmarks*. Cambridge: Cambridge University Press, 1998.

VW   *Vom Wesen der Wahrheit: Zu Platons Höhlengleichnis und Theätet*. Frankfurt: Klostermann, 1988 (GA 34).

WB   "Wissenschaft und Besinnung." In Martin Heidegger, *Vorträge und Aufsätze*, Frankfurt: Klostermann, 2000 (GA 7). Translated (from the first *Vorträge und Aufsätze* edition) by William Lovitt as "Science and Reflection," in Martin Heidegger, *The Question Concerning Technology and Other Essays*. NY: Harper and Row, 1977.

Bibliography of Major Secondary Studies Devoted to Heidegger's Philosophy of Technology

Heidegger's philosophy of technology has generated an extensive secondary literature, including numerous full-length monographs. A good sampling of the latter is listed below. Yet I have come away from reading the secondary literature with the conviction that Heidegger's writings on technology largely remain terra incognita. It is not so much that, for example, the following books are in error, although I do indeed not agree with any of them completely. It is more a matter of their unwillingness to engage Heidegger's work on a fundamental level. While they all have something to say, not one of them, in my view, exhibits the close reading Heidegger deserves and repays. Very little separates the most penetrating of the following studies from the least, and so, rather than rank them, I list them here simply in alphabetical order.

Cavallucci, Valerio. *Heidegger tra metafisica e tecnica.* Venezia: Arsenale Cooperativa, 1981.

Guery, François. *Heidegger rediscuté: Nature, technique et philosophie.* Paris: Descartes & Cie., 1995.

Loscerbo, John. *Being and Technology: A Study in the Philosophy of Martin Heidegger.* The Hague: Nijhoff, 1981.

Lovitt, William, and Harriet Brundage Lovitt. *Modern Technology in the Heideggerian Perspective.* Lewiston, NY: Edwin Mellen, 1995.

Mazzarella, Eugenio. *Tecnica e metafisica: Saggio su Heidegger.* Napoli: Guida, 1981.

Milet, Jean-Phillipe. *L'Absolu technique: Heidegger et la question de la technique.* Paris: Kimé, 2000.

Platte, Till. *Die Konstellation des Übergangs: Technik und Würde bei Heidegger.* Berlin: Duncker & Humblot, 2004.

Romano, Bruno. *Tecnica e giustizia nel pensiero di Martin Heidegger.* Milano: A. Giuffrè, 1969.

Rosales-Rodríguez, Amán. *Die Technikdeutung Martin Heideggers in ihrer systematischen Entwicklung und philosophischen Aufnahme.* Dortmund: Projekt Verlag, 1994.

Ruggenini, Mario. *Il soggetto e la tecnica: Heidegger interprete "inattuale" dell'epoca presente.* Roma: Bulzoni, 1978.

Schirmacher, Wolfgang. *Technik und Gelassenheit: Zeitkritik nach Heidegger.* Freiburg: Karl Alber, 1983.

Seubold, Günter. *Heideggers Analyse der neuzeitlichen Technik.* Freiburg: Karl Alber, 1986.

Zenklusen, Stefan. *Seinsgeschichte und Technik bei Martin Heidegger: Begriffsklärung und Problematisierung.* Marburg: Tectum, 2002.

One book on Heidegger deserves special mention:

Zimmerman, Michael E. *Heidegger's Confrontation with Modernity: Technology, Politics, and Art.* Bloomington: Indiana University Press, 1990.

This latter is an exemplary work of scholarship regarding the historical and political context of Heidegger's philosophy of technology. It says very little about the actual content of that philosophy, and I disagree strongly with what it does say about the content. But by uncovering the background of Heidegger's writings on technology, it complements my own work, and I therefore do not hesitate to recommend, even urge, readers of my book to take up Zimmerman's.

Index

Abse, Dannie, 231

abstraction: essence as, 157, 200; science as, 98, 119–20, 122

active letting (*das Ver-an-lassen*), 32–35, et passim. *See also* occasioning (*das Veranlassen*)

aei on (*ἀεὶ ὄν*). *See* eternal being

aesthetics, as metaphysical theory of art, 186–91

agriculture, 76–77

airliner, as ephemeral, 86

aletheia (*ἀλήθεια*): the goddess, 2–8, 50–51, 225, 233n4; as name for Being in general, 65; as a negative and passive word, 171–72; vs. the positive word "truth," 54; as self-offering of Being, 148; as transformed into *homoiosis*, 190; translated into modern languages, 49–54. *See also* truth

aletheuein (*ἀληθεύειν*), 58–64

Anaximander, 233n2

ancient technology: as an abetting, nurturing, 31–33; as bringing-forth, 35–40; as a letting, 32–35; as a gearing into nature, 40–44; as *poiesis*, 65; as pro-ducing, 47–48, 65; as the theory of the four causes, 15–19

anemo-energy, 74, 77

Apollo, 230

apostasy, history as, 3, 5

apprenticeship, for practicing *poiesis*, 227–28

appulse, 179

architect, 45–46

architecture, 196–200

arete (*ἀρετή*), 63–64

Aristotle, 1, 11, 15–29, 37, 45–46, 57–64, 68, 158, 233n2

"Around the World in Eighty Hours," 188

art: and aesthetics, 187–90; appreciation of, 187–88; as a disposable, 183, 187; as fundamentally poetry, 181, 194–201; as higher than though same in essence as technology, 183, 202–6; as highest form of *poiesis*, 192–93; humanistic vs. ontological view of, 186–87, 201; and inspiration, 201; intertwining with philosophical thinking, 210; Kant's definition of, 205; as paving the way to contemplation, 227; piety in, 14, 187, 227; as place of radiant appearance of Being, 193; role of in phenomenology, 228; saves by bringing home to us *poiesis*, 194, 206; as translation of *techne*, 9, 69, 191

atomic energy, 76, 113

241

Bestand
84

Use : 30-1, 70 (science & use) useless, 217, 220

pre given: 92, 166 (Being & Bestowal)

vocation: 130

prety: 207

Ontological for its own sake: 216

Lord: 222